Islamic Finance and Sustainable Development

The interest in improving Environmental, Social and Governance (ESG) outcomes among stakeholders of Islamic banking and finance has become front and centre in the discussions relating to Islamic sustainable finance.

This book offers an expansive overview of the relevant issues, global initiatives and trends in the management, governance, and operation of Islamic sustainable impact finance. It identifies the models and mechanisms required to achieve sustainable impact finance in the context of Islamic investment and project development and collects and observes the latest approaches in maintaining and fulfilling the principles of Shariah-compliance in Sustainable Development Goals and Environmental, Social and Governance-oriented projects. The book also explores conventional financing instruments, which are being used in modern practice.

While Islamic sustainable finance provides a positive change in the Islamic banking and finance industry globally, implementing it is not without its challenges. Such challenges, such as the fulfilment of Shariah-compliance requirements, both legally and jurisprudentially, and the application and development of modern innovative products and hybrid models of classical products are highlighted and addressed in the book. The book delves into the current management practices of Islamic banking and finance, which promote Islamic sustainable impact finance and outlines strategies for meeting sustainable investments and projects. Other factors, such as the latest technology, regulations and social, political and economic policies are also considered. Evidence is provided via case studies from selected countries that participate actively in the Islamic banking and finance industry globally.

The book will attract a wide audience from researchers, scholars, and students to stakeholders of Islamic banking and finance, regulators, policy makers and Shariah-compliant practitioners.

Mohd Ma'Sum Billah is Senior Professor of Finance at the Islamic Economics Institute, King Abdul Aziz University, Kingdom of Saudi Arabia.

Rusni Hassan is Professor of Finance and the Dean at the IIUM International Institute of Islamic Banking and Finance, International Islamic University, Malaysia.

Razali Haron is Associate Professor of Finance at the IIUM International Institute of Islamic Banking and Finance, International Islamic University, Malaysia.

Nor Razinah Mohd Zain is Assistant Professor of Law at the IIUM International Institute of Islamic Banking and Finance, International Islamic University, Malaysia.

Islamic Business and Finance Series

Series Editor: Ishaq Bhatti

There is an increasing need for western politicians, financiers, bankers, and indeed the western business community in general to have access to high quality and authoritative texts on Islamic financial and business practices. Drawing on expertise from across the Islamic world, this new series will provide carefully chosen and focused monographs and collections, each authored/edited by an expert in their respective field all over the world.

The series will be pitched at a level to appeal to middle and senior management in both the western and the Islamic business communities. For the manager with a western background the series will provide detailed and up-to-date briefings on important topics; for the academics, postgraduates, business communities, manager with western and an Islamic background the series will provide a guide to best practice in business in Islamic communities around the world, including Muslim minorities in the west and majorities in the rest of the world.

The Global Halal Industry
A Research Companion
Hussain Mohi-ud-Din Qadri

The Law of Riba in Islamic Banking
Conventional and Unconventional Approaches to Interest-Free Financing
Edited by Hasan Gürak and Neelambar Hatti

Islamic Sustainable Finance
Policy, Risk and Regulation
Edited by Mohd Ma'Sum Billah, Rusni Hassan, Razali Haron and Nor Razinah Mohd Zain

Islamic Finance and Sustainable Development
A Global Framework for Achieving Sustainable Impact Finance
Edited by Mohd Ma'Sum Billah, Rusni Hassan, Razali Haron and Nor Razinah Mohd Zain

For more information about this series, please visit: www.routledge.com/Islamic-Business-and-Finance-Series/book-series/ISLAMICFINANCE

Islamic Finance and Sustainable Development

A Global Framework for Achieving Sustainable Impact Finance

Edited by: Mohd Ma'Sum Billah, Rusni Hassan, Razali Haron and Nor Razinah Mohd Zain

Routledge
Taylor & Francis Group
LONDON AND NEW YORK

First published 2024
by Routledge
4 Park Square, Milton Park, Abingdon, Oxon OX14 4RN

and by Routledge
605 Third Avenue, New York, NY 10158

Routledge is an imprint of the Taylor & Francis Group, an informa business

British Library Cataloguing-in-Publication Data
A catalogue record for this book is available from the British Library

Library of Congress Cataloging-in-Publication Data
Names: Mohd. Ma'sum Billah, 1968– editor.
Title: Islamic finance and sustainable development : a global framework for achieving sustainable impact finance / edited by Mohd Ma'Sum Billah, Rusni Hassan, Razali Haron and Nor Razinah Mohd. Zain.
Description: Abingdon, Oxon ; New York, NY : Routledge, 2024. | Series: Islamic business and finance | Includes bibliographical references and index.
Identifiers: LCCN 2023055365 (print) | LCCN 2023055366 (ebook) | ISBN 9781032743073 (hbk) | ISBN 9781032743103 (pbk) | ISBN 9781003468653 (ebk)
Subjects: LCSH: Finance—Islamic countries. | Sustainable development—Islamic countries.
Classification: LCC HG187.4 .I833 2024 (print) | LCC HG187.4 (ebook) | DDC 332.10917/67—dc23/eng/20240214
LC record available at https://lccn.loc.gov/2023055365
LC ebook record available at https://lccn.loc.gov/2023055366

ISBN: 978-1-032-74307-3 (hbk)
ISBN: 978-1-032-74310-3 (pbk)
ISBN: 978-1-003-46865-3 (ebk)

DOI: 10.4324/9781003468653

Typeset in Times New Roman
by Apex CoVantage, LLC

This book is dedicated to the remembrance of my most beloved parents Allamah Mufti Nur Mohammad (r) and Ustazah Akhtarun Nisa' (r) who have nourished me with their love and wisdom. May Allah (swt) shower them with His Love and Mercy and grant them Jannat al-Ferdaus. I would also like to dedicate this book to my lovely wife Dr Khamsiah Nawawi (Head, OSHE-Hospital UKM) and our heart-touching kids Dr Ahmad Mu'izz Billah (Head of Surgical Department and Medical officer at the Mukah Hospital, a Government hospital under the Ministry of Health, Malaysia), Ahmad Mu'azz Billah (OP-Cadet-RMC, BSc Hons. Formerly affiliated with the JPM, Putrajaya and currently serves at Accenture, Malaysia), Ahmad Muniff Billah (OP-Cadet-RMC. Winner of Gold Medal Award 2023 in his outstanding innovative research project and currently pursuing with his BSc Honors in Aviation Management and Piloting, MSU) and Akhtarun Naba' Billah (Pursuing with her LLB Honors, IIUM and Winner of Dean's List), for their continuous supports and sacrifices.

May all be blessed with *Muwaddau Wa Rahmah, Qurratu A'yun* and *Mardhaati Allah* (swt) in the life and the next.

This book is also dedicated to the Ummah and the whole of humanity.

Mohd Ma'Sum Billah, PhD

A special dedication to my parents, my extended family, my teachers and Murabbi who inspired, guide and shape me to be the person I am today. A special thanks also to the Institute of Islamic Banking and Finance (IIUM) team members for their unwavering support in bringing the Institute to a higher level. May Allah provide us with the fortitude and dedication to contribute to the well-being of our institution and to the Ummah.

Rusni Hasan, PhD

Infinite gratitude to my loving parents, family and my teachers for their care and wisdom. May Allah (SWT) grant them the best reward. Also, for the endless support and trust entrusted in me by the Institute of Islamic Banking and Finance (IIUM) for their mission to be the Centre of Excellence.

Razali Haron, DBA

This book is dedicated to the loving memory of my parents, Sayiran Binti Hassan Raza and Haji Mohd. Zain Bin Haji Harun. My greatest gratitude goes to my husband, Mohd. Yusmadi Bin Mohd. Yunan for teaching me the value of being patience. Thank you also to all my respected teachers, especially Prof. Dr. Mohd Ma'Sum Billah and Prof. Dr. Engku Rabiah Adawiah Engku Ali. May Allah bless them always, Ameen.

Nor Razinah Mohd Zain, PhD

Contents

Figures and Tables

Figures

Tables

About the Editors

Mohd Ma'Sum Billah, DBA, PhD, MBA, MCL, MMB, LLB (hons)

Senior Professor of finance, insurance, fintech and investment, Islamic Economics Institute, King Abdulaziz University, Kingdom of Saudi Arabia. Billah has concurrently been affiliated as adjunct-professor, examiner, assessor and reviewer in numerous reputable universities in the West, Middle East, ASEAN and African countries. Earlier he was a member of the Audit Board of ACIG (approved by the Saudi Monetary Authority/Central Bank of Saudi Arabia), Saudi Arabia. Billah has served and contributed to both academic as well as corporate industries and international organizations for more than 25 years with management, teaching, research, solution proving and sharing of strategic and technical know-how towards the advancement of Islamic finance, fintech, business, investment, capital market and insurance *(Takaful)*, besides *Halal* standard. Billah has published more than 40 books and chapters in books, along with more than 200 articles in international, regional and local reputable journals and social media. Most of his books were published by top global publishers, namely: Thomson Reuters, Sweet & Maxwell, Palgrave Macmillan, Springer, Routledge, Edward Elgar and others. Most of his books and articles are used as among the lead references (solutions to reality) by universities, industries, professional firms, governments, policy makers, regulators, NGOs, academia, researchers and students of higher learning in different parts of the contemporary world. He has presented at more than 300 conferences, seminars, executive workshops, professional developments and industrial training in different parts of the world. In addition, he has also been affiliated with corporate, academic and financial industries including central banks, international corporate organizations, governments and NGOs in his capacity as a board member, director, advisor, strategic decision maker, transformer and reformer with strategic solutions and technical know-how. Among the areas of his interest and contributions are: Islamic finance, insurance (*takaful*), crowd-funding, investment, *Zakat, Waqf*, capital market (*Sukuk*), social finance, SDGs, petroleum finance, trade, fintech, e-Commerce, Crypto-asset, cryptocurrency, industrialization, privatization, PPP, benchmarking and national entrepreneur models, standards, policies strategies and technical know-how.

Rusni Hassan, PhD

Prof. Datin Dr. Rusni Hassan, who is listed in the Top 10 Most Influential Women in Islamic Business and Finance globally, serves as the Dean of IIUM Institute of Islamic Banking and Finance, International Islamic University Malaysia (IIUM). She is an active researcher and expert trainer in IBF. Having nearly 30 years of experience in academia, she has taught, published and supervised academic works, especially in the areas of Shariah, governance and legal aspects of Islamic banking and finance. Her publications include books on Islamic Banking and Finance, chapters in books and articles published in local and international journals. She is listed as a Top 10 contributor for research in Islamic Finance in Scopus database. Industry-wise, she is actively involved as the Chairman and member of Shariah Committee and Board of Director of Islamic financial institutions, both locally and internationally. Her work and contributions to Islamic Finance have been internationally recognized by the Government of Maldives, where she was awarded the National Recognition for Outstanding Contribution of Females to Develop and Sustain Islamic Finance Industry in Maldives in 2018. She has been listed among the Top Women in Islamic Finance since 2013 and was listed in the Top 50 Most Influential Women in Islamic Finance 2018; Top 10 Most Influential Women in Islamic Business and Finance in 2019, 2020, 2021 consecutively and as Women Influencer 2022 by Cambridge IFA.

Razali Haron, DBA

Razali Haron obtained a DBA (Finance) from UKM in 2012 and is currently an Associate Professor at the IIUM Institute of Islamic Banking and Finance, International Islamic University Malaysia (IIUM). Prior to joining IIUM in 2003, he had extensive industrial experience for almost 13 years in covering the capital market, portfolio management, unit trust industry and merchant banking in Malaysia. He served as a member of the IIUM Investment sub-Committee from 2012–2021. His research area includes corporate finance, capital market and portfolio management. Razali has published his research works with reputable international publishers such as Emerald, Elsevier, Sage, Springer, Inderscience and Palgrave Macmillan. As an active researcher, he has been awarded with many awards by IIUM, among others: The Best Researcher Award (2014), Best Indexed Journal Article (2014), Highest Citation in Citation Index Journal (Social Science) (2015 & 2022), Top 250 Contributors to IIUM Research Performance 2015–2017 (2018), Highest Number of Publications Award (2019) and Top 30 Contributors to IIUM Research Performance (2019 & 2021). He is currently the Deputy Dean (Postgraduate & Responsible Research) of the Institute. He has edited three research books: *Islamic Fund and Wealth Management* (2019-IIUM), *Banking and Finance* (2020-IntechOpen, UK) and *Islamic Social Finance and Economic Recovery After a Global Health Crisis* (2021-IGI Global). Very recently, his co-authored paper (with Anwar Hasan) on Bitcoin Currency has been awarded with the Highly Commended Paper in the 2020 Emerald Literati Awards. Razali is currently the Editor-in-Chief of *Journal of Islamic Finance* (IIUM) and Associate Editor of *The Capital Market Review*

(Malaysia Finance Association) and Advisory Editorial Board Member of *Journal of Open Innovation: Technology, Market, and Complexity* (Elsevier).

Nor Razinah Mohd Zain, PhD

Nor Razinah Mohd Zain, PhD is currently working as Assistant Professor of Laws at IIUM Institute of Islamic Banking and Finance and International Islamic University Malaysia. She received her LLB (Honours), Masters of Comparative Laws (MCL), and PhD in Laws from International Islamic University Malaysia (IIUM). She is also an Advocate and Solicitor of the High Court of Malaya (Non-Practicing). Since 2014, she has worked with Ahmad Ibrahim Kulliyyah of Laws, Harun M. Hashim Law Centre, and Kulliyyah of Economics & Management Sciences (KENMS). Her specialization focuses on Comparative Banking Laws, Islamic Banking and Finance, Dispute Resolution, Alternative Dispute Resolution, Business Law and Sustainable Finance Law. Currently, she is one of the appointed Fellows under IIUM's Sejahtera Centre that emphasizes Sustainable Development Goals' community-oriented engagements. She has contributed to several research projects from 2014 to 2023. Her recent participation can be found in recent research projects including: "Humanitarian Sukuk: Developing an Alternative Financial Tool in Addressing Refugee Crisis" (2019 to 2022), sponsored by the Ministry of Higher Education (Malaysia), and "Musharakah as an Islamic Financial Structure for Venture Capital: Its Potentials and Possible Applications for Small and Medium Enterprises (SMES) in Malaysia" (2021 to 2022), sponsored by Bank Rakyat (M) Berhad. She has written more than 70 research works (including articles and chapters). In her leisure time, she enjoys reading.

Acknowledgements

> There is no strength and power except in *Allah (swt)*, To Him comes the praise, the Savant, the Wise, the Omniscient, the most beautiful names belong to Him. May the blessing of Allah (swt) and peace be upon *Muhammad (saw)* and all the Prophets (*aws*) from the first to the last.

I am humbly privileged to acknowledge King Abdulaziz University, Kingdom of Saudi Arabia and its prestigious Islamic Economics Institute for supporting us with every facility in research, academic, human capital and professional development activities outreaching the global *Ummah*. It is also a great honour for me to humbly acknowledge His Excellency Professor Dr Hana bint Abdullah Al-Nuaim, the Acting President of King Abdulaziz University, Professor Dr Amin Yousef Mohammad Noaman, the Vice President of King Abdulaziz University and Dr Mohammad Abdullah Naseef, the Dean of the Islamic Economics Institute (IEI), King Abdulaziz University (KAU), Dr Faisal Mahmoud Alatbani (Vice Dean, IEI-KAU), Dr Hasan Mohammad Makhethi (Vice Dean, IEI-KAU), Dr Abdullah alUtaiby (Head, Department of Insurance, IEI-KAU), my talented colleague Mr Mohammed Alabdulraheem (Lecturer in fintech and Islamic finance, IEI-KAU), Mr Mukhlesur Rahman Chowdhury, former adviser (with the rank and status of a minister) to the President of Bangladesh, Mr Sayak M Rahman (prolific writer and columnist), Mr Nazmul Bari (CEO-Green Max Inc), Mr A M Nazrul Islam Chowdhury (prolific writer, columnist and political analyst), Dr Abdul Aziz (prolific journalist) and Mr Sayed Salim Reza (politician and businessman). I would like to express my full-hearted thanks with appreciation to universities, institutes, academies and professional firms whose direct and indirect supports with knowledge, experiences and resources are full-heartedly recorded.

Mohd Ma'Sum Billah, PhD

I would like to acknowledge International Islamic University Malaysia (IIUM) and Institute of Islamic Banking and Finance, IIUM for their support with every facility in research, academic, human capital and professional development activities outreaching the global Ummah. It is also a great honour for me to humbly acknowledge Honourable Rector Tan Sri Dzulkifli Razak and the University

Management Committee, especially Deputy Rector (Responsible Research and Innovation) Prof Dr Ahmad Hafiz Zulkifli and Prof Ahmad Faris Ismail, Deputy Rector (Academic & Internationalisation), for their unwavering support to us especially in research and publication. My special thanks and appreciation go to every single member of the Institute team, especially my Deputy Dean (Responsible Research and Innovation), Associate Professor Dr Razali Haron, and Dr Nor Razinah Mohd Zain, who are also the co-editors of this book. This book would not be possible without the support, assistance and facilitation of respected Prof Dr Ma'Sum Billah, the lead editor, to whom my gratitude and full-hearted thanks goes. My heartfelt acknowledgement to all individuals, researchers, scholars, institutions and organizations who are passionate about research and publication, especially in Islamic banking and finance to serve the industry and ummah.

Rusni Hassan, PhD

My acknowledgement goes to the Institute of Islamic Banking and Finance and IIUM for the continuous support in producing high-impact research. It is also a great honour for me to humbly acknowledge Honorable Rector Tan Sri Dzulkifli Razak, and the Deputy Rector (Responsible Research and Innovation) Prof Dr Ahmad Hafiz Zulkifli and Deputy Rector (Academic & Internationalisation) Prof Ahmad Faris Ismail, for their endless support to the Institute on research and publication. My special thanks to the Dean of the Institute, Prof Dr Rusni Hassan, for her excellent leadership and guidance, as well as the support from Dr Razinah Mohd Zain. This book would not be feasible without the guidance and facilitation from the respected Prof Dr Ma'Sum Billah, to whom the Institute is very grateful. Lastly, my appreciation to all authors for their full cooperation in ensuring the success of the publication.

Razali Haron, DBA

I hereby would like to take this chance to acknowledge the great support that I received from the International Islamic University Malaysia (IIUM), with a special dedication to the Institute of Islamic Banking and Finance and their research teams/staffs. Thank you to my respected Prof. Dr. Mohd. Ma'Sum Billah for the learning opportunity that he gave me. Thank you also to Prof. Dr. Rusni Hassan (the Dean of the Institute) and Assoc. Prof. Dr. Razali Haron. I was inspired through the great efforts shown by the team from Sejahtera Centre focusing on SDGs activities in IIUM campus, MKitchen team, Centre for Islamization of Knowledge Integration (CENTRIS) and Network for Education and Research on Peace and Sustainability (NERPS), Hiroshima, who are constantly sharing their knowledge and wisdom. Thank you also to all my students who never stop motivating me with their questions.

Nor Razinah Mohd Zain, PhD

Foreword

Since the initiative of global effort of the United Nations with Millennium Development Goals (MDGs) in 2000, which was subsequently replaced by Sustainable Development Goals (SDGs) in 2015 to tackle the indignity of poverty, the United Nations has continued to serve as a universal call for a sustainable future while promoting equality, human rights and justice for all. Moving towards 2030, it is affirmed that financial sectors and their relevant stakeholders have vital roles in making impactful sustainable finance and creating positive trends and changes which are relevant to meeting SDGs. This is not limited to the investors per se, but it extends to includes practices of the financial sector internally, and the community that is externally served. Looking closely to Islamic banking and finance and its related sectors such as Takaful and the Islamic capital market, they stand out as having high potential in attaining sustainable finance and to create positive impacts in multi-layered levels. Instead of reinventing the wheel, Islamic sustainable finance is properly rooted back in the principles of Shari'ah and its financing mechanisms that can be seen in practice as applied throughout Islamic banking and financial industries today. With the continuous expansion of Islamic banking and finance across the globe, it offers a rather unique perspective of sustainable finance in the modern context.

This book is timely, and it accurately contributes to understanding the unique perspective of Islamic sustainable finance and possible changes that it can bring. In order to fully comprehend and value the practical implementation of Islamic sustainable finance, it is imperative to possess a comprehensive publication, such as this book, that encompasses global case studies and contemporary methodologies of Islamic sustainable finance. This book is aimed at contributing as a significant reference, to creating changes in the minds of readers, while considering the diverse range of stakeholders across various geographical regions that are keenly interested in this field. The primary emphasis in this book is directed to engaging in discussions pertaining to global initiatives, developments within Islamic sustainable finance and the presence of classical instruments within contemporary practices. It also highlights the apparent challenges associated with the implementation of Islamic sustainable finance within the respective industries. Obviously, Islamic banking and finance have many suitable financing mechanisms for the implementation of Islamic sustainable finance and its impacts, while it comprehensively emphasizes sustainable development.

Upon a careful examination of the book's content, it becomes evident that the discourse presented in this book is skilfully crafted and meticulously edited by esteemed editors with intellectual efforts. The book also benefits from the valuable contributions of devoted individuals who possess a wealth of expertise in their respective domains. Without a doubt, this book will serve as an essential resource for understanding the discourse and the relevant relationships that exist between Islamic finance, sustainable development and Islamic sustainable finance in the contemporary reality. I would like to extend my congratulations to editors, contributors and the publisher for their praiseworthy efforts in producing a book of exceptional relevance.

Prof. Emeritus Tan Sri Dato' Dzulkifli bin Abdul Razak
Rector International Islamic University Malaysia (IIUM) Malaysia

Preface

Islamic sustainable finance is a concept emerged from the continuous process of integration between classical and modern discourses of Islamic banking and finance with the understanding relating to sustainability and sustainable development agendas. While the notion of sustainable impact finance captures the attention of relevant stakeholders, such as investors, bankers, practitioners, etc., it is important to look back, analyse and share the viable practices of Islamic sustainable finance that are utilised successfully in giving tremendous impacts to societies, communities and selected countries. As prioritised under the main components of sustainable development agendas, i.e., environmental, social and economy, the practices of Islamic sustainable finance and the relevant financing mechanisms are not only emphasised on sustainable impacts from those three perspectives; they are also contributing to Shariah-compliance initiatives and empowering ethical investments and businesses. Currently Islamic sustainable finance and its practices are going beyond borders and jurisdictions. Thus, it is important to capture those different practices from global initiatives and international trends. The practices of Islamic sustainable finance remain unique due to existence of combinations between modern and classical instruments as approved by Shariah principles. While it has huge potential to grow further in the future, it is important to embrace the challenges that may exist within Islamic banking and finance and its closely related industries, i.e., Islamic capital market. By having such a view, the sharing provided in this book attempts to identify the international initiatives and trends of Islamic sustainable finance across borders, appreciate the application of classical instruments or mechanisms in the modern Islamic sustainable finance and address visible challenges that exist in Islamic banking and finance and Islamic capital market. ***This book, titled "Islamic Finance and Sustainable Development: A Global Framework for Achieving Sustainable Impact Finance," is organised into Three Crucial Parts with eighteen important chapters and a specific introduction and index at the end.***

Part I provides a discussion relating to Islamic sustainable finance from global initiatives and trends. Within this Part, the chapters are divided into five important chapters. Chapter 1 explores Islamic sustainable finance from Gulf experiences. Chapter 2 evaluates Islamic sustainable finance from experiences of African countries. Chapter 3 focuses on Islamic sustainable finance from experiences of

SAARC. Chapter 4 analyses Islamic Micro-financing for SMEs towards its sustainability from Libyan experience. Chapter 5 discusses sustainability through Zakat from the experience of the Islamic banking industry in Malaysia.

Part II is concerned with practices of classical instruments in the modern setting of Islamic sustainable finance, which stands out with eleven chapters. Chapter 6 highlights the instruments of Islamic sustainable finance. Chapter 7 provides a bibliometric analysis on the emergence of Zakat in sustainability. Chapter 8 assesses the role of Zakat in building up a sustainable investment. Chapter 9 looks closely at Zakat governance towards sustainable finance. Chapter 10 evaluates the effectiveness of Zakat management towards sustainability. Chapter 11 discusses Islamic sustainable finance: how does Waqf matter? Chapter 12 identifies the practice of Al-Rahnu that leads towards Islamic sustainable finance. Chapter 13 discusses Bay' Al-Salam that leads towards Islamic sustainable finance. Chapter 14 appreciates the practice of Al-Musharakah that leads towards Islamic sustainable finance. Chapter 15 evaluates Hibah al-Ruqba and its contribution to sustainable economy. Meanwhile, Chapter 16 evaluates the practice of SRI Sukuk that leads towards Islamic sustainable finance.

Part III looks at the issues and challenges that may exist within the Islamic banking and finance and Islamic capital markets in implementing Islamic sustainable finance. It consists of two main chapters. Chapter 17 explores issues and challenges of sustainable finance from the experience of Islamic banking industry. Finally, Chapter 18 identifies issues and challenges of sustainable finance in the Islamic capital market.

The motivation that triggers this research book is inspired by the realisation of the importance of exposing the practices of Islamic sustainable finance and its relevant instruments or mechanisms from the real related industry. While there is still an apparent scarcity of literature relating to Islamic sustainable finance, the collection of research works that can be found in this book may open up a richer discussion relating to the conceptual studies of Islamic sustainable finance and its practices in the real world. It is important to highlight that certain regions have preferences in selecting the classical instruments that can be used for modern practices of Islamic sustainable finance. Such trends are shown and explored here. In their applications, it is also important to appreciate the emerging issues and challenges in implementing Islamic sustainable finance where steps or processes should be considered in overcoming them. However, due to the inherent limitations of human perception, it is plausible to consider the presence of imperfections inside this book. Thus, we express our sincere gratitude for the readers who kindly notify us of any further enhancements.

Contributors

Nik Anis Idayu Nik Abdullah is a PhD candidate at the Institute of Islamic Banking and Finance, IIUM. She has a master's in accountancy and Association of Chartered Certified Accountants (ACCA) studies from Universiti Teknologi MARA (UiTM). She has published articles and research papers on topics related to environmental, social, and governance (ESG) and corporate finance. With over a decade of academic experience as a lecturer in UiTM, she continues exploring the associations between ESG practices and their impact on firms through empirical studies and data-driven analysis.

Pg Mohd Faezul Fikri Ag Omar (PhD candidate) is a lecturer in Shari'ah and Islamic Finance at the Universiti Malaysia Sabah (UMS). He obtained a bachelor's degree in Ulum Islamiyyah wal Arabiah from Al-Azhar University, Cairo, Egypt, and a master's degree in Islamic Economics (Islamic Finance) from Universiti Kebangsaan Malaysia (UKM). He teaches courses such as Usul Al-Fiqh, Al-Qawaid Al-Fiqhiyyah, Fiqh Al-Muamalat, fundamentals of Islamic finance, Arabic for Islamic finance, Islamic accounting, and microeconomics. His area of research includes zakat and taxation, Fiqh and Usul Al-Fiqh, Islamic social finance and philanthropy. He is currently pursuing his PhD in Islamic banking and finance at the Institute of Islamic Banking and Finance, IIUM.

Mohamed Aslam Akbar, PhD is an Assistant Professor in Shari'ah and joined IIUM in 2019. He obtained his diploma in Arabic language and a degree of Alimiyyah in Shari'ah from Jamiah al-Uswah al-Hasanah, Tamil Nadu. In 2002, he went to Deoband and received Fazil Daura-e-Hadith (kutub al-sittah, the six canonical authentic books of Hadith) with Ijazah and Sanad-e-Faraghat (the graduate degree) from Jamiah Islamiyyah Darul Uloom Deoband, Delhi. In 2009, Akbar earned his master's degree in Usul al-Din from the Kulliyyah of Islamic Revealed Knowledge and Human Sciences at IIUM and subsequently completed his PhD in philosophy, ethics and contemporary issues, specializing in wisdom studies in Qur'an and Sunnah with particular reference to an unpublished manuscript of Ali al-Muttaqi al-Hindi, from the International Institute of Islamic Thought and Civilization (ISTAC) in 2016. Upon graduation, he worked as a post-doctoral research fellow at IIUM, where he conducted preliminary research in identifying and assessing economic thought in the early period of Muslim scholarship with special reference to classical Arabic manuscripts. Mohamed Aslam Akbar is a citizen of India and currently lives and works in Malaysia. He teaches undergraduate and postgraduate courses in Islamic commercial jurisprudence, Islamic economic thought and sustainable development and conducts research on the classical works of Muslim scholarship in economic thought and Maqasid al-Shariah-based developments.

Syuhaeda Aeni Mat Ali, PhD in Law from IIUM. She practiced in civil litigation for six years before becoming an academician on the Faculty of Law, Universiti Teknologi MARA. She is experienced in teaching both postgraduate and undergraduate courses. Her areas of interest are Islamic banking and finance, Islamic capital market, Takaful and Waqf, personal bankruptcy, corporate insolvency and Business law. She has written several articles published in both local and international journals. She has received best paper awards at local and international conferences in Islamic banking and finance.

Md Atiullah PhD Candidate at the University of Malaya (UM). He obtained his bachelor's and master's degrees in economics and finance from IIUM in 2014 and 2019, respectively. Atiullah has published his research works in reputable journals and is currently pursuing his PhD at the UM in banking credit and global financial crisis.

Akhtarzaite binti Abdul Aziz, PhD is currently an Assistant Professor in the Department of Fiqh and Usul al Fiqh, AbdulHamid AbuSulayman Kulliyyah of Islamic Revealed Knowledge and Human Sciences, IIUM. She graduated from IIUM in LLB in 1995 and completed LLB (Shariah) in 1996. She also holds a master's degree (2000) and PhD (2005) in Fiqh and Usul al Fiqh from the same university. Her research interest is in contemporary issues in Islamic jurisprudence, particularly in Islamic banking, Islamic capital market and Takaful, as well as Halal management industry. She is currently a member of Maybank Islamic Berhad Shariah Advisory Committee, Pru Bsn Takaful Shariah Advisory Committee, and Bank Kerjasama Rakyat Shariah Advisory Committee.

Farah Herneeda binti Bahar obtained her master's degree in Fiqh and Usul Fiqh from IIUM in 2020 and is currently an Assistant Vice President, Group Compliance at Alliance Bank Malaysia Berhad. She has 14 years of experience in Islamic banking and finance covering product development, Shari'ah advisory and regulatory advisory. Farah has obtained certifications from AICB, including Executive Banker (2015) and Professional Banker (2018). She also obtained certification as an Islamic Financial Planner (2022) from IBFIM.

Mohd Ma'Sum Billah, DBA, PhD, MBA, MCL, MMB, LLB (hons) Senior Professor of finance, insurance, fintech and investment, Islamic Economics Institute, King Abdulaziz University, Kingdom of Saudi Arabia. Billah has concurrently been affiliated as adjunct-professor, examiner, assessor and reviewer in numerous reputable universities in the West, Middle East, ASEAN and African countries. Earlier he was a member of the Audit Board of ACIG (approved by the

Saudi Monetary Authority/Central Bank of Saudi Arabia), Saudi Arabia. Billah has served and contributed to both academic as well as corporate industries and international organizations for more than 25 years with management, teaching, research, solution proving and sharing of strategic and technical know-how towards the advancement of Islamic finance, fintech, business, investment, capital market and insurance *(Takaful)*, besides *Halal* standard. Billah has published more than 40 books and chapters in books, along with more than 200 articles in international, regional and local reputable journals and social media. Most of his books were published by top global publishers, namely: Thomson Reuters, Sweet & Maxwell, Palgrave Macmillan, Springer, Routledge, Edward Elgar and others. Most of his books and articles are used as among the lead references (solutions to reality) by universities, industries, professional firms, governments, policy makers, regulators, NGOs, academia, researchers and students of higher learning in different parts of the contemporary world. He has presented at more than 300 conferences, seminars, executive workshops, professional developments and industrial training in different parts of the world. In addition, he has also been affiliated with corporate, academic and financial industries including central banks, international corporate organizations, governments and NGOs in his capacity as a board member, director, advisor, strategic decision maker, transformer and reformer with strategic solutions and technical know-how. Among the areas of his interest and contributions are: Islamic finance, insurance (*takaful*), crowd-funding, investment, *Zakat, Waqf*, capital market (*Sukuk*), social finance, SDGs, petroleum finance, trade, fintech, e-Commerce, Crypto-asset, cryptocurrency, industrialization, privatization, PPP, benchmarking and national entrepreneur models, standards, policies strategies and technical know-how.

Jarita Duasa, PhD is a Professor of Economics at the Department of Economics, Faculty of Economics and Management Sciences, IIUM. Her research niche areas are international economics, international finance, economic development, applied economics, environmental economics, food security and social finance. She is actively involved in research and has won several awards in research and publication. Among them are the 2006 Quality Award in research at the faculty level, the Outstanding Researcher for the category of Social Sciences and Humanities in 2011 at the university level, PENCIPTA 2009, IRIIE (IIUM Research, Invention and Innovation Exhibitions) for several years as well as the High Impact Responsible Innovation Award (Social Science) 2023. Her work is made possible by her receipt of support in the form of grants from various agencies and ministries at national and international levels. These include grants from the Malaysian Institute of Integrity (IIM), International Centre for Education in Islamic Finance (INCIEF), Permodalan Nasional Berhad (PNB), FRGS, ERGS and TRGS from Ministry of Higher Education, East Asia Development Network (EADN), PPZ and others. She has published several articles in cited refereed journals as well as books and chapters in books. Her contribution is widely recognized in the country and abroad through the appointment of Evaluation Officer of Science Fund projects by MOSTI, a panel judge in Creativity,

Research and Innovation Exhibition, a panel interviewer of Public Service Department's Training Scholarship, Editor of IJEMA, editorial board member of several local and international journals, and invited speaker at conferences local and abroad.

Mohammad Habibullah, PhD is currently an Academic Fellow at the Institute of Islamic Banking and Finance, IIUM specializing in Shari'ah, mu'amalat, Islamic social finance (zakat and waqf management), Islamic wealth management, Islamic jurisprudence, and Islamic commercial law. He obtained his master's and PhD in Islamic Revealed Knowledge and Heritage (Qur'an and Sunnah) from the IIUM. He was a recipient of the Rector Scholarship Award in 2014 from IIUM during his PhD program. Habibullah also completed his post-doctorate at the Institute. He is lecturing on various subjects for master's and PhD students at the Institute, such as Islamic jurisprudence, Islamic commercial law, and Islamic social finance. Habibullah has published in reputable journals and reputable publishers for book chapters. He has presented more than 20 conference papers at local and international conferences.

Nurhaiyyu Abdull Hamid completed her master's in accountancy and Association of Chartered Certified Accountants (ACCA) studies from Universiti Teknologi MARA. Before joining the academic field, she gained valuable practical experience working with the Ministry of Finance, specifically in the Tax Department, for nearly three years. This experience gave her deep insights into the intricacies of tax regulations and the practical application of accounting principles within a governmental context. She is currently a Senior Lecturer at Universiti Teknologi MARA, where she teaches accounting information systems and corporate finance. With nearly ten years of teaching expertise, she plays a vital role in shaping the future generation of accounting professionals.

Hichem Hamza, PhD is currently a Professor of Islamic Economics and Finance at the Islamic Economics Institute-King Abdulaziz University in Jeddah. He holds a master's and a Ph.D. in Sciences of Economics from the University of Auvergne – France. He began his academic experience at the Higher School of Commerce in Tunis – Manouba University, where he taught on financial markets, Islamic finance, risks of Islamic banking and economic analysis for undergraduate and postgraduate students, and he further taught in many other Tunisian universities. In 2016, Dr. Hamza joined the Institute of Islamic Economics at King Abdulaziz University as a faculty member, along with his participation in many academic projects and educational program design for graduate studies and research activity in the field of Islamic economics and finance. Among his research interests: Islamic finance and banking, monetary systems and endowments. Dr. Hamza has published many research papers in refereed journals and has participated in many international seminars and conferences.

Razali Haron, DBA is an Associate Professor and Deputy Dean (Postgraduate & Responsible Research) of the Institute of Islamic Banking and Finance, IIUM. Prior to joining IIUM in 2003, he had extensive industrial experience for almost

13 years covering the capital market, portfolio management, unit trust industry and merchant banking in Malaysia. He served as a member of the IIUM Investment sub-Committee from 2012–2021. His research area includes corporate finance, capital market and portfolio management. Razali has published his research works with reputable international publishers such as Emerald, Elsevier, Sage, Springer, Inderscience and Palgrave Macmillan. As an active researcher, he has been received many awards from IIUM, among others: the Best Researcher Award (2014), Best Indexed Journal Article (2014), Highest Citation in Citation Index Journal (Social Science) (2015 & 2022), Top 250 Contributors to IIUM Research Performance 2015–2017 (2018), Highest Number of Publications Award (2019) and Top 30 Contributors to IIUM Research Performance (2019 & 2021). He is currently the Deputy Dean (Postgraduate & Responsible Research) of the Institute. He has edited three research books: *Islamic Fund and Wealth Management* (2019-IIUM), *Banking and Finance* (2020-IntechOpen, UK) and *Islamic Social Finance and Economic Recovery After a Global Health Crisis* (2021-IGI Global). Very recently, his co-authored paper (with Anwar Hasan) on Bitcoin Currency was awarded the Highly Commended Paper in the 2020 Emerald Literati Awards. Razali is currently Editor-in-Chief of Journal of Islamic Finance (IIUM) and Associate Editor of The Capital Market Review (Malaysia Finance Association) and Advisory Editorial Board Member of Journal of Open Innovation: Technology, Market, and Complexity (Elsevier).

Aznan Hasan, PhD is a Professor at the Institute of Islamic Banking and Finance, IIUM. He received his first degree in Shari'ah from the University of al-Azhar (BA Hons), Egypt, and a master's degree in Shari'ah from Cairo University, Egypt, with distinction (Mumtaz). He then obtained his PhD from the University of Wales, United Kingdom. Currently, he is Deputy Chairman of the Shari'ah Advisory Council (SAC) of Securities Commission, Deputy Chairman of the Shari'ah Supervisory Board of Bank Nizwa (Oman), a Board member of Higher Shari'ah Authority of UAE Central Bank, and a Shari'ah Board member of AAOFI. He had served as a member of the SAC of Bank Negara Malaysia (2006–2008 and 2010–2013). He is also the Chairman of the Shari'ah Committee and Non-Independent Non-Executive Director of Maybank Islamic, and member of the SAC for Employees Provident Fund. He also serves as a Shariah consultant/adviser to Maybank Investment Bank, Hong Leong Investment Bank, Public Investment Bank, Malacca Securities Bhd, CGS-CIMB Securities Berhad, UOB Kayhian Securities and Inter-Pacific Securities Bhd. Aznan Hasan also serves as the Chairman of the Shari'ah Committee at Etiqa Family Takaful Berhad, Etiqa General Takaful Berhad, Bank Pembangunan Malaysia Berhad, and Amanah Hartanah Bumiputra.

Rusni Hassan, PhD is a Professor and Dean at the Institute of Islamic Banking and Finance, IIUM. She graduated with LLB (Honors), LLB (Shari'ah) (First Class), Master of Comparative Laws (MCL) and PhD in Law. Her area of specialization includes legal, governance and Shari'ah aspects of Islamic banking and finance. She is an active researcher and expert trainer in IBF. Her publications include books on Islamic banking and finance, chapters in books and articles published in local and international journals. She is listed as a Top 10 contributor for research in Islamic finance in the Scopus database. She is on the Shari'ah Committee for several Islamic financial institutions in Malaysia and the Maldives. Her works and contributions to Islamic finance were also been recognized internationally when she was listed among the Top Women in Islamic Finance starting in 2013. The most recent was the Top 10 Most Influential Women in Islamic Finance 2018, 2019 and 2020 by Cambridge IFA.

Zainab Belal Lawhaishy, PhD in Islamic banking and finance from the Institute of Islamic Banking and Finance, IIUM in 2023. Since 2016, she has worked as a freelance project manager for private and public financial institutions and universities. She also joined IIUM Shariah Advisory Services Sdn. Bhd. (ISAS) in 2017–2018. Her research areas include the regulations of Islamic banks, corporate governance, takaful, Islamic microfinance, and modern Islamic finance rulings. Zainab has published her research work with reputable international publishers such as Emerald. She is also a certified Shariah Advisor and Auditor (CSAA), AAOIFI, 2021.

Nur Farhah Mahadi, PhD obtained her bachelor's and master's degrees in Islamic Revealed Knowledge and Heritage (Fiqh and Uṣul al-Fiqh) from IIUM and pursued her PhD (Philosophy in Islamic economics and banking) at Yarmouk University, Jordan. She is the Head, Shari'ah Advisory of International Islamic Finance and Insurance (IIFIN) Consulting Sdn Bhd and has conducted Shari'ah auditing for Takaful and Retakaful companies in Kuala Lumpur and Singapore. She has conducted several training courses under IIUM Shari'ah Advisory Services Sdn. Bhd (ISAS), namely Certificate in Shari'ah for Takaful Practitioners (CSTP), Certificate of Islamic Banking and Finance (CIBF) and Short-Course of Islamic Banking and Finance (SCIBF). In 2022, she was invited to be a keynote speaker by the College of Law, Prince Sultan University, Riyadh, CIBEST IPB University in collaboration with Bank Syariah Indonesia, the Ministry of Religion State Islamic Religion Institute (IAIN) Pontianak Faculty of Ushuluddin, Adab and Dakwah, and State Islamic University of North Sumatra, Indonesia. In August 2022, she was invited as a discussant on the 6th Annual Islamic Finance Conference (AIFC); "Islamic Finance Role in MSMEs Empowerment: Boosting Capability and Fostering Inclusiveness for Sustainable Future", organized by Fiscal Policy Agency – Ministry of Finance with Department of Islamic Economics, IPB University.

Syed Marwan, PhD is currently an Assistant Professor and Coordinator at the Institute of Islamic Banking and Finance, IIUM. He obtained his PhD in Islamic banking and finance from the Institute, researching the area of social impact. Prior to that, he completed the Chartered Islamic Professional (CIFP) at the International Centre for Education in Islamic Finance (INCEIF) after graduating with a degree of Commerce (Economics & Finance) from the University of Melbourne. His industrial experience includes working at Kuwait Finance

House (KFH) Research as an analyst and at the Maybank Group as a fellow under the CEO@faculty program. His research interests are in Socially Responsible Investment (SRI), Social Impact Bonds (SIB) and impact measurement. He has published multiple papers in these areas and has embarked on research projects, namely "Social Impact Performance Measurement Model for Islamic Financial Institutions: Integrating Sustainable Development Goals (SDGs), Value-Based Intermediation (VBI) and Maqasid Shariah" and "Humanitarian Sukuk: Developing an Alternative Financial Tool in Addressing Refugee Crisis", both funded by the Fundamental Research Grant Scheme (FRGS).

Musthafa Mu'adz Bin Mohammad Masruh is a dedicated professional with a strong background in Shari'ah and Islamic studies. With a combination of working experience and educational achievements, Musthafa has developed extensive knowledge in his field. Currently, Musthafa serves as a Shari'ah Research & Secretariat at Agrobank, Malaysia, where he has been working since 2021. In this role, he conducts research and supports the administrative aspects of Shari'ah compliance within the bank. Prior to his current position, he also worked as an Arabic translator at the Ministry of Islamic Affairs Saudi Arabia during Hajj periods, where he utilized his language skills to facilitate communication and translation. He gained valuable experience as a Treasury Manager in Pondok Moder Darussalam Gontor from 2008 to 2009. This role involved managing treasury-related activities and contributing to the financial operations of the organization. In terms of education, Musthafa holds a bachelor's degree in Shari'ah Islamic law from the Madinah Islamic University in Saudi Arabia, which he completed in 2014. He further pursued his studies at the same university, obtaining a higher diploma in Dakwah and Islamic culture in 2015. Continuing his academic journey, Musthafa completed a master's degree in Fiqh jurisdiction at Islamic Madinah Islamic University in 2020.

Imron Mawardi, PhD is currently a Lecturer in the Islamic Economics Department, Faculty of Economics and Business, Universitas Airlangga, and serves as Vice Dean of the Faculty of Advanced and Multidisciplinary Technology, Universitas Airlangga. Imron completed his undergraduate studies in the Department of Soil Science, University of Jember, then continued his master's studies in Management Science at Universitas Airlangga and received a PhD in Islamic Economics at Universitas Airlangga. Before joining the academia, he worked in journalism such as PT Jawa Pos, Harian Jatim Mandiri, and Harian Surabaya Pagi. He also served as President and Director of PT Pintu Abadi Sejahtera and PT Surabaya Mandiri Sejahtera.

Nur Hafizah binti Miszairi completed her bachelor's degree in 2022 with a Rector List Award in Fiqh and Usul al-Fiqh at IIUM. She represented IIUM in the Intervarsity Young Motivator Competition (IMAC) in 2019 and was one of the finalists at the national level. She served as an enthusiastic internship student at Dakwah Department, Jabatan Agama Islam Wilayah Persekutuan. She is currently pursuing a master's degree in Fiqh and Usul al-Fiqh at IIUM and teaching Islamic studies at a private tutoring company in Malaysia.

Mustafa Omar Mohammed, PhD is presently an Associate Professor at the College of Economics and Management, al-Qasimia University, UAE. He is also an Executive Council Member of the Sharjah Center for Islamic Economics, al-Qasimia University. He is a managing editor of Al-Qasimia Journal of Islamic Economics and has been a journal editorial member and on the reviewer panel to 11 academic entities. He was the former Director of Center for Islamic Economics at the Kulliyyah of Economic and Management Sciences, IIUM. He also served as the Head of the Department of Economics at KENMS. He obtained his PhD (Finance) from Universiti Sains Malaysia (USM) in 2011. He has more than 100 publications to his credit. Most of his research works are published by reputable international publishers including Emerald, Elsevier, Sage, Routledge, and Palgrave Macmillan. He has co-edited six books in the field of Islamic economics. Mustafa has won several awards in teaching, research, and publications. He was awarded the Top 30 Contributors to the IIUM Research Performance for Outstanding Achievement for the Year in 2019; two Gold Medals for Research Invention and Innovation in 2012; best conference paper awards in 2021, 2019, 2013, 2009, and 2008; and Best Teacher Award at the Kulliyyah Level in 2003. He has ample experience in translations. He undertook projects for MIFC, BNM, IBFIM, AIBIM, IFSB, ISRA, and other international organizations. He is also involved in consultancy and training on Islamic economics, fintech, banking, and finance.

Mohamed Asmy Bin Mohd Thas Thaker, PhD obtained his bachelor's in economics (Hons), master's in economics and PhD in economics from the IIUM. He joined IIUM in October 2014 as an Assistant Professor in the Department of Economics and was promoted to Associate Professor in 2019. He specializes in economic development, SMEs Islamic economics, Waqf, Zakat and Islamic banking and finance. He has published close to 100 articles in highly reputable journals and received various national and international research grants. His research outputs are recognized internationally and have earned several awards, such as the Distinguished Paper Award, Best Paper Award and Emerald Literati Award. He has also received several awards at faculty and university levels, such as the High Impact Responsible Research Award, High Citation in Indexed Journal Award, Active Researcher Award, Promising Young Researcher Award and High Joint Publication Award. Currently, he is the Head of Department of Economics, Research Fellow of Centre of Islamic Economics, IIUM and Life Member of Malaysian Economic Association.

Nor Razinah Binti Mohd Zain, PhD is currently an Assistant Professor at the IIUM Institute of Islamic Banking and Finance, IIUM. She has actively participated and published on dispute resolution, Islamic banking, Islamic social finance, and Islamization of knowledge since 2013. She was trained in mediation for conflict solution and trauma conciliation by Prof Dr. Johan Galtung, the Founder of Peace Research Institute Oslo, Norway in 2014. Prior to joining IIiBF, she was an Advocate and Solicitor of the High Court of Malaya (Non-Practicing). She is currently the acting Editor for Journal of Islamic Finance and Islamization Coordinator for IIiBF. She is also an active member of the International Council of Islamic Finance Educators (ICIFE) and Association of Shari'ah Advisors in Islamic Finance (ASAS). Recently, she and her team successfully proposed the use of dispute resolution to the Malaysian government, which led to the establishment of the National Unity and Reconciliation Council in overcoming interfaith and interracial disputes. She also has researched fintech as well as smart contracts and their impacts on regulations and Shari'ah principles. She contributed a chapter of a book titled "Settlement of Islamic finance disputes in the United Arab Emirates" in an edited book titled *Dispute Resolution in Islamic Finance*, 2019. Her latest research on Islamic Social Finance can be found in the Global Islamic Finance Report 2019, organized by the Cambridge Institute of Islamic Finance.

Mir'atun Nisa' completed her bachelor's degree from the Islamic Economics Study Program, Universitas Airlangga in 2022. She has participated in many essay writing competitions, scientific papers, business plans, and international conferences. She is also active as a research assistant at the Islamic Economic Department, Universitas Airlangga. She is currently preparing for her master's study.

Azman bin Mohd Noor, PhD is currently a Professor at the Institute of Islamic Banking and Finance, IIUM. He has been lecturing on Islamic jurisprudence and Islamic finance at IIUM since 2005. He completed his degree in Islamic law in 1997 at the Islamic University of Madinah, Saudi Arabia. He did his MA in Islamic criminal law in 2000 at the Universiti Kebangsaan Malaysia and MA in Muamalat (Islamic Law of Transactions) in 2001 at the Department of Fiqh and Usul al-Fiqh, IIUM. He obtained his PhD in Islamic Law in 2005 from the University of Edinburgh, Scotland. His areas of research interest are in Islamic law of transactions, Islamic banking and capital market, Takaful and Retakaful, Waqf and Zakat.

Fatimah Mohamad Noor, PhD in Islamic banking and finance from the Institute of Islamic Banking and Finance, IIUM. Her research primarily focuses on the captivating realms of mualamat, waqf, and governance. In her doctoral study, she delves deep into the realm of corporate waqf institutions, aiming to shed light on the practice of good governance. Her ultimate objective is to identify effective approaches to address the governance challenges faced by the waqf institutions. Notably, Fatimah also holds an MA (2017) and BA (2014) in Islamic Revealed Knowledge, specializing in Fiqh and Usul Fiqh, both of which were obtained from the same university. During her master's program, her research revolved around the intriguing topic of the purification methodology of Shari'ah-compliant stocks. Furthermore, she contributed a chapter to a published book, enriching the discourse on this vital subject. Driven by her passion for disseminating knowledge, Fatimah actively cultivates a diverse range of scholarly publications. Her primary focus lies in the intricacies of waqf, its governance challenges, and other thought-provoking matters related to muamalat. She has also contributed her knowledge to several book chapters published by international publishers such as Palgrave Macmillan and IGI Global.

Ahmad Azam Othman, PhD obtained his LLB (Hons), LLB (Shari'ah)(Hons), MCL degrees from IIUM and PhD from University of Wales, UK and joined IIUM in 2001. He currently serves as an Assistant Professor in the Department of Islamic Law of AIKOL, IIUM. He was the Director of Harun M. Hashim Law Centre of Ahmad Ibrahim Kulliyyah of Laws (AIKOL), IIUM from 2011 to 2012 and Head of Department of Islamic Law of AIKOL from 2006 to 2008. He has vast experience in teaching postgraduate as well as undergraduate courses. Besides this, he is an internal examiner and supervisor to a number of PhD theses and master's dissertations in various areas, including Islamic banking, Islamic microfinance, Islamic capital market, Takaful and Waqf.

Anwar Hasan Abdullah Othman, PhD is currently an independent researcher. He was a former Deputy Dean for Responsible Research and Innovation and Assistant Professor at the Institute of Islamic Banking and Finance, IIUM. He was previously a postdoctoral researcher at the IIUM. He obtained his PhD (Finance) from IIUM in 2015. He is currently an editor for the Turkish Journal of Islamic Economics, as well as an associate editor for the European Journal of Islamic Finance. Additionally, he is an associate editor for Al Qasimia University and Journal of Islamic Economics, a former editor for the Journal of Islamic Finance and an associate editor for the International Journal of Al-Turath in Islamic Wealth and Finance. Previously, he worked as a lecturer at the Universiti Kebangsaan Malaysia (UKM) and lectured at the Lincoln University College in Malaysia. He has published in areas such as monetary policy, cryptocurrency, micro and macroeconomic policies, asset pricing, unit trust funds industry, Islamic banking and finance and Asian stock markets. Anwar has membership in many research organizations. In addition, he has participated in several local and world economic forums on business, economics, finance and social science. Anwar has extensive experience in data analysis software and statistical models and supervised several master's and PhD candidates at the Institute of Islamic Banking and Finance, IIUM.

Nur Harena Redzuan, PhD is currently an Assistant Professor at the Institute of Islamic Banking and Finance, IIUM. Before joining academia, she gained extensive experience in the Islamic banking industry by working closely with the Shari'ah advisory and product development team. Her research interest is Islamic banking products, housing financing models, and Islamic social finance. Nur Harena is a prolific researcher and has published several articles in local and international peer-reviewed journals. She was also awarded multiple research grants from the university, national and international levels in the Islamic finance area. She regularly engaged in the industry by providing training and research in Islamic banking and finance. She has been recognized as one of The Top 150 Most Influential Women in Islamic Business and Finance for 2020, 2021, and 2022 by Cambridge IFA. Nur Harena is currently the Editor of the Journal of Islamic Finance.

Raja Rehan, PhD is a Post-Doctoral Fellow at the Institute of Islamic Banking and Finance, IIUM. He attained a PhD in Finance from the University Kuala

Lumpur (UniKL), Malaysia. Besides this, he holds an MS and MBA in finance from Karachi, Pakistan. Before this, he had extensive academic and industrial experience. He is also an Associate Professor at ILMA University, Karachi, Pakistan, and the Editor-in-Chief of the ILMA Journal of Social Sciences Economics (IJSSE). He worked as a research assistant on a research project at the University of Kuala Lumpur. Also, he served as a finance and accounts executive for almost 12 years, covering the areas of funds management, portfolio management, and building of financial statements and their analysis in the industrial sector of Pakistan. As an active researcher, he has published in reputable international and local publications. His areas of expertise include capital structure, capital markets, energy economics, financial crisis, Islamic finance, and financial technologies.

Yakub Alim Remi obtained his BA (Arabic and Islamic Studies) from the Al-azhar University in 2019 and his HND (Banking and Finance) from Kwara State Polytechnic in 2012. He is currently a master's student in Islamic banking and finance at the Institute of Islamic Banking and Finance, IIUM.

Romzie Rosman, PhD is an Associate Professor at the Institute of Islamic Banking and Finance, IIUM. He is a member of the International Council of Islamic Finance Educators (ICIFE); associate member of the Association of Shariah Advisors in Islamic Finance (ASAS); and associate member of the Malaysian Institute of Accountants (MIA). He is also an Adjunct Professor at the Management and Science University and a Visiting Research Fellow at the Accounting Research Institute, Universiti Teknologi MARA. He graduated with a BA (Hons) in Accounting and Finance from Lancaster University, United Kingdom, in 2000. He was awarded a Master of Business Administration (Islamic Banking and Finance) in 2005 and a PhD (Islamic Banking and Finance) in 2012 from the IIUM. He has published in the Journal of Economic Cooperation and Development, Pacific-Basin Finance Journal, and Journal of Islamic Accounting and Business Research. He is also the Editorial Board Member of the International Journal of Islamic Business and Associate Editor for the Journal of Islamic Accounting and Business Research. His research interests include accounting, Islamic finance and Islamic social finance.

Auwal Adam Sa'ad, PhD is an Assistant Professor at the Institute of Islamic Banking and Finance, IIUM. Auwal completed his LLB Shari'ah at the Islamic University Madinah, Saudi Arabia. He also completed his master's in comparative laws and doctor of philosophy in laws from Ahmad Ibrahim Kulliyyah of Laws, IIUM. His PhD research was on sukuk assets regulations in Islamic capital markets. He is an alumnus of the Cambridge Judge Business School, where he studied "Fintech Innovation: Disrupting the Financial Landscape" in the class of 2021. He is currently working as a Shari'ah consultant to Capital House SA Switzerland on blockchain sukuk applications. Prior to his appointment at the Institute, he was a Lecturer on the Faculty of Management, Universiti Sains Malaysia (USM), and Ahmad Ibrahim Kulliyyah of Laws IIUM. Auwal serves as visiting lecturer at the Islamic University of Minnesota USA and the University of Technology Brunei, where he teaches Islamic capital markets as well as Islamic financial technology (i-Fintech). His areas of research are Islamic fintech, Islamic banking and finance, blockchain sukuk, smart contracts, Central Bank Digital Currency (CBDC), metaverse technology and Islamic finance, Islamic capital markets, Islamic economics, Islamic commercial law, business law, crypto assets regulations and AI applications and artificial neural networks in Islamic banking and finance.

Siti Saffa' Shaharuddin is a PhD candidate at the Institute of Islamic Banking and Finance, IIUM, specializing in Islamic social finance, sustainable finance, and sukuk. With research experience in Green Sukuk, Zakat institutions, and financial exclusion, she aims to contribute to the field and promote responsible Islamic finance practices.

Ashurov Sharofiddin, PhD is currently an Associate Professor at the Institute of Islamic Banking and Finance, IIUM. He completed his bachelor of economics from the International University of Africa, Sudan (2007) and master's degree (Islamic finance) from IIUM (2011). He obtained his PhD in Islamic banking and finance from Sultan Abdul Halim Muadzam Shah International Islamic University (UniSHAMS), Malaysia in 2018. He teaches about money and banking, research methodology, quantitative and qualitative method, principle of economics, principle of accounting, Islamic economics, Zakat for social financing, and financial management analysis for Arabic and English sessions. He is supervising postgraduate students in the field of Islamic banking, Islamic social finance, governance, risk management, and monetary systems. He has published more than 30 papers in reputable journals and participated in international conferences.

Mukhtar Arif Siraj (PhD candidate) completed his master's in Islamic banking and finance from the Institute of Islamic Banking and Finance, IIUM, and bachelor's degree (Islamic Economics) from Universitas Darussalam Gontor, Indonesia. Mukhtar is currently a PhD candidate at the Institute focusing on Shari'ah-compliant investments. He has published his research works in reputable journals.

Muhammad Umar A (PhD candidate) graduated with a degree in Shariah from the OIC Islamic University in Niamey in 2011, then continued his education at the IIIBF Bayero University in Kano, Nigeria, where he studied for his master's degree in Islamic banking and finance (MSc). He is a PhD candidate at the Institute of Islamic banking and Finance, IIUM. Currently he serves as the Head of the Department of Islamic Studies and Lecturer at Federal University Dutsin-Ma. He has published papers in both national and international journals and presented papers at international conferences.

Abubakar Usman, PhD is a research fellow at the Institute of Islamic Banking and Finance, IIUM. He holds dual masters from IIUM and the Institute of

Diplomacy and Foreign Relations (IDFR), and a PhD from the Institute of Malaysian and International Studies (IKMAS), Universiti Kebangsaan Malaysia. His areas of expertise include globalization and development, Islamic finance and development, violent extremism, foreign policy, Islam and politics, diplomacy and strategic studies, and African international relations.

Tika Widiastuti, PhD is a Lecturer on the Faculty of Economics and Business, Universitas Airlangga. She completed her bachelor's degree in the Development Economics Study Program, Universitas Airlangga, then got her master's degree in the Middle East and Islamic Study Program, specializing in Islamic Economics, at University of Indonesia and a PhD in the Study Program of Islamic Economics at Universitas Airlangga. She once served as Chair of the Center for Social Fund Management (PUSPAS) Universitas Airlangga for 2017–2020 and currently serves as Vice Dean of Faculty of Vocational Studies, Universitas Airlangga. She is active as a researcher and publishes articles in reputable international journals, reputable national journals, popular writings, books, copyrights and other scientific works.

Siti Ainatul Mardhiah binti Yusof is a PhD candidate in Islamic banking and finance at the Institute of Islamic Banking and Finance, IIUM. Previously, she graduated with a bachelor's in business administration (Islamic Finance) (Honours) from UniSZA, and with a master's degree in Islamic banking and finance (MIBF) from UiTM. Her primary research concerns mobile banking services of Islamic banks and their customers' awareness and protection. She has actively participated in presenting her research works at both national and international conferences. Her recent research paper titled "The Application of Mobile Banking Services by Malaysian Islamic Banks: An Evaluation on the Customers' Main Concerns" was presented at the 10th ASEAN International Conference on Islamic Finance 2022 (AICIF).

Nurul 'Iffah binti M A Zaaba, PhD (Islamic Banking and Finance) from IIUM in 2023 and currently a Lecturer at UCSI University, Kuala Lumpur branch. Her research area includes corporate zakat of Islamic banks from the reporting and the distribution. Being an active student, 'Iffah has been awarded with scholarships for both her master's and doctorate degrees. She was also listed as the recipient of the Rector's List Award during the 32nd IIUM Convocation Ceremony. Very recently, her co-authored papers (with Rusni Hassan) on zakat have received the Best Paper Award and Best Presenter Award in the 10th ASEAN International Conference on Islamic Finance (AICIF) 2022 and the 10th International Conference on Entrepreneurship, Business & Technology (InCEBT 2022), respectively.

Nor Syahirah Zain (PhD candidate) graduated with a bachelor's in accounting (Hons) from IIUM in 2012 under the scholarship of Bursa Malaysia. Upon graduation, she served the capital market for 3 years before furthering her master's in Islamic finance at INCEIF under the scholarship from Yayasan Khazanah. Thereafter, she worked with a management consulting company where she actively contributed to numerous transformation projects at the national and organizational levels, demonstrating her expertise in guiding clients through strategic planning and execution, managerial finance and business turnaround. Currently, Syahirah is a PhD candidate at the Institute of Islamic Banking and Finance, IIUM under the sponsorship of Maybank, one of the largest banks in Malaysia. Her dedication to her research has recently been recognized, with her latest paper receiving the Best Paper Award at the esteemed 10th ASEAN International Conference on Islamic Finance (AICIF) in 2022. Her research area includes waqf, impact measurement, sustainability, accountability and SRI sukuk.

Habeebullah Zakariyah, PhD is an Assistant Professor at the Institute of Islamic Banking and Finance, IIUM, specializing in Islamic law and muamalat transactions. He graduated with an LLB (Hons) in Shari'ah and Law from Omdurman Islamic University, Sudan. He was awarded a Master of Arts and PhD in Islamic Jurisprudence (Islamic Finance) from the IIUM. His research interests include Islamic finance, Islamic social finance, contemporary issues in Islamic law and Islamic social finance. He has published more than 40 articles and book chapters in reputable journals. Habeebullah has participated in more than 30 national and international conferences.

Introduction

History witnesses that there has been a consistent pattern of humanity's failure to effectively address the issue of sustainability in relation to available resources. This failure has resulted in a multitude of challenges, such as poverty, health disparities, educational deficiencies, social inequality, and hindered economic progress. In the contemporary period characterised by a multitude of uncertainty, our collective existence remains intricately entangled with a plethora of pressing and imperative challenges. One of the key concerns is the optimal use of resources in order to ensure their sustainability for the benefit of future generations. Achieving a harmonious equilibrium in resource utilisation is imperative to prevent adverse impacts on both human well-being and the environment. This necessitates the conservation of seas and forests while effectively utilising the existing resources and concurrently addressing the issue of climate change resulting from the disparity between economic and environmental endeavours.

The United Nations has acknowledged the relevance of this issue by adopting the 17 Sustainable Development Goals (SDGs) in 2015.These goals are also referred to as "Global Goals". By 2030, these objectives are intended to serve as an all-encompassing call to action for concerted group efforts to end world poverty, protect the environment, and ensure global peace and prosperity. The SDGs are interdependent, meaning that actions made in one area have repercussions on results in other domains. In addition, the pursuit of development calls for the integration of social, economic, and environmental sustainability. The fundamental concept of sustainability posits that present choices ought not to hinder the capacity to uphold or enhance future living conditions, including the administration of economic systems. In order to effectively accomplish the Sustainable Development Goals in any given environment, it is imperative to harness the collective potential of creativity, innovation, expertise, technological advancements, and financial resources from all sectors of society.

In light of the present issue, it is crucial to ascertain the manner in which Islam addresses the challenge of sustainability and the solutions it offers for its determination. Islam places significant emphasis on the concept of sustainability. Indeed, the concept of *Maqasid al-Shari'ah* aligns most closely with contemporary notions of sustainability. This can be taken from the evaluation of Islamic sustainable

DOI: 10.4324/9781003468653-1

finance from its local to global initiatives and visible trends that can be traced from Islamic banking and finance. It can also be appreciated from the Islamic capital market's practices. Hence, the title ***"Islamic Sustainable Impact Finance: Issues and Attainable Strategies"*** has been selected with the intention of fulfilling the anticipated expectations.

Part I

Islamic Sustainable Finance

Global Initiatives and Trends

1 Islamic Sustainable Finance

Gulf Experiences

Auwal Adam Sa'ad, Abubakar Usman & Raja Rehan

Introduction

The concept of Islamic sustainable development has been the focus of Muslim economists and rulers throughout the history of Islamic civilization. One of the Prophet Muhammad's missions (PBUH) was to enlighten people on the sustainability of the earth's resources. The prophet was recorded to have said: "whenever you encountered an hour (the day of judgement) and you have a sapling in your hand, you should plant it" (Recorded by Imam Ahmad). This is beyond just planting a tree but is to give hope and to showcase the importance of continuity in working, developing and sustaining the resources of this earth even though the earth has already come to an end. The UN's 17 Sustainable Development Goals (SDGs) are tremendously significant in addressing the challenges confronted by our environment and humanity as a whole. The accomplishment of these goals may require extraordinary efforts and resources as well as collaboration across the world, which must include governments as well as private sectors. The financial sector is relatively important and regarded as a driver of a successful sustainable development.

Islamic Sustainable Finance in Saudi Arabia

The Kingdom of Saudi Arabia is considered the largest economy in the Middle East by some margin. The Kingdom is among the pioneer countries that adopted Islamic banking and finance as a system of financing parallel with the conventional system (Aldarabseh, 2019). Saudi Arabia currently holds the largest share of Islamic banking assets at over 30%, more than the total share held by Iran (17%) and Malaysia (11%), which respectively occupy the second and third position in the list. Similarly, Saudi Arabia is behind only Malaysia in terms of developing a robust Islamic economy ecosystem, as reported by Dinar Standard Report (2022). According to the recent reports, Saudi Arabia's Islamic banking and finance has been outperforming its conventional counterparts. It has recorded double-digit development rates (Baeshen & Shaheen, 2021). It has established new Islamic fintech platforms that utilize revolutionary technologies including Artificial Intelligence (AI), blockchain, big data, Internet of Things (IoT) devices (that provide Islamic financial services in the most modern, sophisticated and transparent way) and extensive cloud computing (Ali et al., 2019).

DOI: 10.4324/9781003468653-3

Despite the Covid-19 pandemic outbreak, Saudi Arabia, along with the UAE, Malaysia and Nigeria have made outstanding commitments towards bolstering the Islamic economy, particularly in Halal food sector, Islamic finance and fintech. At the height of the Covid-19 pandemic, many Saudi companies adopted i-fintech; within a year (2020–2021), there was a dramatic increase of the companies adopting i-fintech with the number rising from two in 2020 to 21 companies in 2021 (Glavina et al., 2021).

- In addition to fintech, during the Covid-19 pandemic sovereign sukuk issuance by the Saudi government also increased dramatically, particularly the green sukuk (Zoair & Mohamed, 2022). In fact, despite the challenges of the pandemic, Saudi Arabia managed to retain its leading position in the global sovereign sukuk market with a 28.9% (USD 21.4 billion) share. Likewise, Saudi Arabia is behind only Malaysia and the UAE with USD 9.1 billion or 16.2 percent of the corporate sukuk total market share. All this evidence indicates the sustainability of Islamic finance.
- Islamic sustainable finance in Qatar.

  Qatar is considered one of the richest economies in the Middle East. Its gross domestic product (GDP) in 2019, prior to the outbreak of the Covid-19 pandemic, amounted to 667.8 billion Qatari Riyals (approximately $183.41 billion). Qatar is a tiny city-state in terms of geography. However, in terms of Islamic banking and finance assets, as of early 2020 it accounted for up to 6.1% of the Islamic banking and finance total global assets (Mohammed et al., 2020). The Islamic finance sector in Qatar is classified into four main sectors including Islamic banks, Takaful insurance companies, Islamic finance companies and Islamic investment companies. The sector issues Islamic finance products that include Sukuk, investment funds and Islamic indices. Qatar Islamic banking and finance has earned a positive reputation over the years, particularly in digital innovation. As testaments to its reputable pedigree, Qatar Islamic Bank (QIB) was awarded four times for its leadership in digital innovation at the Digital Bankers Innovation Awards 2022. One of its standout features is its cash management, the "outstanding account opening and onboarding initiative in Qatar" (Hussain, 2022, p. 1). In fact, in April 2022, Masraf Al Rayan (MAR) launched its Sustainable Finance Framework, which was the first of its kind for an Islamic bank in Qatar. The purpose of the framework was to closely follow the launch of Qatar Financial Centre's Sustainable Sukuk and Bonds Framework. This points to Qatar's immense desire and deliberate effort to make itself a key player in the Islamic sustainable space (Kareem, 2022).

Although the size of the Islamic banking and finance sector is approximately half that of the conventional sector, the Islamic sector has been gaining ground and has been growing annually. In 2015, Qatar's Islamic banking and finance assets amount to QR 305 (US$ 96 billion). However, by 2019, total assets made a significant rise to QR 416 billion (US$ 114.25 billion). Such a steady rise is testament to the sustainable alternative Islamic finance provides alongside conventional options. In recent years, Qatar has faced its own political and economic challenges as a result of the political blockade imposed by the four neighbouring Gulf countries, including the Kingdom of Saudi Arabia, the United Arab Emirates, Bahrain and Egypt. The blockade has triggered a huge economic and diplomatic crisis that threatens Qatar's survival. This coincided with Qatar's commitment to hosting the 2022 FIFA World Cup, which required massive financial commitments. Amid all these challenges, the Covid-19 pandemic broke out and devastated not only Qatar's economy but the global economy as a whole. The impact of Covid-19 on Qatar's economy was evident in the shrinking public budget reported by the country's Ministry of Finance. Qatar's government had to curtail public expenditure significantly on major projects from QR26.1 billion in the last quarter of 2019 to QR15.3 billion in the second quarter of 2020 (Mohammed et al., 2020). Similarly, foreign trade (import, export and trade balance) also dropped significantly from over QR24billion in December 2019 to nearly QR13 billion in June 2020 (Mohammed et al., 2020).

Despite such challenges, Islamic financial tools such as zakat, infaq, qard hasan and waqf were proven to be resilient and more sustainable than other forms of financing (Mohammed et al., 2020). Furthermore, despite the crisis, there has been excessive liquidity in the Islamic banks about Farmosa Sukuk, Waqf, Zakat and so on. Policies that are based on the objectives of Shari'ah were found to have great potential for reinforcing Qatar's economy to regain its stability (Mohammed et al., 2020). It was found that Islamic banking and finance is not only registering outstanding performance in terms of profit making, but also in terms of the Capital Adequacy Ratio and Liquidity Coverage Ratio (LCR) (Akkas & Al Samman, 2021; Mohammed et al., 2020). Sukuk has been the dominant among the various Islamic financial instruments functioning in Qatar. The country's maiden Formosa Sukuk was first issued in January 2020. It showed promise from the beginning, which was evident in Qatar's government need to inject QR10 million to Qatar Stock Exchange as part of the stimulus package, but it raised $800 million from the Formosa Sukuk despite initially planning to raise just $650 million (Hidayat et al., 2020; Mohammed et al., 2020). Qatar is also one of the leading countries in terms of corporate sukuk with US$ 2.1 billion, which is equivalent to 3.6% of the total share of corporate sukuk. In addition to Sukuk, other Islamic financial instruments, such as Takaful, Waqf and Zakat, have also shown promise (Mohammed et al., 2020). All these confirmed the potential of Islamic finance as a sustainable alternative to regaining economic stability in Qatar as the Covid-19 pandemic begins to show its end and with the country aiming to recover from the diplomatic crisis that threatened its sovereignty not that long ago.

Islamic Sustainable Finance in the United Arab Emirates

The United Arab Emirates is one of the most successful economies, not only in the Middle East but in the world. The UAE has the second-highest GDP per capita among the GCC, surpassed only by Qatar. The UAE's banking and financial sector is considered the biggest in the GCC. Along with Bahrain, Malaysia,

Indonesia and Saudi Arabia, the United Arab Emirates are the most developed countries in terms of Islamic finance. The Islamic Finance Development Indicator ranked the UAE as the fourth most developed country in Islamic finance during 2020, with seven fully-fledged Islamic banks and various other conventional banks operating Islamic windows (Ahmed & Robinson, 2021). The UAE also holds the second-largest Islamic banking assets globally (behind Saudi Arabia), with $169.2 billion as of the second quarter of 2020 (Domat, 2020). In fact, part of the UAE's rich experience of Islamic banking and finance is Dubai Islamic Bank, which was established over 40 years ago. Currently, the bank holds the second largest assets among Islamic banks in the world (Domat, 2020). In 2006, Dubai declared the restructuring of its main stock exchange, known as the Dubai Financial Market, to become the world's first Islamic stock exchange. Since then, Islamic banking and finance has made outstanding progress. In 2016, the UAE cabinet approved Shari'ah Authority launch, a national regulatory body to set standards for Islamic finance products (Bouyamourn, 2016). As of 2021, the Islamic Financial Services Board (IFSB) reported that over 20% of the banking products in the UAE currently comprise Islamic finance products (Ahmed & Robinson, 2021).

Like most of the leading economies where Islamic banking and finance have been making steady progress, the UAE was massively affected by the Covid-19 pandemic. During 2020 and the first part of 2021, Islamic banking and finance assets growth remained reasonable, with most banks reporting lower profits. According to Ahmed and Robinson (2021), some UAE banks closed some of their branches due to the losses caused by the pandemic. However, during the height of the pandemic, there was a noticeable increase in the issuance of sustainable sukuk, which was expected to continue after the pandemic due to the Islamic finance focus on social roles. An Emirati real estate and retail giant, Majid Al Futtaim, launched the first corporate green sukuk worth US$600 million on the NASDAQ stock exchange in Dubai (Ahmed & Robinson, 2021), with proceeds planned to be used for the financing and refinancing of current and future green projects.

Islamic Sustainable Finance in Kuwait

Kuwait is one of the universal players and is considered a pioneer in the substantial Islamic finance industry. Kuwait's Islamic Finance Services (IFS) are well accepted around the globe. Kuwait also holds one of the major Islamic finance and banking industries which has nearly 46% of the local banking industry (Fitch Ratings, 2021). The Kuwait Finance House (KFH) is one of the principal Islamic banks of the globe and plays a central role in announcing sustainable Islamic finance products to its clients locally and internationally via its offices in Malaysia, Turkey and Bahrain (IMF, 2014). KFH delivers a sustainable Islamic finance model to regulatory bodies and the central government to implement a comprehensive sustainable Islamic financial system that delivers continuous growth. Visibly, there are nearly 30 fintech organizations functioning in Kuwait and presenting Shari'ah finance products to financial markets (Sekar, 2021).

Like the experiences of other countries in the Gulf region, Kuwait's economy has also faced the consequences of the financial crisis and Covid-19 pandemic. The Kuwait Finance House faced liquidity matters throughout the financial crisis of 2007–2008 (Jan & Marimuthu, 2015; Husna et al., 2012). Kuwait's economy is severely suffering because of the rising inflation rate, which rose up to 4.30% at the end of 2021 and was also reported unchanged till the end of January 2022. Notably, the identified rate of inflation in Kuwait is the highest since 2011 (IBRD, 2022). Also, Kuwait Central Statistical Bureau stated that prices of numerous everyday essentials surged rapidly and reached at their peak in January 2022 in comparison with their previous year's states; for instance, prices of food and beverages (6.53% vs 6.89% of December 2021), transportation fares (4.6 % vs 4.5% of December 2021) and household equipment prices (2.4% vs 2.3% of December 2021). (Trading Economic, 2022). As a result, Kuwait's government, which always supports its citizens in several ways and expends a huge fragment of its yearly budget on employees' payments and their welfare, is now encouraging citizens to set up their private minor businesses. On the flip side, numerous privately-owned businesses seemed to close down because of vast losses after the Covid-19 outbreak (Hagagy, 2021).

In view of these factors, it is essential for Kuwait to focus more on a sustainable financial system that can handle the hazardous effects on the country's economy of the former financial crisis and the pandemic. Undoubtedly, the continuous financial disasters indicate the need for an alternate sustainable financial system for Kuwait's economy. Islamic finance is a good choice to deliver continuous and sustainable growth. Though the Islamic financial system is not totally isolated from the crisis, it can be an alternative option that mitigates the undesirable impacts of divergent situations and can always deliver sustainable financial growth for Kuwait's economy (Alhammadi, 2022). Lately, the Central Bank of Kuwait announced a standard for banks to maintain sustainable finance. The banks are clearly instructed to issue sustainability reports or to add a new section on sustainability to their financial reports. Notably, in the initial quarter of 2022, Kuwait's Islamic banking industry holds the largest market segment; i.e. 46% of assets of the country's overall banking sector (Kareem, 2022; Fitch Ratings, 2021). Thus, the existing state is further urging Kuwait's Islamic banking sector to preserve robust sustainability for the continuation of the business. Clearly, Kuwait requires a further Islamic sustainable finance structure to cope with prevailing and foreseen financial fiascos.

Islamic Sustainable Finance in Oman

The development of Islamic finance is still measured at an early phase in the Sultanate of Oman. Despite this, the demand for Islamic finance-based sustainable products is very strong among the 4.7 million Omanis (IMF, 2021). Moody Investor Services indicated that Oman's market is the second-largest growing market of Islamic finance. Thus, in view of the growing demand, the government is providing significant support for evolving a sustainable system. The surge of the coronavirus pandemic and the downward plunge of oil prices in the previous year led the country's economy towards a concealed financial fiasco. However, the evolution of the Islamic sector continued to extend its wings and deliver sustainable growth. According to the Central Bank of Oman (CBO), Islamic banks in Oman have accomplished a milestone and shown vigorous growth of 30% from 2013 to 2020, and now hold 15% of the whole market shares (CBO, 2021). Remarkably, the main cause of the economic recession in Oman is the falling oil prices which have distressed the hydrocarbon industry of the country (Al Jabri et al., 2022). On the flip side, it is anticipated that Oman will run out of oil and other natural resources such as gas reserves in the coming two decades (Warrak, 2022). Indeed, the conditions are very challenging for a nation that generates its most significant profits from the export of crude oil. The growing financial deficits from the fiscal year 2019–2020 and increasing reliance on outside finances forced global credit rating agencies such as Fitch Group, Moody's Investor Services and S&P Global Rating to decrease Oman's position, ranking it to a junk position. Likewise, Gulf Corporation Council, which often offered development assistance funds to Oman, stipulates that the republic's economic situation has become more vulnerable because of the rising negative impact of the Covid-19 pandemic (Abouzzohour, 2021). Consequently, the government of Oman has announced that it will move out gradually from natural resources-generated income and look for other ways to maintain sustainable revenue. Importantly, one of the core objectives Oman's government has been concentrating on is to boost sustainable Islamic finance, particularly in the banking sector (Shaukat & Raisi, 2017).

Notably, Oman was the last country of the GCC to adopt Islamic Banking (Salim & Al Ani, 2015). In 2021, the Omani Islamic banks' funding has displayed steady growth; however, the level of financing is not reasonable (Otman, 2022). Though Oman is among those countries in which Islamic banks attained the targets of high sustainable growth, it is anticipated that Islamic finance in Oman will rapidly grow and start to deliver sustainable growth in the forthcoming years (Osmanovic et al., 2022). Recently, the first Islamic bank of Oman, Bank Nizwa, announced they would raise sustainability-linked Islamic financing, thus paving the way for other banks to adopt Islamic sustainable finance practices. Recently, the Central Bank of Oman announced its plan to launch further Islamic financial instruments for the money market to deliver sustainable growth to the Islamic industry and expand investors' assets (Zawya, 2022). Obviously, the development of sustainable Islamic finance in the Oman banking sector will shape the future of Islamic finance.

Islamic Sustainable Finance in Bahrain

Bahrain, with a total of 1.5 million residents, is recognized as one of the main leaders of the Islamic finance world, particularly in the nations of the Gulf Cooperation Council (GCC). Remarkably, Bahrain holds the second rank in the Middle East and North Africa (MENA) region and is also considered the fourth country mounting sustainable Islamic finance rapidly in the sphere (EDB Bahrain, 2021). Bahrain Islamic Bank (BisB) has signed a three-year roadmap to connect with Sustainability Excellence,. which is a research firm and is also considered a specialist in sustainability-based reporting, to get support in maintaining the bank's sustainability and ESG plans (BisB, 2021). A large number of Islamic foundations are gearing up in Bahrain for innovative and sustainable Islamic finance products (ICD, 2021). Thus, Bahrain has effectively established numerous sustainable finance-related Shari'ah-based products, such as the Islamic exchange of cryptocurrencies, the second main Islamic Real Estate Investment Trust (REIT) in the GCC region and a digital platform of BisB, the first entirely Islamic digital Tejoori rapid finance that allows its clients to conduct immediate transactions in just five minutes (Poon et al., 2020). Also, Bahrain FinTech Bay operates the Global Islamic Sustainable Center of Fintech (GISFC) with the collaboration of its local, international and other regional members. GISFC is a Bahrain-based important platform operating in the Middle East and African countries with an emphasis on Islamic finance-based sustainable fintech. Bahrain's financial sector, which contributes 17.8% to the overall country's GDP, focuses more on maintaining Shari'ah-based sustainable financial growth (Abdulla et al., 2020)

The Covid-19 pandemic harshly impacted Bahrain's capital markets, and all businesses' performance declined to an alarming state. Subsequently, the rapidly rising GDP of the country fell to −4.9%, which is the largest GDP drop in Bahrain's whole history (Manaa & Haq, 2021). Hence, in view of recent settings, the International Monetary Fund has projected that the adverse trend of the country's GDP will continue, but that it may also get better at an identically slow speed (IMF, 2021). Several scholars predict that Islamic finance offers sustainable financial tools to help economies pass securely from the adverse effects of financial and economic fiascos (see Raza Rabbani et al., 2021; Abdul Hadi et al., 2019). Thus Bahrain, which is known as the leading Islamic finance hub and offers several sustainable Islamic fintech products, needs to be focused more on adopting sustainable Islamic finance.

Conclusion

It is imperative that Islamic sustainable finance is practiced by all GCC members, including Saudi Arabia, Kuwait, Oman, Qatar, Bahrain and the United Arab Emirates. Bahrain's financial sector, which contributes 17.8% to the overall country's GDP, focuses more on maintaining Shari'ah-based sustainable financial growth. One of the core objectives of Oman's government is to boost sustainable Islamic finance, particularly in the banking sector. Moreover, the first Islamic bank of Oman, Bank Nizwa, announced that it would raise sustainability-linked Islamic financing. Thus, Bank Nizwa paved the way for other banks to adopt Islamic sustainable finance practices. The Central Bank of Kuwait announced a standard for banks to maintain sustainable finance. The banks were clearly instructed to issue sustainability reports or to add a new section on sustainability in their financial reports. In the UAE, however, during the height of the pandemic, there was a noticeable increase in the issuance of sustainable sukuk, which was expected to continue after the pandemic due to the Islamic finance focus on social roles. Qatar is also one of the leading countries in terms of corporate sukuk with US$ 2.1 billion, which is equivalent to 3.6% of the total share of corporate sukuk. In addition to sukuk, other Islamic financial instruments such Takaful, Waqf and Zakat have also shown promise. As one of the leaders in the Islamic banking and financial sector, the Kingdom of Saudi Arabia has been moving towards innovative and sustainable Islamic finance. It has established new Islamic fintech platforms that utilize revolutionary technologies including Artificial Intelligence (AI), blockchain, big data and Internet of Things (IoT) devices that provide Islamic financial services in the most modern, sophisticated, transparent and sustainable ways.

References

Abdul Hadi, A. R., Hussain, H. I., Zainudin, Z., & Rehan, R. (2019). Analyzing Performance of Shari'ah and Non-Shari'ah Portfolios during the Global Financial Crisis 2007–2008: Malaysia's Experience. In *The Sixth ASEAN International Conference 2019, held in Bali, Indonesia* (pp. 145–157).

Abdulla, Y., Ebrahim, R., & Naser, H. (2020, November). Sustainability in the Banking Sector: The Case of Bahrain. In *2020 Second International Sustainability and Resilience Conference: Technology and Innovation in Building Designs (51154)* (pp. 1–4). IAEME, Chennai.

Abouzzohour, Y. (2021). *One Year into His Reign, Oman's Sultan Must Renegotiate the Social Contract and Prioritize Diversification, Brookings*. www.brookings.edu/blog/order-from-chaos/2021/01/13/one-year-into-his-reign-omans-sultan-must-renegotiate-the-social-contract-and-prioritize-diversification/ (Accessed 8 December 2022).

Ahmed, S., & Robinson, L. (2021). *UAE Islamic Finance: Steady Growth Through Adversity*. www.squirepattonboggs.com/-/media/files/insights/publications/2021/04/uae-islamic-finance/uae-islamic-finance.pdf (Accessed 6 January 2023).

Akkas, E., & Al Samman, H. (2021). Are Islamic Financial Institutions More Resilient Against the COVID-19 Pandemic in the GCC Countries? *International Journal of Islamic and Middle Eastern Finance and Management*, 28

Aldarabseh, W. M. (2019). The Interest in Islamic Finance Contracts in Saudi Arabia as Viewed by Google Trends. *International Journal of Economics and Finance*, 11(9), 9.

Alhammadi, S. (2022). Analyzing the Role of Islamic Finance in Kuwait Regarding Sustainable Economic Development in COVID-19 Era. *Sustainability*, 14(2), 701.

Ali, H., Mohamed, H., Hashmi, H. S., & Hassan, M. (2019). Global Landscape of the Islamic Fintech: Opportunities, Challenges and Future Ahead. *COMSATS Journal of Islamic Finance*, 4(2), 29–53.

Al Jabri, S., Raghavan, M., & Vespignani, J. (2022). Oil Prices and Fiscal Policy in an Oil-Exporter Country: Empirical Evidence from Oman. *Energy Economics*, 111, 106103.

Baeshen, L., & Shaheen, R. (2021). Analysis of Performance of Islamic Banks in Saudi Arabia. *PalArch's Journal of Archaeology of Egypt/Egyptology*, 18(13), 194–202.

BisB. (2021). *BisB Outlines a Three-Year Sustainability Roadmap*. www.bisb.com/en/node/1431 (Accessed 8 December 2022).

Bouyamourn, A. (2016). UAE Cabinet Approves Shari'ah Authority Launch. *The National News*. www.thenationalnews.com/business/uae-cabinet-approves-Shari'ah-authority-launch-1.202169 (Accessed 6 January 2023).

CBO. (2021). *Islamic Banking Assets in Oman Achieve 15% Market Share in June 2021*. https://cbo.gov.om/News/293 (Accessed 17 December 2022).

Domat, C. (2020). Islamic Finance: Just for Muslim-Majority Nations? *Global Finance*. www.gfmag.com/topics/blogs/islamic-finance-just-muslim-majority-nations (Accessed 7 January 2023).

EDB Bahrain. (2021). *Bahrain Ranks Fourth Globally and Second in MENA for Islamic Finance Development Indicator*. www.bahrainedb.com/latest-news/bahrain-ranks-fourth-globally-and-second-in-mena-for-islamic-finance-development-indicator (Accessed 17 December 2022).

Fitch Ratings. (2021). *Kuwait Remains Among the Largest Islamic Banking Markets*. www.fitchratings.com/research/islamic-finance/kuwaiti-islamic-banks-see-slower-growth-resilient-asset-quality-20-10-2021 (Accessed 10 December 2022).

Glavina, S., Aidrus, I., & Trusova, A. (2021). Assessment of the Competitiveness of Islamic Fintech Implementation: A Composite Indicator for Cross-Country Analysis. *Journal of Risk and Financial Management*, 14(12), 602.

Hagagy, A. (2021). *Kuwait's Economic Makeover Under Threat as Small Businesses Fight for Life*. www.reuters.com/world/middle-east/kuwaits-economic-makeover-under-threat-small-businesses-fight-life-2021-08-12/ (Accessed 25 February 2022).

Hidayat, S. E., Farooq, M. O., & Alim, E. A. (2020). *Impacts of the COVID-19 Outbreak on Islamic Finance in the OIC Countries*. Republic of Indonesia: KNEKS.

Husna, H. N., Rahman, R. A., Graff, M., Mirani, M. A., Shah, S. M. M., Alani, J., & Brezinova, O. (2012). Financial Distress–Detection Model for Islamic Banks. *International Journal of Trade, Economics & Finance*, 3(3).

Hussain, A. (2022). *Qatar: Islamic Green Sustainable Finance on the Rise*. https://marketingstorageragrs.blob.core.windows.net/webfiles/IFN_Hussain.pdf (Accessed 20 December 2022).

IBRD. (2022). *The World Bank*. https://data.worldbank.org/indicator/FP.CPI.TOTL.ZG?locations=KW (Accessed 25 February 2022).

ICD. (2021). *Publications, Islamic Development for the Development of the Private Sector*. https://icd-ps.org/en/publications (Accessed 8 March 2022).

IMF. (2014). *International Monetary Fund. Middle East and Central Asia Dept, IMF eLibrary*.

IMF. (2021). *World Economic Outlook, October 2021: Recovery During a Pandemic*. www.imf.org/en/Publications/WEO/Issues/2021/10/12/world-economic-outlook-october-2021

Jan, A., & Marimuthu, M. (2015). Sustainability Profile of Islamic Banking Industry: Evidence from World Top Five Islamic Banking Countries. *International Journal of Economics and Finance*, 7(5), 125–139.

Kareem, M. (2022). *Central Bank of Kuwait Tells Local Banks to Begin Sustainability Reporting*. https://islamicsustainable.com/central-bank-of-kuwait-tells-local-banks-to-begin-sustainability-reporting/ (Accessed 10 December 2022).

Manaa, A., & ul Haq, M. A. (2021). The Effects of SMEs, Population and Education Level on Unemployment in Kingdom of Bahrain. *IKSP Journal of Business and Economics*, 1(2), 23–33.

Mohammed, M. M., Tok, M. E., & Ali, S. N. (2020). The Potential of Islamic Finance in Reinforcing and Regaining Economic Stability in Qatar. *Journal of Economic Cooperation & Development*, 41(4), 191–217.

Osmanovic, N., Puska, A., Thomas, S. S., & Stojanovic, I. (2022). Sustainable Economic Performances of Islamic Banks in Gulf Countries: Bahrain, Oman, Saudi Arabia and the United Arab Emirates. *Journal of Sustainable Finance & Investment*, 1–15.

Otman, A. (2022). Islamic Bank and Sustainable Development Goals in the Arab World: A Case Study of Selected Countries. *Arab Monetary Fund, 94–2022*. https://www.amf.org.ae/sites/default/files/publications/2022-01/islamic-banks-and-sustainable-development-goals-in-the-arab-world-a-case-study-of-selected-countries.pdf

Poon, J., Chow, Y. W., Ewers, M., & Ramli, R. (2020). The Role of Skills in Islamic Financial Innovation: Evidence from Bahrain and Malaysia. *Journal of Open Innovation: Technology, Market, and Complexity*, 6(3), 47.

Raza Rabbani, M., Asad Mohd. Ali, M., Rahiman, H. U., Atif, M., Zulfikar, Z., & Naseem, Y. (2021). The Response of Islamic Financial Service to the COVID-19 Pandemic: The Open Social Innovation of the Financial System. *Journal of Open Innovation: Technology, Market, and Complexity*, 7(1), 85.

Salim, B. F., & Al Ani, M. K. (2015). The Impact of Islamic Banking Challenges and Opportunities on the Market Share: Evidence from Oman. *European Journal of Economics, Finance and Administrative Sciences*, 76.

Sekar, H. (2021). *ETF's in GCC: How far Have They Come? MENA Intelligence, Marmore*. www.marmoremena.com/etfs-in-gcc-how-far-have-they-come/ (Accessed 18 February 2022).

Shaukat, M., & Raisi, A. A. (2017). Risk Sharing Equity-Based Islamic Finance, Macroeconomic Resilience and Significance to Oman as a New Entrant. *Journal of Finance, Accounting & Management*, 8(1).

Trading Economic. (2022). *Kuwait Inflation Rate*. https://tradingeconomics.com/kuwait/inflation-cpi (Accessed 25 February 2022).

Warrak, M. (2022). What Is the Future of Arab Oil by 2050 in a Zero-Emission World? *Mena 2022 Oil and Gas Conference*.

Zawya. (2022). *Exchange-Traded Funds to Be in Strong Demand in 2022, By Refinitiv*. www.zawya.com/mena/en/business/story/ExchangeTraded_Funds_to_be_in_strong_demand_in_2022-SNG_285471662/ (Accessed 30 January 2022).

Zoair, M., & Mohamed, A. (2022, October 31). Smart Sukuk Issuance Platforms based on Blockchain Technology to Finance Small and Medium Enterprises in the Kingdom of Saudi Arabia: Opportunities and Challenges. *Smart Sukuk Issuance Platforms Based on Blockchain Technology to Finance Small and Medium Enterprises in the Kingdom of Saudi Arabia: Opportunities and Challenges*.

2 Islamic Sustainable Finance

Experiences of African Countries

Habeebullah Zakariyah, Nur Farhah Mahadi, Muhammad Umar A & Yakub Alim Remi

Introduction

The notion of sustainability is complex and evolving. Sustainability is closely connected to the field of finance and socio-economic discussion and is a relatively new subject. It is collectively known as "sustainable finance "or "sustainable impact finance". According to the World Bank Group, which closely follows the definition provided by the European Commission, "sustainable impact finance" relates to "the process of taking due account of environmental, social and governance (ESG) considerations when making investment decisions in the financial sector, leading to increase longer-term investments into sustainable economic activities and projects". The discussion on sustainable impact finance can be attributed closely to the sustainable development discourse that emerged from the Brundtland report in 1987. There are many published books and research regarding sustainable impact finance currently available on the market. However, there is no specific book on the topic of sustainable impact finance derived from the perspective of Shari'ah. Whilst Shari'ah provides the world with a unique perspective of a religious worldview, it is apparent that sustainable impact finance should be discussed and tremendously relevant to the growing Islamic banking and finance industry globally. Islamic banking and finance not only offer to their practitioners, customers, shareholders, and investors new and innovative products, but they also offer to the public the possibility of having Islamic sustainable impact finance through the implementation of classical principles and practices. Instead of only focusing on inventing new strategies for facing modern issues and developments, Islamic sustainable impact finance offers a consideration of hybrid innovative strategies that appreciate past practices and evolve towards capturing the best for the future.

There is a clear and growing interest in Islamic banking and finance relating to environmental, social, and governance matters. This is obvious when it comes to businesses, investments, financing, and their relevant decision-making processes, which may include the operation and management of the involved corporate players, investors, and financiers. Simultaneously, while meeting the sustainable impact development agendas as promoted by many governments, the players of Islamic banking and finance are triggered to find the most suitable practices or operations to meet the need for sustainable socio-economic development or business-oriented projects while Shari'ah-compliance requirements must

DOI: 10.4324/9781003468653-4

simultaneously be fulfilled. This brings us to the importance of discussing Islamic sustainable impact finance and its related issues while analysing its achievable strategies. It is indeed timely to have such a research book published on this subject that stands as a needed reference for the growing industry globally. The book shall be an international book whose primary mission is to explore, evaluate, and discover the real and innovative practices of Islamic sustainable finance that can be detected from around the globe. It is important to appreciate the application of Islamic sustainable finance and its instruments in the financial market both globally and locally. This chapter is set to open a new dimension of discussions relating to Islamic sustainable finance and its impacts on the investment world in Africa. The goal of this chapter is to provide an overview of sustainable finance in Africa, with specific reference to Nigeria as a hub of Islamic finance in west Africa.

Islamic Finance and Sustainable Development

Islamic finance expanded at a yearly rate of 17 percent from 2009–2013 and is evaluated to have surpassed USD 2 trillion in 2014. Despite its fast development, there is a need for Islamic banks to fulfil social objectives (Siddiqi, 2004). **Islamic sustainable finance is all out to deal with** man's social injustices **leading to greediness, envy, hatred, and arrogance**. Africa has a large and growing gap between the rich and the poor. It is typical in Africa that a wealthy elite has captured the benefits of economic growth at the expense of ordinary Africans. For instance, an African wealthy man earns 8,000 times more in one day than a poor African who will battle to provide for his basic needs in a year. The African richest man would have to spend $1 million a day for 42 years to exhaust his fortune, while more than 112 million people in 2010 were living in poverty, a rise of 69 percent; the number of millionaires increased by 44 percent during the same time (Emmanuel et al., 2017). Africa needs workable sustainable finance to address the issue of "extreme poverty", which is very pertinent, thus the continent is struggling with **low incomes and the inability to acquire the basic goods and services necessary for survival with dignity. Hence, there are low levels of health and education, poor access to clean water and sanitation, inadequate physical security, lack of voice, and insufficient capacity and opportunity to better one's life. These are basic needs for human beings to live peacefully.** However, the continent is also ravaged by high conflict and economic inequality as a key factor in that conflict, which rendered many people into IDPs and refugees. **As stated by Nelson Mandela:**

> **Overcoming poverty is not a task of charity, rather it is an act of justice. Like Slavery and Apartheid, poverty is not natural. It is man-made, and it can be overcome and eradicated by the actions of human beings. Sometimes it falls on a generation to be great. You can be that great generation. Let your greatness blossom.**
>
> **(Mandela, 2005)**

In Nigeria, Islamic banking and finance is an avenue to provide sustainable finance to achieve SDGs gools. Many efforts have been put in place to establish non-interest banks in Nigeria; as of now, there are four fully-fledged non-interest banks in Nigeria: Jaiz Bank, which was established in 2013 and listed on the Nigerian Stock Exchange in 2017; TAJ Bank, which was granted a license in July 2019 by the Central Bank of Nigeria (CBN); Stanbic Bank, which operates an Islamic banking window; and Sterling Bank, which received regulatory approval in 2020 to restructure and spin off its Islamic window into a standalone non-interest bank serving the personal and corporate segments. On the other hand, there are four Shari'ah-based microfinance institutions: Al-Barakah Microfinance Bank, Tijarah Microfinance Bank, I-Care Microfinance Bank, and Giginya Microfinance Bank. These are instruments to ensure that all financial related matters are geared to address the issues of sustainable development in the country by providing finance in a more efficient and sustainable way.

Global Poverty

There are many African countries listed as having the highest poverty rates based on World Bank :

Table 2.1 Countries With the Highest Poverty Rates

S/No	*Country*	*Rate of poverty in Percentage*
1	South Sudan	82.30%
2	Equatorial Guinea	76.80%
3	Madagascar	70.70%
4	Guinea Bissau	69.30%
5	Eritrea	69.00%
6	Sao Tome and Principe	66.70%
7	Burundi	64.90%
8	Democratic Republic of the Congo	63.90%
9	Central African Republic	62.00%
10	Guatemala	59.30%

Source: World Bank

Demand for Interest-free Financial Products

As awareness of the non-interest financial products grows, so does the demand increase for the Islamic financial industry. Aliyu (2012), in the process of emphasizing the magnitudes of the non-interest financial products, asserts that the monopoly status enjoyed by the conventional system of banking and finance globally changed with the emergence of the Islamic system, which is based on the principles of the Shari'ah (Islamic law). The conventional system, which was formerly the only medium of financial transactions, with impurity nurtures and survives on interest, hatches uncertainty, and multiplies speculation, all for profit. The Islamic financial system is unique as it provides many opportunities to safely invest funds and thus many chances to acquire huge profits, and one is always safe as he operates halal investments (Rarick, 2009). With 38.6% of the population being Muslim, the Republic of Côte d'Ivoire, often known as the Ivory Coast, is the primary economic and financial hub of the West African Economic and Monetary Union (WAEMU). It also supports the booming Islamic banking industry in the region. Ivory Coast, one of the nations with the greatest economic growth rates, is the top exporter of cocoa and cashews, a net exporter of oil, and it has a robust manufacturing industry. According to the World Bank, the nation has seen rapid, strong, and consistent economic growth since 2012. However, the COVID-19 issue severely hurt the nation's economy, causing a decline that started in 2020. However, Ivory Coast's GDP was already starting to slow before the pandemic, which influenced the government to look at Islamic financing to increase domestic investment and draw international capital. The Central Bank of West African States, or Banque Centrale des Etats de l'Afrique de l'Ouest (BCEAO), is the central financial institution for the region. The Islamic Corporation for the Development of the Private Sector (ICD), a subsidiary of the IsDB, is also collaborating with several regional governments to find solutions to the problem of double taxation for Islamic transactions.

The Inter-African Conference on Insurance Markets (CIMA) issued regulations in December 2019 that allow both full-fledged and window-based Takaful and re-Takaful activities with a minimum share capital of XOF3 billion ($5.02 million). Along with the other 13 nations that the CIMA supervises, the Ivory Coast is subject to the rules (Tamano, 2022-IFN). The West Africa country of Senegal, where 96% of the population is Muslim, continues to be a desirable place to invest, especially for Islamic investors. The country also features a competitive banking sector and a generally calm political climate. Fish, phosphate, nuts, and tourism industries all contribute significantly to Senegal's economy, and about a third of its total government spending is on international aid. The economy expanded by more than 6 percent every year between 2014 and 2018, and Senegal's GDP was $24.9 billion in 2020, according to the World Bank. The COVID-19 pandemic has slowed developments in the industries contributing to the GDP of the country, particularly tourism, and unfortunately, roughly half of the population lives below the poverty level (Tamano, 2022-IFN).

Islamic Finance and Social Sectors

Islamic social finance is considered one of the tools used by Shari'ah to table the issue of wealth redistribution. The main instruments consist of zakat, waqf, infaq, and sadaqah. Zakat, for instance, is one of the pillars of Islam and aims to provide a just platform for wealth distribution. One of the ultimate goals of zakat is poverty elevation. This is confirmed by a study conducted by Shirazi & Amin (2009), who elaborated on the possibility of using zakat funds collected by zakat institutions to solve poverty, especially in the Organization of the Islamic Conference (OIC) countries. This study concluded that an average of 1.8 percent to 4.3 percent of GDP annually can be realized. Waqf, on the other hand, is one of the most significant instruments in Islamic development and civilization. This instrument came into existence through Islamic teaching and practices. According to Islahi (1992), a well-established and systematically organized waqf institution was not in practice during the pre-Islamic Arabia system, However, the Prophet (SAW) initiated this kind of waqf as a tool for the betterment of the society and social wellbeing. Since then, waqf institution has played significant roles in many aspects of human life. Historically, waqf institutions provided social welfare services that many countries currently struggle to offer, (Cizakca, 2002, p. 264); unfortunately, the modern state did not reach the potential of waqf. Shaikh et al. stated, "The institution of waqf in the Islamic social finance framework provides a useful vehicle to fill the gap in social intermediation".

It is worth noting that in the Islamic economic system, social security measures such as zakat and waqf are seen as a last resort against the threat of poverty because of their responsive mechanisms; they are intentionally designed to accommodate human development, which is contrary to conventional economics and sustainable in nature. As described by Iqbal and Shafiq, the mainstream economic system is unsustainable in terms of social welfare and less effective at impacting the designed social intervention program. On the other hand, the Islamic economic system focuses on both economic and social justice to improve societal well-being by sharing zakat and waqf institutions to address mutual distribution and redistributing wealth, increasing government revenue, increasing levels of productivity, and employment investments in the economy that will significantly contribute to poverty reduction in the long run (Hassan & Khan, 2007; Raimi, 2015).

The historical event of the establishment and development of Awqaf proceeded during the lifetime of Prophet Muhammad (PBUH), when the very first mosque as an Islamic multipurpose centre was built by him in Madinah on a parcel of land endowed by two orphans, and the individuals and the ruling classes have endowed their valuables for social welfare and other public good as well, which at the same time served as a piece of machinery for sustainable development. Consequently, the evolutionary trend continued its headway through multifarious Islamic eras to meet the basic societal needs and infrastructural development which enumerate the level of Muslims' civilization and intuitive rationale that pave the way for environmental sustainability and infrastructural development in a quest for peaceful and integral coexistence, hence yielding positive results by creating job opportunities, i.e., philanthropic gift to the society. The track history of waqf and its evolution through various Islamic eras is a proven fact on the expansion and improvement of the institution and reveals the extent to which Muslims are politically sophisticated, socio-economically civilized, and how candid they are in their religious activities. *Al-awqaf* (endowments) has various forms, such as the waqf of the Green Meadow in Damascus, which was a waqf for ill animals to graze until they pass away; the milk point, the waqf in Damascus was endowed by Citadel King Nasser Salah al-Din al-Ayoubi to supply mothers with milk and sugar to feed their babies; and the waqf of fruitful gardens for every wayfarer to eat; and the waqf of pots, which was for compensating for broken pots as a result of falling from the hands of house-servants (Al-Ubaidy, 1999).

West African countries are paying more attention to some segments of Islamic social finance; an assessment showed that over 90 percent of the Islamic social finance subscriptions to the phenomenon are religious waqf, mainly on building mosques, while others that have a direct affiliation to the socio-economic benefits to the masses enjoy low subscription (Abdullahi, 2006). The development of waqf through various Islamic eras proved that investment in infrastructure is the best way to enhance productive capacities as there will be a water supply, irrigation schemes, shelter and health care facilities, etc. There would be a high economic return through increased agricultural output, roads, and other necessities which will one day extend to the geographically remote areas (Ogunleye, 2010). The absence of the aforementioned led West African countries to suffer squarely from a deficit of many macroeconomic variables like poverty, unemployment, etc. The institutional structure for waqf in Sudan is through the Diwan of National Waqf and in Nigeria is through the Shari'ah Court of appeal while in South Africa it is the law for non-profit organizations (Hassan, 2019). The National Insurance Commission, which oversees the Takaful industry, established a framework in 2013 that permits operators to offer *al-Mudharabah, wakalah,* and hybrid products in addition to permitting traditional insurers to operate Islamic windows. The agency stated that it would release micro Takaful regulations in 2020 to bring microinsurance services to the nation.

In 2003, African Alliance Insurance was the first to provide Takaful goods. The other legitimate Takaful companies in the nation include Noor Takaful, situated in Lagos; Salam Takaful Insurance Company; Cornerstone Takaful Insurance Company; and the Takaful subsidiary of Jaiz Bank. The Takaful window of SenAssurance Vie, commonly known as SenTakaful, was launched in 2018 and continues to be the only participant in the market. It only provides one product, a life Takaful contract, which supports funding that complies with Shari'ah in the event of the subscriber's infirmity, unemployment, or demise. By adopting specific legislation allowing the issuance of Takaful contracts in 2019, the Inter-African Conference on Insurance Markets supported Takaful and re-Takaful activities in 14 African nations, including Senegal (Tamano, 2022-IFN)

Sustainable Financing Through Sukuk Issuance

When examining sukuk issuance over the years, one sees more focus placed on sustainability and environmental issues, though it also involves investment activities that would generate financial returns for investors. Thus, sukuk can play an important role in supporting social finance. The fact that countries like Malaysia and other emerging economies around the world are relying more on public-private partnerships (PPP) in funding development projects mainly related to health and education means that the use of sukuk is well suited to these areas. After the issuance of socially responsible investment (SRI) Sukuk Ihsan to build schools in Malaysia by Khazanah National Berhad in 2015, recent times saw more renewable energy and environmentally friendly projects leading to a series of green Sukuk issuances. Malaysia has been hailed as the market leader here with the inaugural issuance of green Sukuk worth US$250 million for the construction of a solar energy platform for a clean and sustainable power supply by Tadau Energy Sdn Bhd in 2017. A year later, in 2018, Indonesia issued the world's first sovereign green sukuk amounting to US$1.25 billion aimed at achieving its national emission reduction goals by 2030. The issuance of US$600 million sukuk by Etihad Airways for the transition of the airline towards zero carbon emissions and the US$1.3 billion by Saudi Electricity Company in 2020 also marked the additional new green sukuk in the market. Joining the force is the Islamic Development Bank (IDB) with the issuance of the world's first AAA-rated sustainable development goals (SDG), specifically for funding projects related to good health and sustainable economic growth in the same year. As of July 2020, up to US$6.1 billion had been raised through 12 unique green sukuk issuers, mainly from Malaysia, Indonesia, and the United Arab Emirates (World Bank). Later in September 2020, RM500 million Malaysia Sukuk Prihatin was issued by the government of Malaysia aimed solely at the societal cause, providing the opportunity for the public to participate and contribute to the rebuilding of the nation post-COVID-19. And more recently in March 2021, ISDB issued another US$2.5 billion AAA-rated sustainability sukuk to be allocated for green financing and social development projects.

The Osun State Government (OSG) of Nigeria issued the first sukuk in Sub-Saharan Africa on October 8, 2013, through a Special Purpose Company, for a total of N11.4 billion ($70.6 million). The sukuk matures on October 8, 2020, and was issued at a rate of 14.75% annually at N 1,000 per unit. Following the Osun State Government's issue, interest in ethical finance in Nigeria surged, resulting in three successful issuances by the Federal Government of Nigeria (FGN) from 2017 to 2021, which have all been significantly oversubscribed. In 2022, the Federal Government of Nigeria designated Taj Bank as the receiving agent for a N150 billion Sukuk Bond. With money obtained via sukuk bonds sold in the bond market, FGN plans to repair 44 highways. In June 2020, Minister of Finance Mrs. Zainab Ahmed gave the Minister of Works and Housing, Mr. Tunde Fashola, a symbolic sovereign sukuk cheque for 162.55 billion that had been raised. Each of Nigeria's geopolitical regions was to have eight roads built (Statistical Bulletin Report for 2020 from CBN).

In Nigeria, sukuk has been used as a tool for sustainable financing, and in 2022 the federal government of Nigeria issued a sovereign Sukuk Ijarah facility worth NGN100 billion (US$224.6million), despite Nigerians' low awareness of Islamic sustainable finance instrument. The Debt Management Office of Nigeria confirmed that "The level of subscription is evidence of investors' confidence in the use and impact of sukuk in the construction and rehabilitation of road infrastructure across the country". In the Ivory Coast, the first sukuk facility was a historic sovereign transaction worth XOF150 billion (US$251.16 million), issued in 2015 and fully repaid at the end of 2020. This was followed by a second issuance of the same amount in 2016, arranged by the ICD under a XOF300 billion (US$502.32 million) program. On the West African Regional Stock Exchange, both periodicals were listed (Tamano, 2022-IFN).

In 2017, FGN Roads Sukuk company 1 PLC offered Subscription and was authorized to receive applications for N100,000,000,000 7-Year 16.47% Ijarah Sukuk, due 2024.

In another development in 2021, the same FGN Sukuk Company offered a subscription and was authorized to receive applications for N250,000,000,000 10-Year 13.00% Ijarah Sukuk, due 2031. However, the private sectors are also striving to join the developmental arena of sukuk, as witnessed in the case of one big company in Nigeria called Family Homes Sukuk Issuance Program Plc, which set to mobilize 30 billion to achieve the following objectives:

- The New Urban Agenda and the Global Goals support sustainable cities and communities, zero poverty, good health and well-being, clean water and sanitation, decent work, and economic growth that reduces inequalities. Family Homes Funds Limited is strongly in line with these objectives.
- To accomplish this, FHFL is aiming to: offer solutions to Nigeria's rising urbanization (more than 50% of Nigerians currently reside in urban areas) and limit the growth of slums by providing adequate homes, and promote inclusivity and access to homes for all Nigerians (only 24,414 mortgages were given in 2018).
- Promote economic growth and development by creating jobs and obtaining building supplies locally.

The company employed 14,000 people, and they estimated that if the apprenticeship is implemented the program will generate another 27,000 indirect jobs.

Conclusion

This chapter provides an overview of Islamic sustainable finance and its practices in Africa. It found that one of the objectives of Islamic sustainable finance is to help improve the economic development of a country as well as the well-being of the community. In addition, it is discovered that the most suitable and relevant instruments in the ISF issue are waqf, zakat, microfinance, and sukuk, among others. Other Islamic social finance instruments for sustainable development from African perspectives are to be discussed in future research. Furthermore, policies related to sustainable Islamic finance are expected to be optimized by regulators to reduce poverty, maintain environmental sustainability, and increase economic growth.

References

Abdullahi, S. A. (2006). *An Assessment of the Impacts of Zakah on the Beneficiaries in the Six Local Government Areas of Kano Metropolis (Sponsored Research Project)*. Kano: Kano State Zakkah and Hubusi Commission.

Aliyu, S. U. R. (2012). *Islamic Banking and finance in Nigeria: Issues, Challenges and Opportunities International Institute of Islamic Banking and Finance*. Bayero University, Kano. http://mpra.ub.uni-muenchen.de/42573/

Al-Ubaidy, S. (1999). *Nadwatu Muàssasatu al-Awqaf wa dauriha fi-al-Hifaz ala al-Athaar al Islamiyyah wal-Makhtutat*.

Cizakca, M. (2002). Latest Development in the Western Non-Profit Sector and the Implications for Islamic Awaqf. In Iqbal, M. (Ed.), *Islamic Economic Institutions and the Elimination of Poverty* (pp. 263–287). Leicester: The Islamic Foundation.
Emmanuel, M., Chiara, M., Evelyn, M., & Celestine, O. O. (2017). Inequality in Nigeria, Exploring the Drivers. *OXFAM*. www.oxfam.org/en/research/inequality
Hassan, M. K., & Khan, J. M. (2007). Zakah, External Debt and Poverty Reduction Strategy in Bangladesh. *Journal of Economic Cooperation Among Islamic Countries*, 28(4).
Hassan, Z. (2019). *Regulatory Framework of Islamic Social Finance ISSF 2019 14th International Shari'ah Scholars*.
Mandela, L. (2005). *Make Poverty History A Speech Delivered by Nelson Mandela in London's Trafalgar Square*.
Ogunleye, O. S. (2010). Towards Sustainable Poverty Alleviation in Nigeria. *African Research Review*, 4(2). On Islamic Banking and Insurance.
Raimi, L., Saibu, A., & Shokunbi, M. O. (2015). An Exploratory Study of Zakah and Waqf for Financial Inclusion in Nigeria. *1st International JIMF* (pp. 1–29).
Rarick, C. A. (2009). *Islamic Finance: An Alternative in the Global Financial Market?* http://ssrn.com/abstract=1332793 (Accessed 21 May 2011).
Shirazi, N. S., & Amin, M. F. (2009). Poverty Elimination through Potential Zakat Collection in the OIC-member Countries: Revisited. *The Pakistan Development Review*, 48(4), 739–754.
Siddiqi, M. N. (2004). *Riba, Bank Interest and the Rationale of Its Prohibition*. Jeddah: Islamic Research and Training Institute, Islamic Development Bank Group.
Tamano, N. (2022). *IFN Analysis Islamic Finance News 29/03/2022-IFN Country Analysis – Ivory Coast*.

3 Islamic Sustainable Finance

Its Experiences From SAARC

Mohammad Habibullah, Razali Haron & Md Atiullah

Introduction

In reference to the contemporary global concern, sustainable finance is needed for financial and socio-economic development that brings welfare for the society and alleviates extreme poverty. However, sustainable finance is defined as all financial services, including social and environmental, that provide means for the investors and businesses that bring long-term benefits for the society. The main aim of sustainable finance is to promote social well-being and fair economic development for both present and future generations. A sustainable development takes place through preserving natural resources, environmental quality, and human development in the community. Nevertheless, Islamic finance has been considered a potential socio-economic development means to ease insufficiency by providing sustainable monetary assistance to the needy and destitute. To develop the socio-economic condition of the poor and financially deprived people, the SAARC countries have a greater opportunity to combat poverty through Islamic finance. Islamic finance is growing in popularity in SAARC Muslim countries like Bangladesh, Pakistan, Afghanistan, and the Maldives; however, it has yet to thrive in the Muslim countries, as conventional finance has been well established for decades and the poor are unclear regarding Islamic financial systems. Islamic finance is riba- (interest) free and Shari'ah-based financing, whereas the conventional financial system is interest-based.

Despite the fact that Islamic finance has a certain impact on the GDP, poverty reduction, and economic growth in the SAARC countries, it is rather limited. Islamic finance influences the gross domestic product (GDP), the reduction of poverty, and overall economic growth of most nations, yet sustainable development in SAARC countries will not happen unless these countries can ensure their development associates are ready to cooperate for mutual benefit. To determine the sustainability of setting up viable Islamic finance in SAARC countries, primary and secondary sources as well as the governments' policies are scrutinized using an industrial experiences and solutions approach and policy analysis. The fundamental function of Islamic finance is to propose to the community and businesses financial amenities that support social and financial stability and balanced financial development. Small-scale businesses can sometimes receive medium-term financial help from Islamic Financial Institutions (IFIs) in addition to short-term loans. The SAARC

DOI: 10.4324/9781003468653-5

was established in December 1985, and it consists of seven countries: Bangladesh, Bhutan, India, the Maldives, Nepal, Pakistan, and Sri Lanka. In 2007, Afghanistan joined the organization as the eighth member state. These SAARC countries share their borders with one another and have comparable economic, environmental, and political systems. The guiding principle of the SAARC is to promote social well-being, social security, poverty reduction, and solving common problems through mutual respect and cooperation.

Scope of Islamic Sustainable Finance

Sustainability can only be achieved though financing, and funding is the principal tool of sustainability (Rezaee, 2016). Financial sustainability cannot be achieved without fulfilling the needs of financial demands as well as promoting development goals. With the emergence of the Islamic financial industry around the world, the demand for Islamic banking and financial products is growing rapidly. Consequently, the access to Islamic banking and finance services correlates with the steep climb in preference for these in Muslim and non-Muslim countries alike. However, an obstacle in this growing trend is the fact that Islamic finance is firmly rooted in Shari'ah principles and interest-free transactions, whereas the most established global financial system is interest-based. The primary objective of the Islamic financial system is to attain fairness and justice in the society since without achieving social justice, sustainable progress in the society will not be possible. The Islamic financial system is still lagging behind the conventional financial system due to policy implementation and practices, despite the fact that Islamic financial institutions are more stable than conventional finance due to not being affected by inflation and changing interest rates. In order to alleviate poverty, Islamic finance provides zakat, waqf, and sadaqah as a means of easing difficulty and hardship of the poor, and thus it promotes equality in the standard of living. As the Islamic financial sector is based on Shari'ah law and practices a risk-sharing policy, the investors and shareholders will be risk-free.

Experience of Islamic Sustainable Finance in SAARC

Sustainability emphasizes social, environmental, and financial development, and academics have found that sustainable finance has a remarkable impact on socio-economic development and improvement of societal well-being. Financial sustainability can be achieved by making true financial decisions and productive and efficient financial activities, which reduce the financial burden of the poor (Martínez-Ferrero et al., 2014). Even though Islamic finance is a relatively new industry in the current financial system, yet it plays a significant role in many Muslim countries, especially in SAARC member states like Afghanistan, Bangladesh, Pakistan, and the Maldives, where Muslims are the predominant population: for example, in Afghanistan, 100% of the population is Muslim, and almost 90% in Bangladesh and Pakistan respectively. In Afghanistan, Islamic microfinance has considerably grown in access and popularity among the unbanked population in recent years, where it has significantly contributed to social development as well as reducing extreme poverty.

Apart from the aforementioned, Islamic banking and financial organizations are performing equally and providing Islamic products and financial services to the people, and have acquired more than a 15% market share in the banking industry (IFSB, 2016). Similarly, Islamic microfinance industry has emerged as one of the strongest leading industries in SAARC countries. With the help of Islamic Bank Bangladesh Limited (IBBL), Islamic microfinance bodies are providing financial amenities to the rural poor and unbanked Muslims; subsequently, it leads to social and financial development of the rural communities. Similarly, in Pakistan, Islamic financial services and microfinance have an incredible popularity and have led to a developed Islamic finance industry. Being home to the Muslim majority and a significant unbanked Muslim population, Islamic finance has a comprehensive role in financial development compared to the other nations in SAARC member states. However, in India, the Maldives, and Sri Lanka, the Islamic banking and financial industry is still in its infant stage and its popularity is growing among the Muslim population. On the other hand, other non-Muslim SAARC member states like Bhutan and Nepal have yet to embrace and implement Islamic banking and financial services. As the main goals of SAARC states are to promote social development and poverty alleviation through mutual respect and cooperation, Islamic finance is a potentially comprehensive tool for SAARC countries to attain financial sustainability in South Asia.

Role of Islamic Finance to the Growth of Sustainable Finance

Over the decades, Islamic economic and financial ideas came into reality for social and financial development as well as economic progress and play a significant role in various Muslim countries based on Islamic law and principles. Islamic banking and financial institutions have significantly contributed to financial development and economic growth (Hassan et al., 2011). Gazdar et al. (2019) mentioned that Islamic finance has a positive impact on the economic sector in terms of oil trading, and a strong Islamic financial system leads to significant financial development. In fact, Islamic banking and finance have become an alternative financial means to conventional financial systems (Leon & Weill, 2018). In the current system, the financial market has become more progressive and competitive. As a result, banks and financial institutions are facing tremendous demands from investors and businesses and are facing challenges in sustaining their financial services. Thus, Islamic financial sustainability has drawn much attention to the current financial system in keeping their economic activities parallel to economic and sustainable development. The recent global financial crisis (GFC) in the USA in 2008 has highlighted the importance of the Islamic financial system to create more resilience to protect bank capitals and assets to support sustainable economic growth. Consequently, in the post-GFC, Islamic banking and finance became more stable; Islamic financial institutions have higher liquidity reserve and capital assets than conventional banks and financial institutions (Beck et al., 2010). Hence, Islamic banking and finance have contributed to reducing financial distress in the society.

Elements of Islamic Finance for Sustainability in SAARC

In order to provide Islamic microfinancial assistance to the underprivileged people in SAARC countries, the elements of zakat (Islamic tax), awqaf (Endowment), and takaful (Islamic insurance) are truly the means for sustainability. It will ultimately contribute to economic growth and the increased prosperity of the nations (Akhter & Jaffri, 2009). The primary emphasis of the Islamic financial system is on financial and social justice and improving total societal well-being, in contrast to the conventional economic system, which places additional emphasis on social welfare. However, this does not preclude an individual from pursuing their own interests as long as they fall within the bounds of morality and the larger interests of society. The institutions and tools that make up the Islamic social financial infrastructure focus on social fairness, risk-sharing, and cooperative working ethics. In essence, this infrastructure reduces the possibility that targeted programs will not be sustainable or effective in raising society's standard of living. When employed efficiently, the time-honored Islamic economic instruments of zakat, sadqa, hewalah, waqf, and qard-al-hassan can contribute significantly to the process of sustainable development. Iqbal and Shafiq (2015) show that qard-al-hasan contributes significantly to the promotion of sustainable financial development and improvement of social justice and well-being. However, most of the Muslim population lives in the South Asia region or in the member states of SAARC.

Islamic Endowment in the Indian Subcontinent

Islamic doctrine has always been encouraged by the authorities to have divine ordination to be implemented and observed accordingly. Muslim Sultans (kings) in the Indian subcontinent have frequently attempted to gain some sort of legitimacy by providing different types of patronage to revered religious figures. Endowments (awqf), which were the most prevalent type of benefaction, were practiced throughout the Muslim rulers' regimes. Waqf in SAARC countries was highly significant. By funding their favorite shrines and khanaqahs and designating them waqf under royal patronage, kings of the Sultanate and Mughal periods dealt with endowments in the "classical" manner described earlier, much like West Asian rulers during the same period. By making sufis and ulama economically dependent on awqaf during the time of the centralized system, Mughal emperors were particularly interested in the distribution of deeds, which served as a tool for controlling specific social and political groups (Malik, 2008).

Sustainability Challenges for Islamic Finance

The biggest challenges for Islamic finance in SAARC countries are liquidity management, government securities, stocks, mutual funds, and other products. Currently, many organizations are striving to develop practical solutions to the liquidity issue, including the banks of Malaysia, the Islamic Chamber of Commerce and Industry (ICCI), the International Islamic Financial Market (IIFM), and the Dubai International Finance Centre (DIFC) (Khan & Bhatti, 2008). In comparison with conventional banking systems, Islamic banking and finance is still in its initial stage and has been dealing with a variety of issues and difficulties. The ongoing issue of surplus liquidity plagues Islamic banks. Due to the severe lack of more lasting Shari'ah-compliant investment tools and outlets, they hold around 40% more liquidity than their conventional equivalents. 95% of their resources are invested in rather short-dated ijarah, murabahah, and Al-Musharakah instruments (Islamic Finance News, 2006).

Proposed Framework for Islamic Sustainable Finance in SAARC

Jan et al. (2021) have reiterated that to achieve sustainable development goals (SDGs), Islamic banking and finance transactions are correlated with their financial responsibilities based on Shari'ah principles. On the other hand, Ahmed et al. (2015) put forward that despite having a small number of financial institutions and organizations, they are playing a significant role in Organization of Islamic Countries (OIC) member nations and beyond in achieving sustainable financial development by integrating Shari'ah-based principles and financial strategies. Enhancing commerce, investments, connectivity, governance, infrastructure, and policy implementation are all necessary for the South Asian area to successfully integrate (Fernando, 2021). Additionally, fostering trust and goodwill among the South Asian countries is essential to this integration process. Even though the member countries have high expectations for growth, the SAARC's limited success in promoting the socio-economic development of the South Asian economies points to its weakness. If successful implementation of a regional organization's objectives is a key indicator of that organization's success and credibility, then the SAARC's limited success in this regard indicates such (Fernando, 2021).

Recommendation

South Asian countries have made significant financial sector reforms over the past few decades with the aim of promoting financial sector competition, creating payment and settlement systems, and bolstering regulatory and legal frameworks. The region's financial sector legislation has been strengthened even though the SAARC members are in different phases of change. This study closely analyzes and contrasts the adjustments that the SAARC countries have made to assist them in jointly achieving a high quality of regulatory and financial integration for sustainable financial development in the South Asian region. At the study's conclusion, a few recommendations are offered for additional reforms and collaboration to build an efficient, competitive, and resilient financial sector in the SAARC nations.

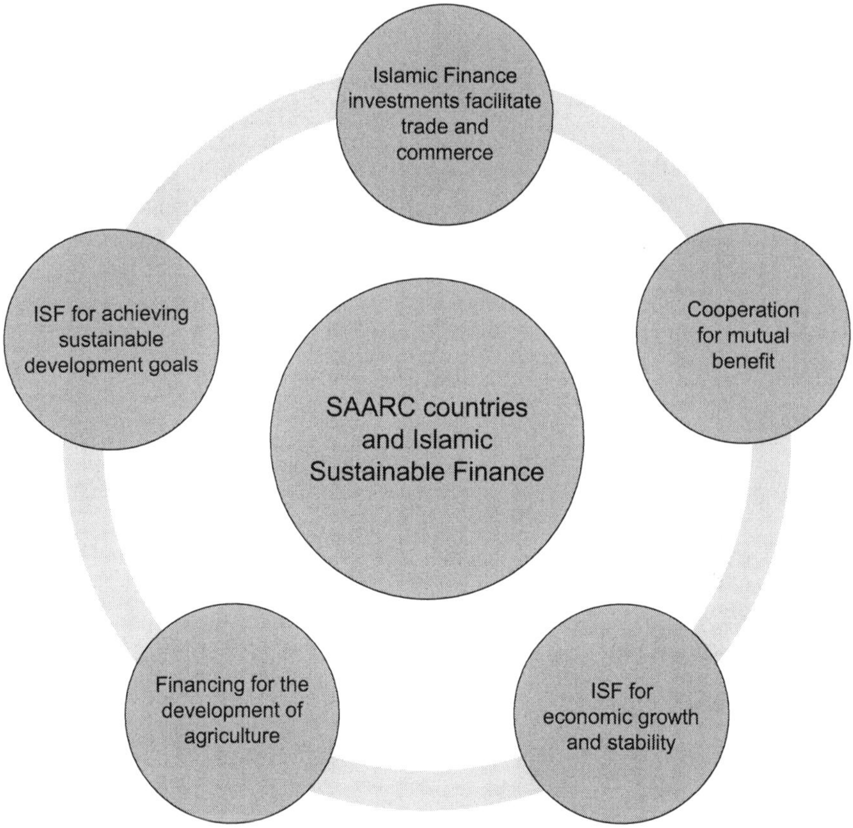

Figure 3.1 SAARC Countries and Islamic Sustainable Finance

Source: Fernando (2021)

Establishing SAARC Islamic Bank

The Islamic Bank's mission is to support the financial and communal advancement of its partner nations and Muslim societies individually and collectively in compliance with the tenets of Shari'ah law. The development of the Islamic banking and finance sector and institutions, the reduction of poverty, and the encouragement of collaboration between the member nations are among the specific goals. To achieve the goal of social and economic development, the member countries may extend their financial activities through capital and share markets and providing financial aid for productive and profitable projects. Moreover, with the setting up of trust funds, the Bank is mandated to create as well as manage special funds for distinct objectives, such as a fund to support Muslim populations outside of member countries.

Establishing of SAARC Regulatory Body for Islamic Finance

Both national and international financial regulations need to be applied in banking and financial institutions. Recent high-profile corporate fraud instances and bankruptcies, together with continuing globalization, have prompted urging for tighter governing standards and an improved importance on the value of proper management in the economic sector (Alexakis & Tsikouras, 2009). Deep concerns about the effects of financial cooperation are acknowledged by SAARC, and its regional activities have been alluded to in discourse. There are indications that member states lack political will, however, as regional activities have primarily focused on nascent strategies such the creation of validations, contracts, and supportive pathways to track and share regional practices (Kumar, 2006). However, the main focus is on several areas that are listed in the SAARC Action Plan on development as well as financial cooperation, and the scope of the activities carried out by the technical committee on economic growth demonstrates the prospect for collaboration between SAARC countries.

The ideas aimed at business collaboration remain all-inclusive and cover critical facets of cooperation such as procedures and acts, investments, education and responsiveness, adaption processes, administration, and competence building. However, SAARC continues to lack involvement with local communities and vulnerable groups, which may be essential as an adaptive mechanism for successfully addressing risks to financial security and the economics of the countries. Since the 1980s, the SAARC has unquestionably been fast to voice its concerns about poverty reduction and economic growth and its effects (Sridharan, 2008). Through a direct relation to financial safety, the SAARC participants have united as a region to guarantee financial security by setting up a regulatory framework/body. In addition to (i) "acting as a regional financial security reserve for the SAARC Member Countries during normal time and emergencies," (ii) "providing regional support to national financial efforts; fostering intercountry partnerships and regional integration and solving regional financial crisis through collective action" will be accomplished by this (Jain, & Singh, 2009).

Conclusion

Islamic finance has experienced several obstacles in its growth trajectory despite making good progress. As the chapter highlights, the development of Islamic banking and finance sector is not evenly distributed within SAARC states. Additionally, Islamic banks must enhance their risk management strategies, corporate governance, and liquidity in countries where they have firm footing. They must create Islamic accounting standards and procedures that are both domestically and globally competitive. They must develop their Shari'ah faculties and legal systems in accordance with accepted global standards. Furthermore, they should take research and development (R&D) earnestly and create comprehensive and unique Islamic Shari'ah-based products. Islamic banks and financial institutions must employ PLS financing in place of the vast majority of murabahah financing (Khan & Bhatti, 2008). They are also urgently needed to address the worsening human resources management crisis. Without proper management of Islamic banking becoming justly dedicated and proficient, it will be impossible to successfully address the issues and challenges facing Islamic banks. Apart from these specific objectives, Islamic banking and finance ought to explore and seize upon the opportunities to expand their operation to non-Muslim majority states as there are clear indications of demand for these. In summary, it has not yet been sufficiently demonstrated that Islamic finance provides more effective and morally sound explanations in the contemporary financial world.

References

Ahmed, H., Mohieldin, M., Verbeek, J., & Aboulmagd, F. (2015). On the Sustainable Development Goals and the Role of Islamic Finance. *World Bank Policy Research Working Paper*, 7266.

Akhter, W., Akhtar, N., & Jaffri, S. K. A. (2009). Islamic Micro-Finance and Poverty Alleviation: A Case of Pakistan. *Proceeding of the 2nd CBRC, Lahore* (pp. 1–8).

Alexakis, C., & Tsikouras, A. (2009). Islamic Finance: Regulatory Framework–Challenges Lying Ahead. *International Journal of Islamic and Middle Eastern Finance and Management*.

Beck, T., Demirgüç-Kunt, A., & Merrouche, O. (2010). *Islamic vs. Conventional Banking: Business Model, Efficiency and Stability*. The World Bank.

Fernando, S. (2021). *Politics, Economics and Connectivity* (p. 20). St. Sebastian Hill, CO: M.D. Gunasena and Company Printers (Private) Limited.

Gazdar, K., Hassan, M. K., Safa, M. F., & Grassa, R. (2019). Oil Price Volatility, Islamic Financial Development and Economic Growth in Gulf Cooperation Council (GCC) Countries. *Borsa Istanbul Review*, 19(3), 197–206.

Hassan, M. K., Sanchez, B., & Yu, J. (2011). Financial Development and Economic Growth in the Organisation of Islamic Conference Countries. *JKAU: Islamic Econ*, 24(1), 145–172.

Iqbal, Z., & Shafiq, B. (2015). Islamic Finance and the Role of Qard-al-Hassan (Benevolent Loans) in Enhancing Inclusion: A Case Study of AKHUWAT. *ACRN Oxford Journal of Finance and Risk Perspectives*, 4(4), 23–40.

Islamic Finance News. (2006). Sukuk-Friendly Regime for UK? *Islamic Finance News*, 3(39), 6.

Islamic Financial Services Industry Stability Report (IFSB). (2016). www.islamicfinance.com/wp-content/uploads/2016/06/IFSI-Stability-Report-2016-final.pdfIFSI-Stability-Report-2016-final.pdf

Jain, R., & Singh, J. B. (2009). Trade Pattern in SAARC Countries: Emerging Trends and Issues. *Reserve Bank of India Occasional Papers*, 30(3), 73–117.

Jan, A., Mata, M. N., Albinsson, P. A., Martins, J. M., Hassan, R. B., & Mata, P. N. (2021). Alignment of Islamic Banking Sustainability Indicators with Sustainable Development Goals: Policy Recommendations for Addressing the Covid-19 Pandemic. *Sustainability*, 13(5), 2607.

Khan, M. M., & Bhatti, M. I. (2008). Development in Islamic Banking: A Financial Risk-Allocation Approach. *The Journal of Risk Finance*.

Kumar, S. (2006). Pakistan and Regionalism. *Strategic Analysis*, 6(1), 122–138.

Leon, F., & Weill, L. (2018). Islamic Banking Development and Access to Credit. *Pacific-Basin Finance Journal*, 52, 54–69.

Malik, J. (2008). Excursus Islamic Endowments. In *Islam in South Asia* (pp. 234–240). Brill.

Martínez-Ferrero, J., Banerjee, S., & García-Sánchez, I. (2014). Corporate Social Responsibility as a Strategic Shield Against Costs of Earnings Management Practices. *Journal of Business Ethics*, 133(2), 305–324.

Rezaee, Z. (2016). Business Sustainability Research: A Theoretical and Integrated Perspective. *Journal of Accounting Literature*, 36, 48–64.

Sridharan, K. (2008). *Regional Organisations and Conflict Management: Comparing ASEAN and SAARC*. Crisis States Research Centre.

4 Islamic Micro-financing for SMEs Towards Its Sustainability

An Experience From Libya

Zainab Belal Lawhaishy, Razali Haron & Anwar Hasan Abdullah Othman

Introduction

Libya is a country in North Africa and is part of the Maghreb region. As a result of the failed coup in 2014, numerous Islamic and local militias control small swaths of territory, and the Libyan Council is incapable of re-establishing control over these mini-states. Indeed, this situation has resulted in the division of Libya into two regions, Tripolitania and Cyrenaica, with the General National Congress (GNA) controlling one and the Libyan National Army (LNA) controlling the other. Both sides are backed by different countries, resulting in the staging of an international conflict with no clear end in sight (AAE, 2020). Time passes, but the central question for Libya's future stability and sustainability and that of the entire region is how to rebuild this country. The conflict has destroyed the majority of the country's hard infrastructure, including bridges and roads, as well as soft infrastructure, including the education system and business mindset. These scenarios were unfortunately common in many regions of Africa during the 1970s because of state collapse or the outbreak of civil war, resulting in the poverty, starvation, and emigration of many solid states. Numerous economists and private institutions used microfinance to advance the development and sustainability of those sectors (The World Bank, 2020).

Libya entered 2021 as a fractured nation seeking recovery and reconciliation. With the conflict intensifying and oil terminals and fields being blocked, the economy posted one of its worst performances in 2020. Beginning in mid-September, a reconciliation between political and military factions provided much-needed relief to the economy, capping the annual GDP decline at 31.3 percent. Although the election of a unity government in early 2021 has reignited hope, the reunification agenda faces formidable obstacles (The World Bank, 2021). Apart from being heavily reliant on the oil and gas sector, Libya's public sector employs the vast majority of the country's workforce (Gunto & Alias, 2013), and the private sector is small and largely informal. While some progress toward a more private sector-oriented economy has been made, significant obstacles remain in actively supporting these aspirations in the emerging private sector (Omar et al., 2020). This is critical, however, because a healthy private sector contributes to an enabling business environment, which in turn fosters entrepreneurship. Constant political upheaval and dramatic fluctuations in oil production have created the ideal conditions for the

DOI: 10.4324/9781003468653-6

emergence of a private sector motivated by necessity. Due to an over-reliance on oil and gas, Libya's inefficient public sector, arguably the country's economy, is one of the least diversified and most fragile sectors in MENA (Abdulsaleh, 2017). Since Islamic microfinance is widely recognized as an extremely effective tool for alleviating poverty and enhancing the well-being of its clients (Ledgerwood, 1999), microfinance appears to be the tool that could have a beneficial effect on the Libyan economy. As access to Shari'ah-compliant financing continues to be a major barrier for the Libyan private sector, Islamic microfinance can be used in novel ways to meet entrepreneurs' financing needs and to sustain their businesses (Burke, 2017).

Additionally, the Libyan government has recognized the significant role of the private sector (MSMEs) in alleviating poverty, decreasing inequality, and minimizing excessive public hiring, hence generating employment (Hamid & Ibrahim, 2018). As a result, the government established Libyan Enterprise and official business incubators to cultivate an entrepreneurial culture and to assist start-ups with business development. Despite this, start-ups and MSMEs continue to face various obstacles, including the lack of a supportive business environment and limited access to funding resources (Gunto & Alias, 2013). In 2019, Namaa Tamweel was launched as Libya's first and only Islamic microfinance institution following a collaboration between the UK Ministry of Development and International Cooperation and ATIB, with Expertise France overseeing the project implementation. Through this project, the partners aimed to invest in microfinance as the primary mechanism for fostering strong entrepreneurial desires among the population, given that the Libyan economy has a high unemployment rate, a sizable informal sector, an increase in entrepreneurial willingness, and difficult access to finance (AAE, 2020).

Nonetheless, Namaa Tamweel has various obstacles, including a higher cost structure and a low achievement rate. Additionally, Namaa Tamweel lacks product innovation and diversity due to its reliance on Murabahah-based financing. Jawan (2019) asserts that involvement in Murabahah or leasing products had a detrimental effect on numerous small projects, even resulting in the failure of several. Due to the absence of unique legislation governing IMFIs in Libya, Namaa Tamweel is required to conform to the Islamic bank's high capital requirements. Numerous studies have investigated the challenges and solutions pertaining to Islamic microfinance initiatives in many countries. However, there is no single study that has examined the challenges facing Islamic microfinance initiatives in financing MSMEs in the State of Libya from experts' perspectives. Therefore, this study attempts to fill the gap in the literature by investigating the challenges and providing solutions to Islamic microfinance Institutions (IMFIs) by interviewing Libyan experts in Islamic finance. The study aims to answer the following research questions by employing a qualitative research approach.

RQ1: What are the challenges facing the introduction of the Islamic microfinance initiative in the State of Libya?

RQ1: What are the proposed solutions to these challenges?

Literature Review

Even though Islamic microfinance has a notable goal of reaching the poor and marginalized segments of society, various microfinance institutions with different operating models and locations are likely to face a variety of challenges. In Pakistan, even though Akhuwat Foundation is considered one of the most successful IMF models in providing interest-free loans to the poor. Nonetheless, it encounters numerous challenges; for instance, lack of innovation in products and restrictions on outreach to other cities due to close monitoring by the board (Mahmood et al., 2015). Malaysia is a shining example of the burgeoning microfinance industry because it is regarded as an Islamic finance hub. Malaysia's most prominent microfinance institution, Amanah Ikhtiar Malaysia, could reach the poorest of the poor. Qard Al-hassan (interest-free loans) were provided to income-generating activities by Amanah Ikhtiar in partnership with several financing institutions, such as Pembiayaan Mikro, Ar-Rahnu by Bank Rakyat and Yayasan Tekun Nasional (TEKUN). This had a tremendously positive impact when compared to Bai' Al Inah (Abbas, 2014). However, it was criticized for imposing 10 percent service charges on loans which it claims to be based on Qard Al-hassan (Saad & Duasa, 2011)). As a result, rather than relying on a single product, it is suggested that the utilization of a variety of Islamic financial instruments such as Al-Musharakah, Al-Mudharabah, Istisna, and Salam. Many commercial banks in Malaysia that provide microfinance products, such as Alliance Bank, CIMB, EONCap Islamic, and Bank Rakyat, lack innovation and are overly dependent on Bay 'Inah (Saad, 2011). It is counterproductive to the goals of microfinance to use Bay 'Inah for personal consumption rather than income-generating activities.

In comparison to other countries, Indonesia has a unique experience because Islamic microfinance has established networks with various entities such as microfinance divisions in Islamic banks, Islamic rural banks, and Islamic financial co-operatives, such as the well-known Baitul Maal wal Tamwil (BMT), which Abbas (2014) considers a major player in the industry. In contrast to other microfinance institutions that are based on interest charges, BMT offers financing products and services based on profit and loss (PLS) schemes (Maggangka, 2015). However, BMT sometimes runs out of deposit funds due to the significant amount of financing granted. Therefore, BMT could adopt other fundraising methods such as cash-waqf (Satar & Kassim, 2020). On the other hand, Islamic microfinance institutions (IMFIs) face stiff competition in Indonesia from conventional microfinance. Despite having the highest proportion of Muslims in the world, Islamic microfinance is still far behind. While Muslim customers prefer Islamic microfinance, they still choose conventional microfinance products for economic and non-economic reasons such as service quality, interest rate, and loan size (Masyita & Ahmed, 2013).

In Bangladesh, the Grameen Bank model is widely regarded as one of the most successful microfinance models in the world, having been awarded the Nobel Peace Prize. Nonetheless, the model is predicated on the concept of charging interest (riba) and charging interest up to a maximum of 20 percent (Ahmed, 2002). Grameen Bank's borrowers were discovered to have borrowed from external sources in some cases to repay their installments, trapping them in an endless cycle of debt (Rahman, 2019). Nonetheless, private commercial banks have historically been unwilling to offer microfinance programs for a variety of reasons, including low financial returns, outreach issues, particularly among the rural poor, and a lack of human resources to manage the programs (Anwarul Islam et al., 2014). Regrettably, Islamic microfinance is scarce in the country, accounting for less than 2 percent of the total market (around 24 billion borrowers). Bangladesh, according to Saad, has the most extensive conventional microfinance outreach, serving approximately 8 million clients.

Research Methodology

The qualitative methodology is used to explore the challenges and provide solutions for Islamic microfinance in the state of Libya. Introducing Islamic microfinance into Libya is expected to bring about numerous benefits such as empowering the youth, alleviating poverty, and achieving overall economic growth. The reason for selecting a qualitative methodology is to have a complete and detailed description of experts' opinions on Islamic microfinance challenges and proposed solutions to confirm the validity of the outcomes.

Population, Sampling Technique, and Sampling Size

The study population is Libyan experts, including Shari'ah scholars, academicians, practitioners, government officials, and consultants. Purposive sampling is used in this study; the researcher is extremely selective in selecting those who will participate. The interviewees are chosen using expert sampling, a subset of purposive sampling (Etikan & Bala, 2017). The "researcher seeks the consent of experts or those known experts in the area of the study and begins the process of collecting information directly from those individuals or group of respondents" (Etikan & Bala, 2017, p. 2). Additionally, expert sampling is used for two primary purposes: to elucidate the perspectives of individuals with specific expertise and to increase the validity of research findings (Muhammed, 2012). Selecting an adequate and appropriate sample size is crucial in any research. However, this is dependent on the study approach used; for example, in a quantitative approach, the sample size can be established in advance based on the data analysis technique utilized. Nonetheless, with purposive sampling, the sample size is determined by saturation, the point at which no new data or themes are generated, and data collecting may cease (Kappal & Rastogi, 2020).

Research Tool: Semi-structured Interviews

The primary data for this study was gathered through face-to-face and internet-based semi-structured interviews (via Skype). Semi-structured interviews, according to Alshenqeeti, are more adaptable than other types of interviews. The interviewer asks pre-determined questions, and the interviewee is permitted to elaborate on their answers by addressing relevant problems linked to the study's goals. The researcher

Table 4.1 List of Interviewees

Participants	*Position*	*Experience*	*Rank*
Interviewee 1 (A1)	A former Islamic Financial Sector Manager, currently a General Manager of Islamic Banking Affairs	7 years and more	PhD
Interviewee 2 (A2)	SMEs Expert, a former Accountant and Auditor, currently holds Academic position and serves as a board member of several conventional and Islamic Banks	7 years and more	PhD
Interviewee 3 (A3)	A former head of SMEs development program, Investment expert, SMEs expert, and currently serves as a member of the board of directors of some local and international companies	7 years and more	PhD
Interviewee 4 (A4)	A Shari'ah expert, currently serves as Shari'ah Advisor at several Islamic Banks and lecturer of Islamic Banking and Finance	7 years and more	PhD
Interviewee 5 (A5)	SMEs expert, researcher in Islamic Finance, Academic experience	7 years and more	PhD
Interviewee 6 (A6)	A former head of strategic planning division at Investment companies, held a senior position at Islamic Microfinance Institution, currently serves as a head of IT department at investment company.	5–7 years	Master's Degree
Interviewee 7 (A7)	Co-founder and CEO of start-ups and SMEs company. Currently holds a senior position in Islamic microfinance Institution	5 years	Master's Degree

needed to hear from Libyan specialists on the problems that Islamic microfinance institutions would face when it comes to financing MSMEs in the country. The specialists also gave the researcher some suggestions for resolving the problems. This procedure is extremely time- and cost-effective. Most importantly, it is the most efficient method for achieving the study objectives and answering the research questions in this type of research. It is one of the most effective strategies in the absence of primary data sources (Dudovskiy, 2016). The responders' names were encrypted to safeguard their privacy. The details of the interviewees are listed in Table 4.1.

Validity and Reliability

Reliability and validity of research instruments are very significant concepts in scientific research findings. In the qualitative approach, validity means that the researcher checks to confirm the accuracy of the findings by applying specific procedures, while reliability refers to the research's consistency across different researchers and projects (Creswel, 2008). The researchers have adopted a constructivist paradigm, as the questions' design has been driven by researchers' knowledge and experience. Furthermore, each semi-structured interview question must be linked to the primary or secondary research objectives/questions (Shaw, 2020). Therefore, interview questions were identified and adapted from relevant theory related to issues and challenges raised in introducing of Islamic microfinance and modified according to this research objective (Muhammed, 2012; Maulana, 2018). To validate the content, before the research taken place, a draft of the questions was piloted on two Islamic microfinance experts and two academicians. Consequently, valuable feedback was obtained, and minor modifications were made accordingly to ensure consistency is achieved across each interviewee's inquiry area. The interview is conducted with participants considered the most expert group to ensure the research outcome's validity.

Data Analysis

Thematic analysis is a frequently utilized type of qualitative data analysis within and outside of psychology. Braun and Clarke (2006) demonstrated that thematic analysis can be employed independently of other data analysis methods. According to Braun and Clarke (2006), since it is not limited to theory or epistemologies, thematic analysis is very versatile, diversified, and it fits into a broader range of methodologies. The researcher used NVivo 12 Plus Software to perform coding and analysis stages. NVivo allows the researcher to be more creative in their analysis while also relieving the strain of coding more effectively and efficiently by making retrieval much easier (Zamawe, 2015). Basit agrees that NVivo is more versatile in terms of coding. Furthermore, the usage of NVivo allows for fast reform and reorganization of the code and node structure, facilitating a more accurate and transparent data analysis process. As a result, it enhances the accuracy of qualitative investigations (Bazeley, 2009).

Qualitative Results and Findings

This section provides themes/parent-nodes and sub-categories/child-nodes generated from the data analysis process. All themes, categories, and sub-categories were generated from participants' responses obtained through open-ended questions used in interviews. The data was analyzed using a systematic approach with NVivo 12 Plus. A total of 4 main themes and 28 sub-themes were generated from the data analysis process.

Theme 1: Government-Related Challenges

Governments play a vital role in supporting new initiatives, particularly Islamic microfinance institutions worldwide. However, this is not the case in Libya, as those institutions are encountering numerous challenges. In response to RQ1, interviewees indicated several challenges, such as lack of legislation, lack of government support, political instability, inefficient chambers of commerce, lack of economic diversity, reliance on governmental appointments, and unstandardized institutions. Thus, all those challenges are considered as categories/child-nodes for theme 1.

Lack of Legislation

One of the main challenges is the unavailability of laws and legislation pertaining to Islamic microfinance institutions (IMFIs) in Libya. More than 50 percent of the participants mentioned this challenge during the interviews. Participant A6 answered this question by saying: "There is no legislation and laws in Libya, although CBL is very cooperative in setting those laws." There is no specific legislation regarding Islamic microfinance in Libya, and legislation and laws have not been enacted yet. This result is confirmed by a previous study by Maulana (2018), which concluded that legislation issues are among the challenges facing BMT in Indonesia.

Lack of Government Support

About 50 percent of the experts who were interviewed argued that the government does not support those initiatives. Participant A5 stressed the importance of government support by mentioning that: "Without government support, all other parties will find it almost impossible to make any progress in this direction." The present findings seem to be consistent with other research which found that the government plays an imperative role in Islamic microfinance development (Abbara et al., 2019).

Inefficient Chamber of Commerce

The chamber of commerce could have played a fundamental role in dispute resolution. However, this is not the case in Libya. Participant A2 mentioned the inadequacy of the Libyan Chamber of Commerce and pointed out that "the chamber of commerce is also inefficient as there are many disputes that can be resolved through the customs of the chamber of commerce courts."

Lack of Economic Diversity

Regarding economic fragility, when compared to the average fragile context, Libya indicates weaker GDP growth, higher unemployment, and heavier dependency on resource rent (OECD, 2018). As interviewee A1 put it: "the problem is that the nature of our economy, with its over-reliance on oil production." The Libyan government has finally realized that and is attempting to diversify its industrial sector to reduce its reliance on the volatile oil sector (Abdesamed, 2014).

Political Instability

As political change has a very significant impact on any business, participant A5 acknowledges the importance of political stability and states that: "The current political situation has a devastating impact on the economy in general and on the financial system in particular." The findings of (Echchabi & Abd. Aziz, 2012) are consistent with the results of this study. The researchers showed that political stability and financial and economic conditions are among the factors impeding the adoption of Islamic banking in Morocco.

Over-Reliance on Governmental Appointments

A huge portion of the Libyan budget is spent on salaries due to the increased number of corrupted official appointments and hiring more than needed. Interview A1, who worked in the largest bank in Libya for more than a decade, said: "The majority of Libyan people rely on salaries."

Unstandardized Institutions

Libya has multiple governments and two central banks in the country's west and east, in addition to poor and corrupted administrations and financial sectors. In respect to this issue, participant A3 said that: "We have two CBL in Libya, two Libyan Audit Bureau, and half of the banking transactions follow the West and the other half adopt the East."

Theme 2: Challenges Related to Islamic Microfinance Institutions (IMFIs)

Islamic microfinance institutions (IMFIs) in Libya are facing many challenges in developing and sustaining their businesses. Even though IMFIs have started gaining recognition and proven ability as a viable alternative to conventional microfinance (Cross, 2015), there are still some issues that need to be tackled. Studies reveal that lengthy financing approval (Kustin, 2015), lack of accessibility, and high administration costs (Rahman & Dean, 2013). The following section represents the experts' view on the main challenges for IMFIs in Libya.

Incompetent Human Resource

There is no doubt that there is a lack of experts and expertise concerning the operation of IMFIs in Libya. Most of the interviewees agreed on this challenge. Interviewee A5 stated: "There is also the issue of experience and the know-how of bankers/staff regarding the accounting treatment of these models." This finding concurs with Abbara et al. (2019), who discovered that a lack of human resources is one of the impediments to the development of Islamic microfinance in Turkey.

High Operating Costs

This challenge is specifically related to Islamic equity-based microfinance in terms of selecting the client, follow-ups, etc. Half of the interviewees were concerned about the high operation costs relating to Islamic equity-based microfinance. Participant A1 pointed out: "Costing challenge, in terms of how to identify the appropriate client, check their records, ensure the reliability of guarantees or Al-rahn provided. The technical aspects are also very important for the success of any project." According to Jawan (2019), one of the obvious challenges confronting Libyan MSMEs is the high cost of funding. The findings of this study corroborate those of a previous study, which concluded that one of the challenges experienced in Islamic microfinance is high administration costs (Abdul Rahman & Dean, 2013).

Risk-Averse

Islamic banks and financial institutions are risk-averse and avoid providing equity-based financing and prefer to fund MSMEs rather than start-ups due to the high risk involved. In this context, interviewees shared their perspectives on this issue. According to participant A4, who works as a *Shari'ah* Board Member at some Islamic banks in Libya, "Otherwise, banks and other profit-maximizing institutions are risk-averse and prefer to go for debt-based contracts such as Murabahah and Tawarruq."

Complicated and Lengthy Procedures

In terms of selecting, approving, and granting financing to their clients, A1 said: "Lengthy and complicated procedures to get financing in Libya." Participant A6 agreed with that by saying: "the process of granting financing is a bit lengthy."

Conflict of Interests

Some conventional banks' staff are not willing to get out of their comfort zones and learn about Islamic banking products and services, while others are afraid of being downgraded. Therefore, they are resistant to change and adjust their mindset to Islamic financial products. Participant A2 added: "The majority of leaders and managers were raised in conventional banking environments . . . and used to interest rates and then shifted to Islamic banks with the same conventional banking mentality."

Lack of Creativity and Innovation

Islamic banks and financial institutions' products and services, in Libya as in other regions, are missing the element of innovation and relying excessively on one product. Participant A6 blamed the Libyan government by saying that "the government is still working in the traditional way and using the traditional mentality."

Lack of Accessibility to MSMEs

In the past, an attempt was made to finance MSMEs projects in Libya, but reachability was a huge challenge, especially for people who live in villages. Participant A1 said, "Accessibility challenges; there are difficulties in terms of accessing the services to the target clients or micro-investors and marketing their products."

Theme 3: Challenges Related to the Potential Clients (MSMEs)

Access to funds has been a major issue concerning MSMEs, not only in Libya but also in other countries (Abdesamed, 2014). Numerous issues have emerged related to the potential clients or SMEs' owners in Libya. Several issues were highlighted by the experts interviewed. Some of these issues are mostly spoken about in past studies, such as agency problems, while others are specifically related to the Libyan context: for instance, lack of awareness and acceptance, lack of mutual trust, and low investment motive.

Agency Problems

Most past studies discussed this issue, which is specifically related to equity-based financing (partnership contracts). Participant A5 agreed with that statement, stating that "the credit risk of equity-based financing is higher than that of debt-based financing because of moral hazard problems."

Lack of Awareness and Acceptance

Some potential clients do not have an adequate understanding of Islamic finance generally and Islamic microfinance specifically. Therefore, awareness is needed to raise public understanding of this initiative. Participant A6, who speaks from his own experience, said: "How to implement Islamic microfinance culture in Libyan society. As the microfinance concept is very new to us, we tried to educate people about it." The findings of this study confirms Masyita and Ahmed (2013), stating that most clients are not aware of Islamic financing modes. Muhammed (2012) indicated that awareness problems could be one of the challenges encountering Islamic microfinance in Nigeria.

Lack of Trustworthiness

There is a mutual lack of trust between financial institutions and potential clients. Participant A5 stated that "there is a lack of trust between banks and customers." These findings are in alignment with Abdulaziz (2016), who indicated that Bank Al Tanmcya's involvement with SMEs is primarily motivated by their perceived profitability. However, the relative information asymmetry of SMEs and their weak financial infrastructure, as evidenced by their absence of credible collateral and the unavailability and unreliability of financial statement information, as well as prevailing economic instability and the centralization of the bank's organizational structure, have a negative impact on the bank's involvement.

Low Investment Motive

Some clients are more inclined to spend or consume rather than invest their funds. In conjunction with this, interviewee A1, whose institution attempted to provide financing for investment purposes, made a prefunding statement by saying:

> I have also noticed in some cases that some Libyans are not interested in commodities such as cars, boats, etc., but in cash. Unfortunately, they tend to sell the commodity after possessing it and spend the cash instead of investing it in productive activities.

Theme 4: Proposed Solutions

Respondents were asked to suggest some solutions to overcome those challenges. The next section provides solutions to most of the prevailing challenges discussed in the previous section.

Government Support

Government support is crucial for the development and sustainability of IMFIs. All six participants unanimously agreed that government support is the key ingredient for the development, sustainability, and success of IMFIs in Libya. Participant A5 commented: "In my opinion, the government is by far the most important player in the development of microfinance in Libya."

Cultivating Awareness and Financing Culture

To spread the financing culture in Libya, a small number of interviewees suggested that: "Nonetheless, we need to spread this financing culture and increase awareness in Libyan society. We want the investment culture to spread in Libya." (A1)

Collective Work of All Stakeholders

About half of those who were interviewed indicated that economic development should be the collective responsibility of all parties. One interviewee stated that:

> economic development should be a collective responsibility of all, i.e., government and private sector." The former provides monetary support, and the

latter administers and supervises projects. It requires lots of collective work from all the leaders, managers, and all parties involved. (A2)

Encouraging Investment and Production

Some participants expressed the belief that the financing provided should be channeled to investment and production activities rather than consumption. Participant A2 commented, "I am against giving financing for consumption purposes but for channeling financing to productive activities that contribute to economic growth."

Regulatory and Institutional Framework

A minority of participants (20 percent) indicated the importance of issuing legislation concerning IMFIs in Libya. Interviewee A5: "ensuring an adequate regulatory and institutional framework is in place." This result agrees with Abdulsaleh (2017), who showed that enabling conditions such as a well-defined regulatory framework are needed to support the growth of Libya's MSMEs.

Training and Technical Support

A small number of interviewees spoke about the importance of training and empowering staff: "There is also a need for continuing hands-on training for bankers/staff" (A5). Another interviewee stated: "We have undergone very intensive training on customer service, financial analysis, and Islamic microfinance concepts" (A6). This finding is consistent with Abdual Rahman and Dean (2013), who suggested the development of enabling law and policy environment.

Setting up Takaful and Agency Companies

Concerning the high operation costs and lack of mutual trust in equity-based contracts, participant A4 stressed the importance of accompanying the development of IMFIs with the involvement of takaful companies. However, this problem can be overcome by takaful companies, which ensure the success of SMEs by minimizing follow-ups and operational costs. In addition, participant A1 proposed the engagement of agency companies to overcome the moral hazards and agency problems by providing the supervision needed.

Political Stability

As far as political stability is concerned, interviewee A5 affirmed: "Developing a system like this would not be possible without a solid political system in which a stable government is willing and committed to supporting the implementation of microfinance that is in accordance with Islamic teachings." Abdulsaleh (2017) also indicated it is possible to use Islamic finance to support the growth of MSMEs in a stable political climate.

Strategic Planning

One individual alluded to the notion of adopting clear and realistic strategies by:

> having a real vision, mission, and strategic plans. An Islamic bank must have a strategic plan for at least four years with a clear vision and mission and know how to react when crises and setbacks hit. (A2)

Conclusion

The study examined the obstacles for business sustainability that Islamic microfinance programs face when financing MSMEs in the State of Libya. Additionally, it provides suggestions for overcoming these obstacles. A qualitative research approach was used, and primary data were gathered through semi-structured interviews with Libyan exports. The study's findings indicate that numerous barriers exist to the development of Islamic microfinance in Libya. The study demonstrates that the development of the Islamic microfinance sector is hampered by a lack of government support, excessive public sector hiring, which discourages the development of MSMEs, an inefficient chamber of commerce, and the lack of a legal framework. There are additional challenges that Islamic microfinance operators face, such as high operating costs, a lack of creativity and innovation in product development, and a lack of competent human capital. The final challenges are related to the potential clients; for instance, lack of awareness and trust, agency and moral hazard problems, and reluctance to share profit. Furthermore, this study suggests that the first challenge to be handled is the regulation issue, as the current Islamic microfinance operator had to comply with the existing banking laws which decree high capital requirements, which defeats the effort to develop Islamic microfinance in Libya. To overcome the agency problem and moral hazard issues in equity-based contracts, the study proposes the engagement of agency companies and takaful operators to act as guarantors for MSMEs and contribute to the development and revival of Islamic microfinance. In general, the development of Islamic microfinance necessitates the collaboration of all stakeholders, including the government, Islamic microfinance operators, MSMEs, the Central Bank of Libya, and the Ministry of Economy.

References

AAE. (2020). *Libya: Microfinance in Post-Conflict Scenarios*. Retrieved March 22, 2022, from https://aaeafrica.org/home/libya-microfinance-in-post-conflict-scenarios

Abbara, D., Shehi, Q., & Bukari, B. O. (2019). Prospects and Challenges of Islamic Microfinance in Turkey Prospects and Challenges of Islamic Microfinance in Turkey. *Research Gate*. https://doi.org/10.13140/RG.2.2.12868.37768

Abbas, K. (2014). *The Role of Islamic Microfinance in Poverty Alleviation Based on the Perceptions of the Key Players in the Market: The Case of Pakistan (Issue November)*. International Islamic University Malaysia.

Abdesamed, K. H. (2014). *Financing of Small and Medium Enterprises (SMEs) in Libya: Determinants of External Formal Financing Conventional and Islamic Perspective*. http://ddms.usim.edu.my/bitstream/123456789/8224/1/409001925.pdf

Abdulaziz, M. A. A. (2016). *Bank Financing for Small and Medium-sized Enterprises (SMEs) in Libya*. https://researchrepository.griffith.edu.au/bitstream/handle/10072/365835/Abdulsaleh_2016_01Thesis.pdf?sequence=1

Abdul Rahman, R., & Dean, F. (2013). Challenges and Solutions in Islamic Microfinance. *Humanomics*, 29(4), 293–306. https://doi.org/10.1108/H-06-2012-0013

Abdulsaleh, A. M. (2017). The Introduction of Islamic Finance in Libya: Capturing the Opportunities for SMEs Development. *Journal of Emerging Economies and Islamic Research*, 5(1), 40–48. www.jeeir.com/v2/images/2017V5N1/JEEIR2017_V5N1_3abdulsaleh.pdf

Ahmed, H. (2002). Financing Microenterprises : An Analytical Study of Islamic Microfinance Institutions. *Islamic Economic Studies*, 9(2), 27–64. www.isdb.org/irj/go/km/docs/documents/IDBDevelopments/Internet/English/IRTI/CM/downloads/IES_Articles/Vol 9-2.HabibAhmed.FinancingMicroenterprises.dp.pdf

Anwarul Islam, K. M., Alam, I., & Hossain, S. A. (2014). Examination of Profitability between Islamic Banks and Conventional Banks in Bangladesh: A Comparative Study. *Research in Business and Management*, 1(1). https://doi.org/10.5296/rbm.v1i1.4894

Bazeley, P. (2009). Integrating Data Analyses in Mixed Methods Research. *Journal of Mixed Methods Research*, 3(3). https://doi.org/10.1177/1558689809334443

Braun, V., & Clarke, V. (2006). Using Thematic Analysis in Psychology. *Qualitative Research in Psychology*, 3(2), 77–101. https://doi.org/10.1191/1478088706qp063oa

Burke, P. Y. (2017). Pilot for a Microcredit Offer in Libya: "Namaa" Business Plan. *SLEIDSE*. https://doi.org/10.1016/b978-0-12-809372-6.00074-8

Creswel, J. W. (2008). The Selection of a Research Approach. In *Research Design: Qualitative, Quantitative, and Mixed Methods Approaches* (pp. 3–22). https://doi.org/45593:01

Cross, A. (2015). *The Viability of Islamic Microfinance: Financial Sustainability and Outreach Capabilities of Firms in the Middle East and North Africa*. https://pdfs.semanticscholar.org/19bf/f651f169581fbc724603d24f8ea47f412548.pdf

Dudovskiy, J. (2016). *Axiology – Research Methodology*. Research Methodology.

Echchabi, A., & Abd. Aziz, H. (2012). The Relationship between Religiosity and Customers' Adoption of Islamic Banking Services in Morocco. *Arabian Journal of Business and Management Review (Oman Chapter)*, 1(10), 89–94. https://doi.org/10.12816/0002190

Etikan, I., & Bala, K. (2017). Sampling and Sampling Methods. *Biometrics & Biostatistics International Journal*, 5(6), 5–7. https://doi.org/10.15406/bbij.2017.05.00149

Gunto, M., & Haji Alias, M. (2013). SMEs Development in Malaysia: Lessons for Libya. *Prosiding Perkem*, 3, 1521–1530.

Hamid, A., & Ibrahim, N. (2018). The Effect of Education Level and Experience on SMEs Performance in Libya. In *International Journal for Studies on Children, Women, Elderly and Disabled* (Vol. 4).

Jawan, K. H. (2019). The Role of Small Enterprises in the Development of Libyan Society and Economics. *International Journal of Scientific and Research Publications (IJSRP)*, 9(1), 896–906. https://doi.org/10.29322/ijsrp.9.01.2019.p85111

Kappal, J. M., & Rastogi, S. (2020). Investment Behaviour of Women Entrepreneurs. *Qualitative Research in Financial Markets*, 12(4), 485–504. https://doi.org/10.1108/QRFM-04-2020-0053

Kustin, B. (2015). *Islamic (Micro)Finance: Culture, Context, Promise, Challenges* (Issue August). https://docs.gatesfoundation.org/Documents/Islamic(Micro)FinanceCulture,Context,Promise,Challenges.pdf

Ledgerwood, J. (1999). Microfinance Handbook: An Institutional and Financial Perspective. *The World Bank*. https://openknowledge.worldbank.org/bitstream/handle/10986/12383/18771.pdf?sequence=1&isAllowed=y

Maggangka, M. (2015). *Shari'ah Appraisal in Islamic Microfinance Institutions in Riau Archipelago, Indonesia: Bmt's Products and Services (Issue September)*. International Islamic University Malaysia.

Mahmood, H., Fatima, M., Khan, M., & Qamar, M. (2015). Islamic Microfinance and Poverty Alleviation: An Empirical Ascertainment from Pakistan. *Journal of Islamic Economics, Banking and Finance*, 11(2), 85–105. http://ibtra.com/pdf/journal/v11_n2_article6.pdf

Masyita, D., & Ahmed, H. (2013). Why Is Growth of Islamic Microfinance Lower Than Its Conventional Counterparts in Indonesia? *Islamic Economic Studies*, 21(1), 35–62. https://doi.org/10.12816/0000239

Maulana, H. (2018). Factors Influencing Behaviour to Participate in Islamic Micro Finance. *International Journal of Islamic and Middle Eastern Finance and Management*, 11(1), 109–130. https://doi.org/10.1108/IMEFM-05-2017-0134

Muhammed, A. D. D. (2012). *Challenges of Microfinance and the Prospects of Developing and Introducing an Islamic Micro-Investment Model in Nigeria* (Issue October).

OECD. (2018). *Country Case Studies: Building Economic Resilience in Lebanon and Libya* (Issue December).

Omar, A., Ali, F., & Imhamed, S. (2020). Exploring Entrepreneurial Framework Conditions in Libya: A National Experts' Perspective. *Journal of Entrepreneurship, Business and Economics*, 8(1), 15–53.

Rahman, R. A. (2019). Women and Microcredit in Rural Bangladesh. In *Women and Microcredit in Rural Bangladesh*. https://doi.org/10.4324/9780429503023

Rahman, R. A., & Dean, F. (2013). Challenges and Solutions in Islamic Microfinance. *Humanomics*, 29(4), 293–306. https://doi.org/10.1108/H-06-2012-0013

Saad, N. M. (2011). Selecting High-income Generating Activities for Micro-entrepreneurs: The Case Study of Amanah Ikhtiar Malaysia. *International Journal of Humanities and Social Science*, 1(5), 258–264. www.ijhssnet.com/journals/Vol._1_No._5;_May_2011/29.pdf

Saad, N. M., & Duasa, J. (2011). An Economic Impact Assessment of a Microcredit Program in Malaysia: The Case of Amanah Ikhtiar Malaysia (AIM). *International Journal of Business and Society*, 12(1), 1–14.

Satar, N., & Kassim, S. (2020, August). Issues and Challenges in Financing the Poor: Lessons Learned from Islamic Microfinance Institutions. *EJIF – European Journal of Islamic Finance*, 15, 1–8.

Shaw, A. (2020). *A Checklist for Developing Semi-Structured Interview Questions*. Strategic Planet Ltd.

The World Bank. (2020). *Libya Economic Outlook* (Issue Oct). papers3://publication/uuid/A06FF86D-B542-4A14-9345-8F957AD9E8C9

The World Bank. (2021). *Libya Economic Outlook.*

Zamawe, F. C. (2015). The Implication of Using NVivo Software in Qualitative Data Analysis: Evidence-Based Reflections. *Malawi Medical Journal*, 27(1), 13–15. https://doi.org/10.4314/mmj.v27i1.4

5 Sustainability Through Zakat

An Experience of the Islamic Banking Industry of Malaysia

Nurul 'Iffah binti M A Zaaba & Rusni Hassan

Introduction

In the beginning, the word sustainable only referred to the avoidance of plastic containers and implementing recycling programs (Banks Editorial Team, 2020). The word sustainable was not associated with banking until recently (Banks Editorial Team, 2020). Sustainable banking involves a change in thinking from profit maximization to recognizing that social and environment factors must be taken into consideration while designing financial products and services, where it is called the "triple bottom line" (Honzik, 2020). It evolves around three important agendas, which are the environment, ethical values and community involvement (Banks Editorial Team, 2020). The sustainability reports emerged globally due to the introduction of Global Reporting Initiative (GRI)'s G4 Sustainability Reporting Guidelines in 2013 (RESPECT International, n.d.). From there, many institutions started to produce their own reports. However, banks have been a bit slower than other industries to join the sustainability effort (Almuraikhi & Nobanee, 2022; Innig, 2021). An important point mentioned in the guidelines by GRI is that voluntary donations must be reported under the community investments (Global Reporting Initiative (GRI), 2013), where zakat-related information matters. Thus, zakat and sustainability share a common pillar where both contribute to community development. Zakat is a dependable source of funding (Obaidullah & Shirazi, 2015) that is calculated and paid annually. The size of zakat funds globally can reach up to US$1 trillion per year (Rehman & Pickup, 2018). In Malaysia, business zakat is recorded among the highest collection (Rahman, 2012) where it is reported that Islamic banks' zakat payment amounted to nearly RM30 million in 2018 (Zaaba & Hassan, 2020), and it is possible that the amount has increased over the years.

For countries like Malaysia, sustainability reports have not yet been mandated to be published (Smith, 2020), but surprisingly, Islamic banks and their group/parent companies publish their own reports (Kunhibava et al., 2018). It is a plausible effort made by the banks' group or parent companies. By disclosing more information, the public can be more convinced to conduct financial transactions with Islamic banks (Zaaba & Hassan, 2022). Literature on Islamic banking and sustainability is still lacking and is mostly conceptual in nature (Aliyu et al., 2017; Almuraikhi & Nobanee, 2022; E-Vahdati et al., 2019; Jan et al., 2018; Mohammed &

DOI: 10.4324/9781003468653-7

Nobanee, 2021). On the other hand, Zyadat (2016) and Shodiq (2021) assessed the sustainability reporting and its influence on Islamic banks in Jordan and Indonesia respectively. Some others focus on sustainability related to corporate social responsibility (CSR) (Nor & Asutay, 2011; Nor & Hashim, 2014). Although zakat is seen as part of Islamic banks' CSR contribution, it is actually important to discuss zakat apart from CSR since Islamic banks differ from their counterparts in that manner (Abd Samad et al., 2017). Thus, this study explores two objectives: 1) whether Islamic banks view zakat as an important element in their sustainability reports and 2) whether zakat is widely distributed as part of a sustainability agenda.

Methodology

This study applies secondary data collection where sustainability reports were collected from the banks' websites, as they is easily available and accessible. It focuses on licensed Islamic banks listed by Bank Negara Malaysia (BNM) (Bank Negara Malaysia, n.d.).

Results and Discussion

Zakat as Part of the Sustainability Report/Statement

Since sustainability reports are collective efforts between Islamic banks and their group, Table 5.1 shows the banks' group or individual banks that have published the report/statement, as well as whether the banks published the reports as a standalone report or as part of their annual reports.

Table 5.1 shows that all banks published their sustainability reports. This indicates that the banks are participating in the sustainability efforts, contradicting what has been claimed by Innig (2021) as well as Almuraikhi and Nobanee (2022). It is a plausible effort made by Islamic banks, since the banks should not wait for the sustainability report to be obligatory and mandated (Sibio & Bhowmik, 2021).

It is also important to note that the reporting on sustainability is improving compared to the existence of only 5 sustainability reports back in 2015–2016 (Kunhibava et al., 2018). In Malaysia, sustainability reports are under the responsibility of the banks' group or parent companies, except for Bank Islam Malaysia Berhad and MBSB Bank Berhad, where the banks make the effort on their own (Bank Islam Malaysia Berhad, 2022; MBSB Bank Berhad, 2022). The banks either publish a standalone report or report it as a part of their annual reports, as shown in Table 5.2. Most of the banks published standalone reports on sustainability, which are named a Sustainability Report. If the banks incorporated the information on sustainability with the annual report, it is named a Sustainability Statement. However, it is quite different for Al-Rajhi Bank, since the bank reported information on sustainability as part of their ESG (Environmental, Social

Table 5.1 Existence of Sustainability Report/Statement

No.	*Banks*	*Sustainability Report/Statement Issued by*	*Sustainability Report (Stand-alone report)*	*Sustainability Statement/ESG Report (Part of annual reports)*
1.	Al Rajhi Banking & Investment Corporation (Malaysia) Berhad	Group		✓
2.	Affin Islamic Bank Berhad	Group		✓
3.	Alliance Islamic Bank Berhad	Group		✓
4.	AmBank Islamic Berhad	Group	✓	
5.	Bank Islam Malaysia Berhad	Individual bank		✓
6.	Bank Muamalat Malaysia Berhad	Individual bank		✓
7.	CIMB Islamic Bank Berhad	Group	✓	
8.	Hong Leong Islamic Bank Berhad	Group	✓	
9.	HSBC Amanah Malaysia Berhad	Group		✓
10.	Kuwait Finance House (Malaysia) Berhad	Group	✓	
11.	Maybank Islamic Berhad	Group	✓	
12.	MBSB Bank Berhad	Individual bank	✓	
13.	OCBC Al-Amin Bank Berhad	Group	✓	
14.	Public Islamic Bank Berhad	Group		✓
15.	RHB Islamic Bank Berhad	Group	✓	
16.	Standard Chartered Saadiq Berhad	Group	✓	

and Governance) Report. Table 5.2 shows the effort of reporting zakat as part of the banks' sustainability reports.

Table 5.2 shows that not all banks mentioned their zakat as part of their sustainability reports, and 4 banks do not mention their zakat at all. This is normal for HSBC Holdings plc and Standard Chartered, since their Islamic banks are not obliged to pay zakat (HSBC Amanah Malaysia Berhad, 2022, p. 21, 29; Standard Chartered Saadiq Berhad, 2022, p. 22).

Table 5.2 Zakat in the Sustainability Report/Statement

No.	*Banks*	*Zakat is Mentioned*	*Total search results that match the word 'zakat'*
1.	Al Rajhi Banking & Investment Corporation (Malaysia) Berhad	✓	4
2.	Affin Islamic Bank Berhad	✓	16
3.	Alliance Islamic Bank Berhad	✓	7
4.	AmBank Islamic Berhad	✓	5
5.	Bank Islam Malaysia Berhad	✓	6
6.	Bank Muamalat Malaysia Berhad	✓	1
7.	CIMB Islamic Bank Berhad	✓	4
8.	Hong Leong Islamic Bank Berhad	✓	14
9.	HSBC Amanah Malaysia Berhad	X	-
10.	Kuwait Finance House (Malaysia) Berhad	✓	11
11.	Maybank Islamic Berhad	✓	26
12.	MBSB Bank Berhad	✓	8
13.	OCBC Al-Amin Bank Berhad	X	-
14.	Public Islamic Bank Berhad	X	-
15.	RHB Islamic Bank Berhad	✓	16
16.	Standard Chartered Saadiq Berhad	X	-

On the other hand, Public Islamic Bank Berhad and OCBC Al-Amin Bank Berhad do pay their zakat (OCBC Al-Amin Bank Berhad, 2022, pp. 16 & 44; Public Islamic Bank Berhad, 2022, p. 69), but it is unfortunate that Public Bank Berhad and OCBC Group do not report it as part of their sustainability report. The search is also performed to show that zakat has been regularly mentioned in the reports and is substantial information. Thus, zakat information can be considered as one of the important agendas of banks' sustainability reports.

Zakat Information in the Sustainability Reports

In total, only 12 banks disclosed their zakat contribution in the sustainability reports. For further explanation, this section will elaborate the information regarding zakat in their sustainability reports and/or sustainability statements.

Table 5.3 shows the information banks disclosed on their zakat contribution or distribution in their sustainability reports. It is shown that the banks are actively paying and distributing their zakat fund for various occasions, including during COVID-19. Moreover, collaboration with NGOs helps the banks in achieving wide and effective distribution. It is shown in the Table 5.3 that Islamic banks are the

Table 5.3 Zakat Contribution and Distribution of Islamic Banks

No.	*Banks*	*Zakat Contribution*	*Zakat Distribution*
1.	Al Rajhi Banking & Investment Corporation (Malaysia) Berhad	The bank paid SAR 1,699 million of zakat in 2021 (Al Rajhi Bank, 2022, p. 117) to the General Authority of Zakat and Tax (p. 128). The bank also employed qualified experts to ensure compliance with all rules and regulation regarding Zakat and tax (p. 128).	X
2.	Affin Islamic Bank Berhad	The bank contributed more than RM6 millions of zakat to the improvement of the underprivileged (Affin Bank Berhad, 2022, pp. 145, 164 & 180).	The bank contributed RM595,000 to Angkatan Tentera Malaysia as well as to asnaf in Selangor and Kuala Lumpur under 'Program Seorang Sekampit Beras,' organized by Association of Islamic Banks in Malaysia (AIBIM) and Bank Negara Malaysia (BNM) (pp. 168 & 169).
3.	Alliance Islamic Bank Berhad	The banks' zakat allocation for 2022 amounted to RM400,000.	Alliance Bank helps the community by providing financial assistance through bank crowdfunding platform SocioBiz and zakat (Alliance Bank Malaysia Berhad, 2022, p. 30). Zakat is given to the banks' partners, such as Yayasan Kebajikan Negara and Yayasan Pembangunan Ekonomi Islam Malaysia (YaPEIM). The bank also channeled their zakat to communities during COVID-19. Moreover, the bank worked together with People Systems Consultancy to support the asnaf entrepreneurs financially in expanding their business. And by working together with YaPEIM, the bank funded the renovation of the entrepreneurs' premises and purchase of equipment in obtaining Halal certification. The bank also helped students at Universiti Teknologi MARA (UiTM) by settling their outstanding tuition fees (pp. 49 & 51).

(*Continued*)

Table 5.3 (Continued)

No.	*Banks*	*Zakat Contribution*	*Zakat Distribution*
4.	AmBank Islamic Berhad	The bank contributed RM991,087 in 2022 (AmBank Group, 2022, pp. 9 & 29).	The bank held monthly programs for the society and Non-Government Organizations (NGO) by using various modes of communication including zakat contribution (pp. 16 & 52).
5.	Bank Islam Malaysia Berhad	X	Sadaqa House of the bank has continued to be the platform for the bank's philanthropic social finance activities using zakat fund and waqf (Bank Islam Malaysia Berhad, 2022, pp. 124 & 126). The bank contributed RM600,000 in zakat through the bank's program 'Projek Bantuan Rumah, Baiti Jannati' (p. 132). The bank made RM5,000 zakat contribution to Masjid Jamek Kampung Baru during AMAL Ihtimam Ramadan program (p. 132). The bank distributed RM23,000 in zakat funds during AMAL Ihtimam Korban at an army camp named Kem Kementah (p. 133).
6.	Bank Muamalat Malaysia Berhad	X	Tabung Mawaddah, an internal charitable fund that comprises various funds including zakat (Bank Muamalat Malaysia Berhad, 2022, p. 99).
7.	CIMB Islamic Bank Berhad	CIMB Islamic Bank contributed RM5.6 million of corporate zakat in 2021 (CIMB Group Holdings Berhad, 2022, p. 71).	X
8.	Hong Leong Islamic Bank Berhad	X	The bank facilitated Zakat-related transactions to their customers, including zakat payment using debit card and JomPAY to allow customers to pay their zakat outside office hours (Hong Leong Bank Berhad, 2022, p. 49).

9.	Kuwait Finance House (Malaysia) Berhad	The bank paid KWD 1.5 million of zakat in 2020. (Kuwait Finance House, 2021, p. 114).	One of the social value creations of KFH is via zakat (p. 67). KFH made zakat payments to ensure the bank's economic sustainability (p. 49). KFH supported Kuwait Zakat House, a good deeds program in 2019, and also supported the government during COVID-19 (p. 114).
10.	Maybank Islamic Berhad	The bank contributed RM2.6 billion in tax and zakat in 2021 (Maybank Group, 2022, p. 32), including RM1 million was given to more than 4,000 beneficiaries using MAE (p. 49).	The bank elaborated on their zakat contributions to two different categories, which are given to state religion authorities as well as channeled via community programs (pp. 57 & 70). The bank also contributed RM125,000 and RM300,000 to help the communities during COVID-19 to 20 beneficiaries and a program named 'Maybank Islamic Save a Child's Heart' to 17 patients respectively (pp. 59 & 72).
11.	MBSB Bank Berhad	The bank contributed RM259 millions in tax and zakat to the government in 2021 (MBSB Bank Berhad, 2022, pp. 11 & 15).	The bank mentioned the existence of Zakat Policy, among other policies in achieving Shari'ah compliance (p. 40).
12.	RHB Islamic Bank Berhad	The bank contributed RM6 millions of zakat (RHB Bank Berhad, 2022, p. 59).	The bank participated in MyZakat Working Group under the supervision of AIBIM (p. 26). The bank redistributed RM416,000 of zakat refunds (p. 59). The bank also gave zakat amounting to RM100,000 to Masjid Al-Ghufran Perlis (p. 59).

largest zakat contribution annually since the banks are paying millions of zakat, as claimed by Rahman (2012).

Conclusion

This study has explored Islamic banks in Malaysia in relation to zakat information in the banks' sustainability reports. The information gathered from the banks' reports shows that Islamic banks are indeed using zakat as one of the sources of fund in helping the community. These wide distributions to the underprivileged and people in dire need, especially during COVID-19, proves that zakat contribution and distribution of Islamic banks aligned with the zakat requirement of giving the fund to the asnaf. The practice also aligned with the sustainability agenda by helping the community and most importantly, it achieved the maqasid Shari'ah. In view of different styles of reporting, this study suggests that banks follow the GRI's Sustainability Reporting Guidelines as well as provide comprehensive and detail disclosure. It is also timely for the relevant authorities to mandate the publication of sustainability reports.

References

Abd Samad, K., Said, R., Mohd Nasir, I. N., Mahshar, M., & Kamarulzaman, M. H. (2017). Analysis of the Role of Zakat on Islamic Banking Performance. In *State-of-the-Art Theories and Empirical Evidence* (pp. 275–281). https://doi.org/10.1007/978-981-10-6926-0_18

Affin Bank Berhad. (2022). *Annual Report 2021.*

Aliyu, S., Hassan, M. K., Yusof, R. M., & Nalimi, N. (2017). Islamic Banking Sustainability: A Review of Literature and Directions for Future Research. *Emerging Markets Finance and Trade*, 53(2), 440–470. https://doi.org/10.1080/1540496X.2016.1262761

Alliance Bank Malaysia Berhad. (2022). *2022 Annual Report.*

Almuraikhi, M., & Nobanee, H. (2022). *Sustainability Practices in Islamic Banks* (pp. 1–12).

Al Rajhi Bank. (2022). *Annual Report 2021.*

AmBank Group. (2022). *2022 Sustainability Report.*

Bank Islam Malaysia Berhad. (2022). *Integrated Annual Report 2021.*

Bank Muamalat Malaysia Berhad. (2022). *Annual Report 2021.*

Bank Negara Malaysia. (n.d.). *Financial Sector Participants Directory.* Retrieved December 23, 2022, from www.bnm.gov.my/regulations/fsp-directory

Banks Editorial Team. (2020). *What Is Sustainability in the Banking Industry*? Retrieved December 25, 2022, from banks.com website: www.banks.com/articles/banking/sustainable-banking/

CIMB Group Holdings Berhad. (2022). *Sustainability Report 2021.*

E-Vahdati, S., Zulkifli, N., & Zakaria, Z. (2019). Corporate Governance Integration with Sustainability: A Systematic Literature Review. *Corporate Governance (Bingley)*, 19(2), 255–269. https://doi.org/10.1108/CG-03-2018-0111

Global Reporting Initiative (GRI). (2013). *G4 Sustainability Reporting Guidelines.*

Hong Leong Bank Berhad. (2022). *Sustainability Report 2022.*

Honzik, M. (2020). *What Is Sustainable Banking*? Retrieved December 26, 2022, from ecolytiq website: https://ecolytiq.com/blog-what-is-sustainable-banking/

HSBC Amanah Malaysia Berhad. (2022). *Financial Statements – 31 December 2021.*

Innig, C. (2021). *In Banking, Sustainability Is the New Digital. Now What*? Retrieved December 26, 2022, from Accenture website: https://bankingblog.accenture.com/banking-sustainability-new-digital-now-what

Jan, A., Marimuthu, M., Mohd, M. P. Bin, & Isa, M. (2018). Sustainability Practices and Banks Financial Performance: A Conceptual Review from the Islamic Banking Industry in Malaysia. *International Journal of Business and Management*, 13(11), 61–88. https://doi.org/10.5539/ijbm.v13n11p61

Kunhibava, S., Ling, S. T. Y., & Ruslan, M. K. (2018). Sustainable Financing and Enhancing the Role of Islamic Banks in Malaysia. *Arab Law Quarterly*, 32(2), 129–157. https://doi.org/10.1163/15730255-12322023

Kuwait Finance House. (2021). *Sustainability Report 2019–2020.*

Maybank Group. (2022). *Sustainability Report 2021.*

MBSB Bank Berhad. (2022). *Sustainability Report 2021.*

Mohammed, O., & Nobanee, H. (2021). *The Role of Islamic Banks in Sustainable Development* (pp. 1–8).

Nor, S. M., & Asutay, M. (2011). Re-Considering CSR and Sustainability Identity of Islamic Banks in Malaysia: An Empirical Analysis. *8th International Conference on Islamic Economics and Finance* (pp. 1–17).

Nor, S. M., & Hashim, N. A. (2014). CSR and Sustainability Dimension in Islamic Banking in Malaysia: A Management Insight. *26th International Business Research Conference* (pp. 1–15).

Obaidullah, M., & Shirazi, N. S. (2015). *Islamic Social Finance Report 1436H.*

OCBC Al-Amin Bank Berhad. (2022). *Reports and Financial Statements for the Financial Year Ended 31 December 2021.*

Public Islamic Bank Berhad. (2022). *Financial Statements – 31 December 2021.*

Rahman, A. A. (2012). The Role of Zakat in Islamic Banking Institutions in Developing the Economy of the Poor and Needy in Malaysia. *Tazkia Islamic Finance and Business Review*, 7(2), 256–276. https://doi.org/10.30993/TIFBR.V7I2.16

Rehman, A. A., & Pickup, F. (2018). *Zakat for the SDGs*. Retrieved December 23, 2022, from United Nations Development Programme (UNDP) website: www.undp.org/blog/zakat-sdgs

RESPECT International. (n.d.). *G4 Sustainability Reporting Guidelines – Implementation Manual*. Retrieved December 25, 2022.

RHB Bank Berhad. (2022). *Sustainability Report 2021.*

Shodiq, M. J. (2021). The Influence of Sustainability Report on Islamic Banking Performance in Indonesia. In Barolli, L., Yim, K., & Enokido, T. (Eds.), *Complex, Intelligent and Software Intensive Systems* (pp. 590–597). https://doi.org/10.1007/978-3-030-79725-6_59

Sibio, C. D., & Bhowmik, R. (2021). *Sustainability Reporting: Five Ways Companies Should Prepare*. Retrieved December 28, 2022, from World Economic Forum website: www.weforum.org/agenda/2021/06/sustainability reporting-five-ways-companies-should-prepare/

Smith, S. (2020). *Mandatory Sustainability Reporting: What Countries Have It and Should Other Join*? Retrieved December 31, 2022, from reportadvisor.info website: https://reportadviser.info/news/mandatory-sustainability-reporting-what-countries-have-it-and-should-other-join

Standard Chartered Saadiq Berhad. (2022). *Financial Statements for Financial Year Ended 31 December 2021.*

Zaaba, N. I. B. M. A., & Hassan, R. (2020). Calculation, Distribution and Disclosure of Zakat in Malaysia Islamic Banks. *Journal of Islam in Asia Special Issue Islamic Banking and Finance*, 17(2), 162–181.

Zaaba, N. I. B. M. A., & Hassan, R. (2022). The Practice of Islamic Bank in Zakat Distribution: The Case of Malaysia. In Alareeni, B., & Hamdan, A. (Eds.), *Innovation of Businesses, and Digitalization During Covid-19 Pandemic* (pp. 183–193). https://doi.org/10.1007/978-3-031-08090-6

Zyadat, A. A. F. H. (2016). The Impact of Sustainability on the Financial Performance of Jordanian Islamic Banks. *International Journal of Economics and Finance*, 9(1), 55–63. https://doi.org/10.5539/ijef.v9n1p55

Part II

Islamic Sustainable Finance

Classical Instruments in Modern Practices

6 Instruments of Islamic Sustainable Finance

Romzie Rosman, Nur Harena Redzuan & Siti Saffa' Shaharuddin

Introduction

The current global financial crisis, climate change, and the Covid-19 pandemic have inflicted hardships on many people and raised many concerns about the financial system's stability and sustainability (Sawyer, 2021; Bolton et al., 2021). Sustainable, fair, and balanced development for the current and future generations became the major challenge of our century. As a result, there is a growing movement towards advocating alternative ways to create sustainable outcomes to meet the long-term interests of people worldwide while also adding value to the real economy. For instance, the Environmental, Social, and Governance (ESG) criteria for investment and the Sustainable Development Goals (SDGs) are gaining popularity as the preferred responses to these problems. ESG is an acronym for the three most critical factors in determining a company's sustainability and moral impact over time. As stated by Lontsikh et al. (2022), most ethical financiers employ ESG criteria in their investment analysis. In 2021, nearly one trillion dollars in global financial markets were associated with the ESG agenda. Experts predict that no investments will be made in companies that disregard ESG principles. According to Kamil et al. (2019), the Maqasid al-Shari'ah, the backbone of Islamic finance, has common ideals and principles of environmental and sustainability preservation. Hence, as Gundogdu (2018) highlighted in his study, the Islamic financial system can become one of the mechanisms and systems that offers this alternative to achieve sustainability while also making a significant contribution to the expansion of global financial markets in the long term. The core tenets of Islamic finance have close ties to the concepts of financial stability and social responsibility in terms of Islamic sustainable finance and investment. The principles of Islamic finance provide benefits such as fairness, sustainability, interest in the enterprise of all parties involved, and interest in achieving the desired outcome (Ahmed, 2019).

The fundamental requirement set by Shari'ah law principles determines the sustainability and viability of Islamic finance. Islamic transactions must strictly adhere to what is halal (permissible) and eliminate the haram (forbidden). These requirements are implied by divine rules such as the prohibition of riba (interest), gharar (ambiguity), maisir (gambling), and the trading of non-halal products and services such as pork. Moreover, because Islamic finance principles protect

DOI: 10.4324/9781003468653-9

the Islamic financial system from excessive leverage, speculation, and uncertainty, Islamic finance promotes financial stability and long-term sustainability (Al-Roubaie & Sarea, 2019). Consequently, it is anticipated that an increase in the application of the principles of Islamic finance will eventuate, not only in the financial markets of Muslim countries but also in the markets that are concerned with socially responsible objectives and ethical financial solutions. This is because Islamic finance is based on the belief and the principles of Islamic finance, where financial transactions should be conducted under Shari'ah and ethical principles. The REDmoney Group conducted an Islamic Sustainable Finance and Investment Survey in 2022 (REDmoney Group, 2022). In this survey, over 100 practitioners from the Islamic finance industry were surveyed to understand how their respective organizations adopt Islamic sustainable finance and investment. According to the survey findings, 77% of practitioners believe greenwashing is challenging in the Islamic environmental, social, and governance space. Also, the foremost factor practitioners cite as the primary driver of ESG adaptation within their institution is a desire to make a positive impact. This figure represents 49% of all practitioners who participated in the survey. Approximately 6% of respondents cited pressure from industry peers as the primary reason for implementing ESG practices in their respective financial institutions. Then, 60% of the practitioners surveyed attributed a lack of robust ESG data as the main challenge their institution faces in ESG adaptation. Furthermore, 54% of the practitioners surveyed believe Islamic institutions should consider a company's stance on LGBTQ+ (lesbian, gay, bisexual, transgender, queer, and other) issues when making investment decisions. These data demonstrated the considerations of Islamic financial institutions in implementing ESG practices in line with Maqasid al-Shari'ah and achieving Islamic sustainable finance objectives.

Islamic Sustainable Finance and SDGs

Islamic finance refers to a mode of financing activities that comply with Shari'ah. Islamic finance can ensure that more financial resources are mobilized sustainably for the SDGs in a more inclusive way. There is no finite definition of Islamic sustainable finance. However, Islamic finance is expected to support the sustainable agenda and Maqasid Shari'ah. This is well proven when Islamic social finance instruments adopted by Islamic banking and non-banking institutions are tremendously developed. The instruments such as waqf, zakat, and sadaqah are widely expected to contribute to people's socioeconomic well-being. Based on the OECD development policy paper report in 2020, the report identifies the opportunities that Islamic finance present for donors to contribute to achieving SDGs. There is a need to mobilize innovative financing forms and broaden exposure to alternative financing forms that could be mobilized for development. According to the report, Arab donors could consider harnessing Islamic finance to strengthen partnerships with the OECD development assistance committee members to create more equitable and stable development finance for delivering the SDGs that can significantly impact the partner countries (OECD, 2020). Applying Islamic finance in Muslim-majority contexts may be socially, culturally, and ethically more acceptable than other conventional finance forms, including development finance (OECD, 2020). Accordingly, Islamic finance can promote low systemic risks and a sustainable financing system which is essential for developing countries. Concerning Islamic social finance, there are opportunities to accelerate the delivery of SDGs through Islamic social finance instruments, namely zakat, waqf, sadaqah, and Islamic microfinance. Also, sukuk issuance can be a crucial instrument to finance sustainable investment.

Instruments Affecting Islamic Sustainable Finance

The Islamic banking and finance industry was formally established in Malaysia with the inception of the first Islamic bank, Bank Islam Malaysia Berhad, in 1983. With the existence of the Islamic banking industry for almost 40 years, a comprehensive Islamic financial instrument includes the products and services offered to customers. The products include deposit, investment accounts, home financing, hire purchase financing, personal financing, credit cards, sukuk, and many more. These financial instruments are based on the contract of partnership, profit sharing, trading of assets and commodities, and other contracts that comply with Shari'ah. Moreover, the relationship arrangement is based on actual economic transactions involving a real asset and ownership for the financial transaction. In contracting terms, each relationship is tied to specific contractual obligations where the roles and responsibilities of each party to the transaction are clearly defined and agreed upon up-front. Islamic banking and finance institutions are constantly encouraged to be involved in activities promoting risk-sharing. From the theoretical point of view, a risk-sharing model is expected to be an effective mechanism to promote financial stability since risks are shared between relevant parties in the financial system. Risk-sharing has been regarded as one of the main principles representing the Islamic banking and finance system. In the Islamic financial sector, the provider of funds, in the case of investment account holders, will channel funds to financial intermediaries based on a profit and loss sharing contract. Upon receiving the funds, financial intermediaries use the funds for some asset classes to provide returns in the future.

The European Commission stated that sustainable finance incorporates ESG considerations into financial investment decisions, resulting in longer-term investments in sustainable economic activities and projects. For example, environmental concerns may include climate change mitigation and adaptation, as well as the environment in general, such as biodiversity preservation, pollution prevention, and the circular economy. Moreover, social considerations may include the dimensions of inequality, inclusiveness, labour relations, investment in human capital and communities, and human rights issues. For the governance of public and private institutions, this may include management structures, employee relations, and executive remuneration. Meanwhile, Islamic finance, guided by the Shari'ah principle to protect and preserve the benefits and interests of society, can act as an enabler of sustainable finance. Islamic finance is aimed at a balanced distribution of wealth, whereas Islam encourages all the means that enable a balanced distribution of wealth. Indeed, it is a Qur'anic principle that is established as follows:

> Whatever God restored to His Messenger from the inhabitants of the villages belongs to God, and to the Messenger, and to the relatives, and to the orphans, and to the poor, and to the wayfarer; so that it may not circulate solely between the wealthy among you.
>
> (Al-Qur'an, 59:7)

Islamic finance is a way to enhance sustainable finance by bringing those who are self-excluded based on religious concerns into the financial system. Specifically, the Islamic principles of risk-sharing and wealth redistribution are inherently complementary to the goals of sustainable finance. Based on Maybank in explaining humanizing finance concerning the concept of Islamic wealth management (IWM) from a Shari'ah perspective, it involves 5 cycles from wealth creation to wealth distribution, with some examples of the Islamic financial instruments of each cycle (refer to Table 6.1).

In relation to Islamic financial instruments and sustainable finance, it is necessary to have a model for the sustainable circulation of wealth among the people in society to achieve sustainable financial practices. The wealth cannot be idle from any saving or investment instruments but needs to be well-circulated for the

Table 6.1 Islamic Wealth Management Cycles from Shari'ah Perspective

No	*Cycles*	*Explanation*
1.	Wealth Creation	The creation of wealth through income derived from Halal/Shari'ah-compliant businesses, professions, or trade and savings with Islamic financial institutions.
2.	Wealth Accumulation	The enhancement of wealth by generating returns via Islamic investments and instruments, such as Islamic equities, sukuk (Islamic bonds), as well as Islamic funds.
3.	Wealth Purification	The purification of wealth through the concept of zakat. Zakat is the giving of alms to the poor and needy and is obligatory upon every Muslim who meets the requirements to pay zakat.
4.	Wealth Protection	The protection of wealth through risk management, takaful (Islamic insurance), and Islamic trusts.
5.	Wealth Distribution	The distribution of wealth for future generations. This involves the transfer of wealth or assets (estate planning) through wasiat (will writing), waqf (endowment), and hibah (gift).

Source: Maybank

benefit of the investors. The SDGs and the ESG can only be attained through implementing an all-encompassing strategy that incorporates the collection of funding needed from the public sector, the private sector, and government initiatives. Islamic sustainable finance may support positive economic growth and financial system results by mobilizing those funds. For instance, the flow of funds in microfinancing products for small and micro enterprises would increase business activities and provide a return to the business. It also creates domino effects by creating more job opportunities for the close family members and neighborhood community with the expansion of the micro and small businesses. The activities would foster faster and healthier growth of the country's economy with the adquate circulation of wealth in the society. The people can benefit from sustainable finance by improving the welfare and well-being of the people with proper funds for education and healthcare services. It would increase people's living standards, especially among the poor. It can further support financial development and stability, thus improving the resistance of the financial system to shocks like the Covid-19 pandemic.

Islamic sustainable finance also gives positive benefits to individuals and society. Thus, proper policies supporting sustainable finance should be designed and implemented accordingly. Support from the government is a clear responsibility to ensure the policy is well executed. Hence, the Islamic banking and finance industry can play a significant role in achieving sustainable finance objectives. It is estimated that given the demography of the Muslim population, sustainable finance is key to the industry's further growth. It is believed that by doubling the pool of Muslim customers for Islamic financial institutions, the industry's size will increase more in the future. Also, there is a relationship between sustainable finance and financial inclusion. Individuals and businesses can access valuable and affordable financial products and services that meet their needs in terms of transactions, payments, savings, credit, and insurance which can be delivered responsibly and sustainably. By promoting inclusive and sustainable finance, all segments of society have access to convenient and affordable formal financial services. Thus, it allows the lower-income segments of society to safely save and invest, borrow for productive activities, and buffer themselves against unforeseen shocks. With financial inclusion that supports sustainable finance, Malaysia is one of the highest-earning countries among the middle-income countries that receive financial inclusion. According to Bank Negara Malaysia Report 2015, out of the 22 million adult population in Malaysia, 92% own bank accounts. From the figure, 59% of Malaysian adults have an account at a single institution, while the remaining 33% own accounts at multiple banking institutions (BNM, 2015). This commendable achievement results from the effort of many authorities, including the financial institutions in Malaysia, to ensure long-sustainable growth through higher financial inclusivity.

Wealth Creation

The investment account is chosen as an example to demonstrate alignment between the Islamic financial instrument and sustainable finance for wealth creation.

Investment Accounts

The Islamic bank adopted the profit-sharing tools, also known as the al-Mudharabah contract, as an alternative to the conventional interest-based investment deposit product. The al-Mudharabah contract can be defined as the capital contribution partner and the entrepreneur. The benefit from the investment or project will be based on the agreed-upon profit-sharing ratio. Al-Mudharabah in Islamic banking is an investment deposit based on the Shari'ah parameters set by Bank Negara Malaysia. Besides for-profit and saving, al-Mudharabah can also become one of the instruments to support SDGs and ESG. Those investments can support SDG 8, which aims to promote sustained, inclusive, and sustainable economic growth, full and productive employment, and decent work. In Malaysia, CIMB Islamic has introduced the Sustainable Term Investment Account (Yee, 2022). This focus on assets aligned with micro, small, and medium enterprises (MSME) as defined by Bank Negara Malaysia. These assets include activities that contribute to long-term job creation, economic growth, and societal well-being, as well as activities that contribute to increased access to affordable and responsible financial products and services for vulnerable segments in the start-up and MSME sectors.

Wealth Accumulation

The Investment in Shari'ah Compliance and ESG Shares, as well as the Green Sukuk and Sustainable and Responsible Investment (SRI), are examples that demonstrate the alignment between Islamic financial instruments and sustainable finance for wealth accumulation.

Investment in Shari'ah Compliance and ESG

Shari'ah-compliant securities can be defined as securities of a public-listed company which have been classified as Shari'ah permissible for investment based on the company's compliance with Shari'ah principles according to the required screening methodology adopted by their regulator. For example, in Malaysia, the company must comply with Shari'ah principles regarding its primary business and investment activities and its financial position. Here, the Securities Commission Malaysia adopts a quantitative approach that applies the business activities and financial ratio benchmarks in determining the Shari'ah compliance status. Since these securities are Shari'ah compliance, the investments are expected to meet the sustainable finance objectives in supporting ESG. Investments in Shari'ah non-compliant businesses, such as companies whose primary business is involved in tobacco, alcohol, and interest-based businesses, are avoided. Moreover, as part of the efforts to promote and encourage the adoption of ESG practices in the marketplace, Bursa Malaysia, in collaboration with FTSE Russell, has made available the ESG scores of publicly listed Malaysian companies (Bursa Malaysia, 2023). Notably, in July 2021, Bursa Malaysia and FTSE Russel launched the FTSE4Good Bursa Malaysia Shari'ah (F4GBMS)

Index to cater to investors' needs to invest in ESG and Shari'ah-compliant companies. This investment is both Shari'ah-compliant and supports investors in making ESG investments. Another method of investment that can support ESG can be based on equity crowdfunding (ECF). In Malaysia, equity crowdfunding is an innovative form of alternative fundraising that allows small businesses to raise capital from the public using online platforms registered with the Securities Commission Malaysia (Capital Markets Malaysia, 2022). Since its inception at the end of December 2021, ECF has raised RM420.9 million in funds for 248 issuers. Currently, there is one Islamic crowdfunding option, Ethis Ventures Sdn. Bhd. The approach taken by Islamic crowdfunding is not only Shari'ah-compliant but also in line with ESG and impact investing. Among the companies that raise funds and are open for investment include social enterprises, agribusiness, and waste management that support ESG. Similarly, this type of investment is for both Shari'ah-compliant and ESG-friendly companies.

Green Sukuk and SRI

The approach of incorporating social and environmental goals into investing decisions is known as SRI (Sparkes & Cowton, 2004). As a result, SRI is a strategy that fosters socially responsible business practices and initiatives such as impact investment, shareholder activism, and community investing (Guay et al., 2004). SRI is based on considering or integrating financial returns and responsible investments for society's development. Its objectives and goals are focused on environmental concerns, human rights, community participation, and labour relations. It is anticipated that the experience Malaysia has gained in facilitating the issuance of green sukuk through the development of the relevant framework and ecosystem will become a model for bridging Islamic finance with SRI and the green industry (Kamil et al., 2019). For example, Tadau Energy in Malaysia was the first company to issue green sukuk on July 27, 2017, when it sold bonds worth $58.4 million United States dollars (Keshminder et al., 2021).

In summary, the success of this project can be measured by its contribution to increased economic growth, improved ecological sustainability, and increased social equity in the workforce. The local community benefited from the creation of job opportunities, which resulted in the employment of at least 200 people. Meanwhile, Tadau Energy implemented corporate social responsibility (CSR) programmes to give back to their communities and make a positive impact to light up the lives of over 1000 villagers living in rural areas of Sabah, Malaysia, who did not have access to electricity.

Wealth Purification

Zakat is selected as an example of the alignment between Islamic financial instruments and sustainable finance in this section on Islamic Financial Instruments for the purification of wealth.

Zakat

Malaysia is known for having the most advanced zakat payment and distribution systems in the entire world (Migdad, 2019). Evidently, according to the Federal Territory, the amount of zakat collected from 1.15 million zakat payers reached RM828.67 million in 2021. This figure comprises both zakat harta (property) and zakat fitrah. The total amount of zakat harta collected in 2021 increased by 9%, reaching RM816.48 million, compared to RM751 million in 2020 (The Malaysian Reserve, 2022). This indicated that the Malaysian community has a high degree of awareness of fulfilling the obligation and at the same time supporting those in need. Payment of zakat not only serves as a form of worship but also fulfils various social and economic obligations for Muslims. When a global pandemic strikes, for example, the community can see the role of zakat. Zakat institutions have developed and announced a wide variety of community-supporting initiatives, as evidenced by the many initiatives announced during Covid-19. Almost all daily reports detail the efforts of various zakat institutions in Malaysia that have launched and are supervising support programs to aid the most vulnerable citizens in the aftermath of the pandemic. One of the initiatives taken by zakat institutions is the Lembaga Zakat Selangor. The Lembaga Zakat Selangor (LZS) has disbursed a special allocation of RM 15 million to hawkers, small merchants, and low-wage workers affected by the Covid-19 epidemic (Muhamat, 2020). This will prevent their small businesses from shuttering and being ultimately impacted by the pandemic.

Microtakaful

Islamic Financial Instruments for wealth preservation use micro-takaful to illustrate how the Shari'ah-compliant financial product can be aligned with sustainable finance for wealth preservation. Due to the current inflation of medical costs and unexpected weather, takaful coverage becomes more important to all, primarily to protect the vulnerable society. Microtakaful is aimed at low-income individuals who are partially or entirely excluded from regular takaful products due to resource constraints (Mikail et al., 2017). This shows that microtakaful is one of the best initiatives created for lower society to protect them from uncertain situations and cover their risks because it comes at a price that is both accessible and affordable. In addition to low-income individuals, Ahmed (2016) argued that the microtakaful provision is also a mechanism for small and medium-sized enterprises (SMEs). This is because microtakaful has the potential to close a gap in the provision of microfinance in terms of the requirement for collateral and to offer SMEs sufficient protection against a variety of risks. According to Rapi et al. (2022), microtakaful is one of the essential strategies for reducing poverty. Microtakaful instruments attempt to safeguard the poorest and most vulnerable by empowering them to discover a path out of poverty and providing them with a realistic hope of becoming financially self-sufficient.

However, according to Fauzi and Laldin (2022), the poor society regarded as B40 categories couldn't afford to keep their current microtakaful policy, which was considered expensive. This demonstrates that the correlation of high contribution premium rates has resulted in difficulties in the payment of microtakaful. These challenges must be addressed, since takaful payments must be made for the takaful policy to remain sustainable. Moreover, the microtakaful also faces the issue of harmonizing its social objective with market-based sustainability considerations (Mikail et al., 2017). For example, the institution's ability to continue serving its target audience depends on funding availability. This problem has forced microtakaful to reconsider its target population's identity. Alternatively, having a new tool or model can assist microtakaful in providing funds.

Wealth Distribution

The waqf and sadaqah are selected as examples to demonstrate alignment between the Islamic financial instrument and sustainable finance for wealth distribution.

Waqf

The importance of waqf in reforming and shaping modern Muslim economies cannot be underestimated, given the enormous achievements made in countries such as Malaysia, Singapore, the GCC countries, and others (Abdullah, 2019). As a result, rather than relying on conventional economic theories, which are inherently insufficient in addressing social development, investigation and exploration of the waqf institution's economic potential are warranted. The waqf, for example, was the essential institution for wealth redistribution in Islamic economic history. During the 18th century, total waqf revenue in the Ottoman Empire equaled one-third to one-half of the total state revenues (Karagedikli & Tunçer, 2018). This highlighted waqf as one of several instruments established by Islam that provides real solutions and combats poverty while also improving the state of welfare in society. Despite the current state of waqf institutions being unsustainable, there are best waqf practices in poverty eradication, equitable income distribution, and socioeconomic development that can be seen to improve society's economic position; for example, Waqaf An-Nur Corporation (WANCorp). Regarding socioeconomic development, WANCorp established the Waqaf Business Fund and provided qardul hasan microcredit to small businesses. A total of RM393,600 in microcredit loans was also offered to 250 micro-entrepreneurs. (Saad et al., 2016).

Sadaqah

Sadaqah is a voluntary charitable act towards others and is one of the Islamic social finance instruments for wealth distribution. In Malaysia, Bank Islam Malaysia Berhad (BIMB) made an example of this initiative in 2018. BIMB launched a social finance initiative called Sadaqa House, a charity crowdfunding platform that acts as a meeting point between donors and change-makers and beneficiaries overseen by the bank (Sadaqahouse, 2020). Accordingly, there are three selections of funds:

- Perpetual Fund: where the principal will remain in perpetuity and invested, and only the returns generated will be distributed to charitable causes;
- Direct Fund: where donors can choose to donate directly to charitable projects under Sadaqa House; and
- General Fund: where donors do not specify any specific charitable projects, and it is the discretion of BIMB's Zakat & Charity Committee to decide the distribution according to available and suitable charitable projects.

There are four main sectors aimed by Sadaqa House to channel its funds for sustainable impacts related to ESG. The focus areas are health, environment, education, and community empowerment. This is an excellent opportunity for donors to support ESG; for example, the community empowerment sector enables and strengthens social cohesion and social empowerment within communities.

Challenges and Opportunities of Islamic Sustainable Finance

Several issues are identified from the previous studies and the current practices of the Islamic sustainable finance model, which need further research and deliberation. The related issues are as follows:

Issues of Financial Inclusion

The current banking model is exclusive and only accessible to the bankable group segment. The conventional banking model is implemented to reduce costs, mobilize savings, and encourage investments. Banks are restricted to function as the 'financial intermediary' by managing depositors' money with the profit motive and ensuring cost efficiency in operating the banking business. The banks are risk-averse by looking at the customer profiling on creditworthiness, credit assessment and the ability to provide the collateral. Some segments of society are unbankable; they are excluded from formal financial services with no regular or steady income and are unable to provide collateral. This financial exclusion can lead to poverty traps and inequality in society. Financial inclusion also ensures that individuals and businesses have access to and can take advantage of various suitable financial resources. Formal financial inclusion begins at the simplest level by getting a deposit or transaction account with a bank or other financial entity. The account can be used to make and receive payments and to store or save money. Financial inclusion often requires access to adequate credit from structured financial institutions and insurance policies that help people properly handle risks, such as crop damage. In short, inclusion contributes to the promotion of sustainable and inclusive finance, where all sectors of society have access to convenient and accessible structured services, and it also provides opportunities for lower-income segments of society to save and invest securely for productive activities and a buffer against unexpected shocks.

Utilization of Zakat for Microfinance and Microtakaful

There are differences of opinion among the Shari'ah jurists regarding the permissibility to utilize the zakat fund for microfinance. The view of the jurists that do not allow the utilization of zakat funds has some justification. The justification for zakat is exclusivity to the eight *asnaf* categories, which are excluded from the recipients of the microfinance. Using zakat for microfinance will result in the deferment of zakat distribution to asnaf, while it is wajib al-faur (immediately) to distribute the zakat to the recipients. Investment of zakat funds can result in no transfer of ownership to asnaf. Moreover, investment in the zakat fund can expose it to the risk of loss, which can neglect the immediate need for asnaf. The second view among jurists is allowing the utilization of zakat funds for microfinance. The justification is the distribution to the zakat recipients of the poor, and it should be based on the amount which is enough to meet their needs and the dependents of the family based on the ijtihad (effort) of the authorities. If the poor person is engaged in work involving skills, he should be given capital expenditure to purchase the necessary equipment. If he is good at trading, he should be provided with the required capital. If he is in agriculture, he should be given agricultural land whose produce will be sufficient for the long term. Based on this concept, it is permissible to use zakat funds in micro-enterprises such as weave and sewing houses or workshops for small businesses owned by the needy. The jurist members should be more open to differing opinions of fiqh and consider the current fatwa related to the issue of using zakat funds for the benefit of people. It is proposed to collaborate more with financial institutions that have expertise in managing financing products.

Collaboration with Zakat and Waqf Organizations

The industry players focus on advancing the positive socioeconomic impact of Islamic finance. From Malaysia's perspective, Islamic financial institutions, in collaboration with State Islamic Religious Councils (SIRCs), join efforts in allowing the waqf and zakat funds to be beneficially utilized. Collaboration efforts between these institutions could aid in mobilizing wealth with Islamic banking and finance products. To achieve its goal of providing the best possible service to all members of society, particularly the underserved, zakat and waqf are built on philanthropic values. The vision is to ensure that all members of the community, particularly the underserved, have access to high-quality essential services and that they are assisted in meeting their needs in the pursuit of shared prosperity. Zakat and waqf organizations should take an active role in ensuring that the benefits of zakat and waqf properties are distributed to the intended beneficiaries. For instance, proper development of waqf land can aid in preserving and sustaining the benefits for future generations. In addition, the donor receives a continuous flow of rewards for life after death. Islamic social finance mechanisms such as the waqf and zakat are potentially practical tools for eradicating poverty in society. Good management of waqf and zakat property can improve the quality of life for some groups while also ensuring the long-term viability of the wealth.

Lack of Regulatory Standards

Efforts must be accelerated to level the playing field and reduce uncertainty. Information is vital and can be driven by policy and industry adoption. The central bank remains committed to expanding the level of sustainable finance supported by a sustained focus on encouraging the development of innovative delivery systems, products responsive to the needs of the underserved, and effective education, support, and protection for financial consumers. Government plays an essential role in providing the annual budget for the initiatives of sustainable finance.

Awareness of the Public or Customer

Since the inception of the Islamic finance industry, Muslim and non-Muslim investors have had a wide range of financial instruments and assets. As a result, an awareness of the features and distinctions between these instruments and products is necessary for investors, whether Muslims or non-Muslims, to manage their portfolios (Abdullah & Anderson, 2015). There is low adoption of financial services by the people living in the rural areas and the B40 group based on income level. The group's characteristics are lower literacy levels and lower access to information. The income is considered low, irregular, and unpredictable. The need to have a higher degree of awareness and understanding of financial products is the first step towards creating demand and increasing adoption. The strategic policy to raise awareness is to nurture financial value from a young age. It includes reinforcing financial education into the curriculum and co-curriculum in pre-school, primary, and secondary school. It is critical to the strategy's success since shaping the next generation is equivalent to crafting a future for the nation. The strategy includes improving the accessibility to financial management information, tools, and resources. Awareness campaigns and mass media are two methods that can be used to reach out to people and convey easily understandable financial information.

Financial Literacy in the Society

The importance of financial literacy in promoting sustainable finance can be seen in the fact that educated and informed customers lower risk for the institutions and themselves while fostering product innovation. This can be accomplished through the credit counselling and financial education accredited organizations provide. Furthermore, financial education can give the underprivileged the knowledge and resources they need to make better decisions. Financial education also includes imparting the knowledge, abilities, and attitudes necessary for adopting responsible methods of earning, spending, saving, borrowing, and investing money. This might give them more inspiration and optimism to improve their quality of life by taking small, calculated risks.

Conclusion

Islamic finance addresses sustainable finance in two unique ways: through Shari'ah-compliant contracts that provide a viable alternative to conventional investments and some specific instruments of wealth redistribution among society. Both these dimensions have the potential to make a profound impact given the right environment and conditions. The risk-sharing aspects of Islamic finance make it especially suitable for micro and small enterprises often perceived as risky by conventional investors. Also, social solidarity instruments of wealth distribution in an Islamic financial system are explicitly intended to protect wealth. Zakat, waqf, and sadaqah are channels for the promotion of social protection and poverty alleviation in society. One of the legal maxims said to be derived from a saying of the Prophet (PBUH) that "profit comes with liability," implies that Shari'ah distinguishes lawful to profit from all other forms of gain and that entitlement to profit only when there is also the liability or risk of loss. Since the central proposition of Islamic finance is justice, any instrument that is structured based on extracting a rent of the money itself, i.e. interest as a percentage of the principle that was loaned for a specific time period and without the complete transfer of the property rights over the money loaned to the borrower, is eliminated from the financial system. Islam also encourages beneficence over and above these obligatory dues. Still, these instruments for sustainable finance are like mobilizing wealth and returning to others what rightfully belongs to them. Shirking from this obligation causes a misdistribution of wealth and leads to unbalanced wealth in society. In the morality of property rights, Islam unequivocally considers all individuals entitled to a certain standard of life; this entitlement entails the satisfaction of their claim as a matter of equity and justice. In short, the development of Islamic social finance can offer a credible and effective form of wealth distribution, addressing inequality and reducing poverty within societies.

References

Abdullah, M. A. (2019). Waqf and Trust: The Nature, Structures and Socioeconomic Impacts. *Journal of Islamic Accounting and Business Research*, 10(4), 512–527.

Abdullah, M. A., & Anderson, A. (2015). Islamic Financial Literacy Among Bankers in Kuala Lumpur. *Journal of Emerging Economies and Islamic Research*, 3(2), 79–94.

Ahmed, A. (2019). Socially Responsible Investing Interconnect with the Supply Chain Management in Islamic Finance Model. *International Journal of Supply Chain Management*, 8(5), 391–401.

Ahmed, M. H. (2016). Micro Takaful Insurance as a Tool to Guaranteeing Financing and Protecting Micro Enterprises. *Journal of Business & Financial Affairs*, 5(4), 1–11.

Al-Roubaie, A., & Sarea, A. M. (2019). Green Investment and Sustainable Development: The Case of Islamic Finance. *Journal of Islamic Business and Management*, 9(1), 14–24.

Bank Negara Malaysia (BNM). (2015). *BNM Annual Report 2015*. www.bnm.gov.my/documents/20124/6533562/ar2015_en_book.pdf

Bolton, P., Kacperczyk, M., Hong, H. G., & Vives, X. (2021). *Resilience of the Financial System to Natural Disasters*. Centre for Economic Policy Research.

Bursa Malaysia. (2023). *FTSE4Good Bursa Malaysia (F4GBM) Index*. www.bursamalaysia.com/trade/our_products_services/indices/ftse4good-bursa-malaysia-f4gbm-index

Capital Markets Malaysia. (2022). *Equity Crowdfunding (ECF)*. www.capitalmarketsmalaysia.com/digital-equity-crowdfunding-ecf/

Fauzi, P. N. F. N. M., & Laldin, M. A. (2022). Micro-Takāful Scheme for the Protection of Houses Belonging to Low-Income Groups in Malaysia. *ISRA International Journal of Islamic Finance*, 14(3), 303–314.

Guay, T., Doh, J. P., & Sinclair, G. (2004). Non-Governmental Organisations, Shareholder Activism, and Socially Responsible Investments: Ethical, Strategic, and Governance Implications. *Journal of Business Ethics*, 52(1), 125–139.

Gundogdu, A. S. (2018). An Inquiry into Islamic Finance from the Perspective of Sustainable Development Goals. *European Journal of Sustainable Development*, 7(4), 381–381.

Kamil, W. A. R., Bakhor, S. A. S. M., De Luna-Martinez, J., Zhang, W., & Aziz, A. H. A. (2019). Islamic Green Finance: Development, Ecosystem and Prospects. *Disclosure*.

Karagedikli, G., & Tunçer, A. C. (2018). Microcredit in the Ottoman Empire: A Review of Cash Waqfs in Transition to Modern Banking. *Financing in Europe*, 239–268.

Lontsikh, P. A., Golovina, E. Y., Evloeva, M. V., Livshitz, I. I., & Koksharov, A. V. (2022). Implementation of ESG Sustainable Development Concept Criteria Using the Robust Design Methods. In *2022 International Conference on Quality Management, Transport and Information Security, Information Technologies (IT&QM&IS)* (pp. 173–176). IEEE.

The Malaysian Reserve. (2022). *Federal Territory's Zakat Collection Exceeds RM800m in 2021*. https://themalaysianreserve.com/2022/01/11/federal-territorys-zakat-collection-exceeds-rm800m-in-2021/

Migdad, A. (2019). Managing Zakat through Institutions: Case of Malaysia. *Uluslararası İslam Ekonomisi ve Finansı Araştırmaları Dergisi*, 5(3), 28–44.

Mikail, S. A., Ahmad, M. A. J., & Adekunle, S. S. (2017). Utilisation of Zakāh and Waqf Fund in Micro-Takāful Models in Malaysia: An Exploratory Study. *ISRA International Journal of Islamic Finance*.

Muhamat, A. A. (2020). *Covid-19 Outbreaks Dissipates Misconception on Zakat*.

Organisation for Economic Co-operation and Development (OECD). (2020). How Islamic Finance Contributes to Achieving the Sustainable Development Goals. *OECD Development Policy Papers, No. 30*. OECD Publishing, Paris. https://doi.org/10.1787/ac1480ca-en

Rapi, M. Z. H., Salaudeen, A. O., Ravi, M. I. M. R., Wongsangiam, R., & Redzuan, N. H. (2022). Micro Takaful Programs for the Poor: The Malaysian Experience. *International Journal of Accounting*, 7(45), 65–81.

Redmoney Group. (2022). *Islamic Sustainable Finance & Investment (ISFI) Annual Report 2022*. file:///C:/Users/user/Downloads/ISFIAnnual_Report2022.pdf

Saad, N. M., Kassim, S., & Hamid, Z. (2016). Best Practices of Waqf: Experiences of Malaysia and Saudi Arabia. *Journal of Islamic Economics Lariba*, 2(2).

Sadaqahouse. (2020). *About Us*. www.sadaqahouse.com.my/about-us/

Sawyer, M. (2021). Financialisation, Industrial Strategy and the Challenges of Climate Change and Environmental Degradation. *International Review of Applied Economics*, 35(3–4), 338–354.

Sparkes, R., & Cowton, C. J. (2004). The Maturing of Socially Responsible Investment: A Review of the Developing Link with Corporate Social Responsibility. *Journal of Business Ethics*, 52(1), 45–57.

Yee, E. (2022). CIMB Islamic Offers Sustainable Term Investment Account-i to Promote SDG 8. *Businesstoday*. www.businesstoday.com.my/2022/09/19/cimb-islamic-offers-sustainable-term-investment-account-i-to-promote-sdg-8/

7 Emergence of Zakat in Sustainability

A Bibliometric Analysis

Pg Mohd Faezul Fikri Ag Omar & Ashurov Sharofiddin

Introduction

Zakat is among the essential components of Islam. Muslims are convinced that zakat is critical to address social challenges like poverty, insufficient funds for access to education, and a challenging level of livelihood, to name a few. As a result, it is widely believed that zakat should successfully contribute to eradicating poverty and improving socio-economic conditions, hence boosting a country's economic progress (Shaikh & Ismail, 2017; Suprayitno, 2018; Fitriyanti et al., 2019; Zainal et al., 2019). For instance, Muslim countries are expected to significantly benefit from zakat if it is properly administered and managed in terms of collection and distribution. Unfortunately, this is not the situation for many Muslim countries; it has been observed that the Middle East and North Africa regions, where practically all Muslim countries are located, remain impoverished and unequal (World Bank, 2022). Poverty and inequality can have a negative impact on various chances, such as access to better education, increased financial inclusion, improved living conditions, and so on. Furthermore, efforts to fully maximise the potential and contributions of zakat have a long way to go. To address these fundamental concerns, the United Nations introduced a framework of goals dubbed Sustainable Development Goals (SDGs) in 2015 to ensure that the world becomes a sustainable place to live for future generations. The SDGs are a continuation and improvement of the previously defined goals, making them even more inclusive and comprehensive. Using this framework, the UN has set 17 goals comprising various aspects to be scrutinised and addressed for sustainable development. For each goal, many targets are assigned that describe how the goal can be met. With the establishment of SDGs, every nation is expected to contribute to these goals. Table 7.1 depicts the United Nations' SDGs (United Nations, 2022). According to the Islamic Development Bank (2022), there is an urgent need to understand the actual needs of Muslim countries to achieve SDGs, such as eradicating poverty, eliminating hunger, and providing quality education, among others. The bank also recognises the need for improved facilitation of the development agenda, as each country has its own set of development goals suited to the country's needs (Islamic Development Bank, 2022).

DOI: 10.4324/9781003468653-10

Table 7.1 Sustainable Development Goals (SDGs) as identified by United Nations

Agenda/Goal	*Code*
No Poverty	SDG 1
Zero Hunger	SDG 2
Good Health and Well-being	SDG 3
Quality Education	SDG 4
Gender Equality	SDG 5
Clean Water and Sanitation	SDG 6
Affordable and Clean Energy	SDG 7
Decent Work and Economic Growth	SDG 8
Industry, Innovation, and Infrastructure	SDG 9
Reduced Inequalities	SDG 10
Sustainable Cities and Communities	SDG 11
Responsible Consumption and Production	SDG 12
Climate Action	SDG 13
Life below Water	SDG 14
Life on Land	SDG 15
Peace, Justice, and Strong Institutions	SDG 16
Partnership for the Goals	SDG 17

The advent of the SDGs has opened a new discussion horizon on the subject of zakat and sustainability. The zakat mechanism is claimed as being in line with the SDGs. Noticeably, research investigating zakat in relation to sustainability, especially the achievability of sustainable goals, is still in its early stages. More specifically, there is a scarcity of comprehensive studies on the role of zakat towards sustainable development. Furthermore, the role of zakat in fulfilling various goals mentioned in the SDGs has yet to be thoroughly explored, and zakat has yet to attain its fullest sustainable potential. As a result, in order to fill these gaps, the study proposes the following research questions:

RQ1: What are the relevant zakat literatures with regards to sustainability?
RQ2: What are the intellectual structures of research on zakat and sustainability?
RQ3: What are the relevant sustainability goals addressed in zakat research?

Consequently, this chapter aims to offer perspectives on zakat research in relation to sustainability. In order to achieve its purpose and respond to the research questions, the study's objectives are to examine pertinent scholarly works on zakat in relation to sustainability, explain intellectual structures that elaborate zakat and sustainability research, and highlight relevant sustainability agendas addressed in zakat research. The significance of this study lies in showcasing the critical roles of zakat and its contributions to achieving SDGs. To the researchers' best knowledge, this study is the first to use a bibliometric technique to examine research on zakat and sustainability. Therefore, a comprehensive review of existing studies can provide profound insights into the necessity of achieving SDGs through the zakat mechanism. The chapter's organisation begins with the background of the study and literature review on bibliometric studies of zakat research. The discussion is followed by the methodology of the study and results analysis, and discussion of findings. Several focal suggestions for future studies are also elaborated on in the final section of the study.

Literature Review

Bibliometric Studies of Zakat

Ample bibliometric research on the topic of zakat has been undertaken. Alshater et al. (2021) discuss the zakat literature using a bibliometric methodology of 224 Scopus documents. They assert that there is a shortage of research on zakat, and much has to be done. In this work, they also provide numerous research directions. Uyob (2020) analysed 35 research papers on zakat accounting from the Scopus and Google Scholar databases bibliometrically. Although study on zakat has grown steadily each year, he argues that research on zakat accounting is still insufficient and identifies several prospective deficiencies that must be addressed in zakat accounting. Meanwhile, Rusydiana and Nailah (2020) study focuses on zakat and technology, and 440 indexed papers were analysed using Rstudio's Biblioshiny package. According to the findings of their investigation, the number of journal publications on Islamic economics and finance is on the rise, with zakat, Islam, and Indonesia being the most often used keywords. However, given a dearth of studies on zakat and technology, they propose that extensive research be performed on the subject. Anam et al. (2021) examine publications on the term 'zakat' from 41 reputable Scopus-indexed journals and employ software such as Publish or Perish, Mendeley, and VOSviewer for data analysis. They discover the number of zakat-related studies is rising, and common terms include 'zakat,' 'Islam,' 'zakat institution,' and 'poor.' They recommend conducting an additional study on 'compliance,' 'financial inclusion,' 'performance,' and 'social capital,' as these words are understudied and research possibilities do exist.

In addition, Rahman et al. (2021) engage a bibliometric method to examine works on zakat research involving 492 documents from 12 publications in the Scopus database. They discover that zakat research is multidisciplinary and frequently relates to zakat. In addition, they outline several obstacles that zakat must solve to effectively reduce poverty and improve the recipients' quality of life. Apriliyah and Fianto (2022) investigate publications on zakat utilising bibliometric and systematic literature review methods. Publish or Perish and VOSviewer software are used for data analysis. In the paper, the authors suggest that research on zakat is dominated by three subthemes: zakat's role in reducing poverty, zakat compliance, and zakat distributions. They conclude their study by emphasising the need for zakat governing organisations or regulators to re-evaluate their strategies regarding the management, collection, and distribution of zakat. In addition, problems and future directions for zakat research are also highlighted.

Moreover, Bahri et al. (2022) investigate zakat and asnaf entrepreneur research of data acquired from Google Scholar, and their analysis is performed using

PRISMA and bibliometric techniques. According to the study's findings, asnaf entrepreneurship may be examined along four dimensions: life enhancement, financial performance, non-financial performance, and *Maqasid Shari'ah.* They assert that their research has produced a measurement model for the success factors of asnaf enterprises and is helpful for zakat institution management to help nurture entrepreneurial asnaf. Wahyudi et al. (2022) use a bibliometric method to investigate the trends, topics, and social structures of 405 zakat research papers from the Scopus database. Microsoft Excel, VOSviewer, and Publish or Perish are utilised for data analysis. Research on zakat can be found in numerous disciplines, including economics, finance, management, and accounting, as indicated by the findings of their study. Taqi and Rusydiana (2022) examine the development trend of audit zakat research in their bibliometric study on audit zakat research. They investigate 113 published studies in indexed journals using R biblioshiny software. They find that research on the issue is expanding at a rapid rate, the most prolific author is Sofyani H, most publications are articles, and the terms 'zakat' and 'accounting' are frequently used as keywords. They call for zakat institutions to be more transparent and accountable, as achieving these values will boost public confidence in their activities. In addition, Handoko et al. (2022), in their study on previous trends and prospects in zakat research, analyse 635 Scopus-indexed papers from 274 journals. The bibliometric study used Vos viewer software for data analysis. They suggest that the results demonstrate that education, performance, small and medium-sized enterprises, and compliance are contemporary trends in zakat research and that Malaysia, poverty, and zakat institutions are common terms. In addition, they identified around 17 concerns regarding zakat to be addressed in future research.

Even though many researchers have performed bibliometric research on zakat from various perspectives, research on zakat and sustainability is conspicuously absent. In addition, the role of zakat in achieving the SDGs has not yet been thoroughly investigated. Furthermore, documents from databases such as the Web of Science (WoS) are significantly absent from earlier research analyses. In order to overcome these shortcomings, this study employs a bibliometric methodology to examine the literature on zakat and sustainability. The study employs both Scopus and WoS databases for data analysis because they are widely respected for their indexing and data volume, making it more comprehensive than other studies mentioned previously.

Zakat and Sustainability

The study of zakat as it relates to sustainability is a relatively young and intriguing field of research. Researchers have made numerous attempts to delve into this area of study, viewing zakat as a critical tool for developing asnaf and Muslims' socioeconomic standards, which also plays a significant part in achieving SDGs. Shaikh and Ismail (2017) highlight zakat functions that contribute to SDGs in areas such as zero hunger, no poverty, good health and well-being, and reducing inequality. They also felt that zakat might minimise the disparity in income between the poor and the wealthy. Nonetheless, Harianto (2018) stresses in his study on zakat and SDGs that zakat plays a significant role in relieving poverty and assuring the recipients' (asnaf) sustainable livelihood as advocated in SDGs, such as zero hunger, no poverty, quality education, economic progress, and good health and well-being. In addition, Harahap (2018) emphasises the significance of zakat distributions in the form of entrepreneurial aid for achieving the SDG of eliminating poverty. She also opined that the well-being of asnaf may be enhanced, and more socio-economic growth could be experienced if proper management of zakat allocations and entrepreneurship aid with clear poverty reduction goals were implemented. In addition, Suprayitno (2018) argues the significance of the relationship between zakat and sustainable development, which may be exemplified by the substantial impact of zakat on economic growth, consumption, and investment at the macroeconomic level. In his reasoning, he asserted that zakat does impact economic growth, contrary to what many believed due to the low percentage of zakat payments.

According to Fitriyanti et al. (2019), the indirect relationship between zakat and economic growth is undeniably considerable. They argue that sustained economic growth and sustainable livelihoods might be accomplished by giving more significant work opportunities for asnaf to lift them out of poverty. Suriani et al. (2020) also explore optimising zakat to help meet SDGs. They state that through optimising both zakat collection and distribution, zakat institutions should be able to raise awareness of the significance of zakat in alleviating poverty and maximise the ability of zakat to contribute more effectively to the SDGs. Intriguingly, Hudaefi et al. (2020) assert that zakat not only promotes the attainment of the SDG 2 of zero hunger and SDG 1 of no poverty but is also a sufficient mechanism for providing clean water and sanitation to people living in extreme poverty through the construction of latrines. Moreover, Adebayo (2020) suggests that zakat is essential to attaining SDGs in practically all goals relevant to zakat's role. These goals include zero hunger, no poverty, clean water and sanitation, quality education, gender equality, and good health and well-being.

Methodology

The study aims to explain in depth the relationship between zakat and sustainability. The study conducted a bibliometric examination of existing research on zakat regarding sustainability. Although the SDGs are the current primary reference for sustainability and they were only introduced in 2015, the study observes that the principles and values of the sustainability agenda are already embedded in zakat and had been discussed in zakat research much earlier than the establishment of the SDGs.

Data Collection Procedures

The study utilised the Scopus and Web of Science (WoS) databases for bibliometric analysis. Scopus is presently the largest database of research articles, and the addition of the WoS database enriches the study's data. The indexing of both databases is reputable for academic research. For data collection, the study conducted a Boolean search in both databases using the terms 'zakat' AND 'Zakat' and specified the query with several sustainability-related terms, including 'sustainable development,' 'social welfare,' 'poverty alleviation,' 'economic growth,' 'asnaf development,' 'education,' 'hunger,' 'inequality,' 'institution,' 'consumption,' 'environment,' and 'innovation.'" The search query terms were utilised in both the Scopus and WoS databases. In addition, the study restricted its search to journal-only articles. The search yielded 1,109 publications linked to zakat and sustainability concepts, including 962 Scopus items and 147 WoS articles. Texmaker software was used to merge the papers from each search with their respective databases (i.e., Scopus and WoS). Moreover, the study noticed that there might be duplicates of these publications. The research merged both sets of data and used Rstudio to eliminate any duplications. Following the completion of the procedure, 343 documents dating from 1991 to 2022 were deemed appropriate and relevant for the analysis.

Data Analysis

The study utilised the Rstudio program with the Biblioshiny package for data analysis and the presentation of outcomes. In addition, Microsoft Excel was utilised to construct tables as it was more convenient and helped the presentation of the results. Several analyses were conducted to achieve the research objective, including source analysis including Bradford's Law, which explains the topic's source documents, document analyses to elaborate on the frequent keywords used by authors and their trend, and citation and collaboration analyses to determine the relationships between academics and their publications. Thematic analysis elaborates on the sustainability goals addressed in the zakat research. These analyses are essential for providing information on the relationship between zakat and sustainability, thereby assisting scholars in understanding the significance of zakat in accomplishing the SDGs. The overall protocols for data collection and analysis involved four procedures, i.e., Search, Filter, Combine, and Eliminate and Analyze.

Results and Discussion

Relevant Literature Information Analyses

This study provides a general overview and sources analysis, as well as analyses of authors and affiliation to address the first research question. In the sections, the outcomes of these analyses are described and explained.

Annual Scientific Production

The annual distribution of publications published between 1991 and 2022 recorded an average yearly growth rate of 12.54 per cent. It is evident that beginning in 2015, the number of articles on zakat related to sustainability increased dramatically, reaching a high in 2019 and 2020. The report also notes that publications on zakat have addressed concepts connected to sustainability since 2008, despite SDGs not yet being in place.

In term of sources, authors, and keywords used in the zakat publications, the leading journals for zakat and sustainability publications is the Journal of Islamic Accounting and Business Research, Global Journal Al-Thaqafah, and International Journal of Islamic and Middle Eastern Finance and Management, with 20, 12, and 12 documents, respectively. These publications are connected to numerous writers like Saad R., Sawandi N., Wahab, N, and others. Keywords of 'zakat,' 'Malaysia,' and 'zakat institutions' are the most frequently used by the authors in their publications.

Most Relevant Authors

Table 7.2 displays the authors who did the most pertinent studies on zakat related to sustainability. Saad R. and Wahid H. are the most prolific authors, having authored 16 and 10 works, respectively.

Intellectual Structures Analyses

This study employs keyword and co-occurrence analyses and co-citation network analysis to address the second research question. The outcomes of these analyses are detailed and discussed in the sections.

Most Frequent Words

'Zakat' is the most frequently used term, followed by 'Malaysia.' The frequent use of the word Malaysia suggests that more research on zakat has been undertaken in Malaysia. Poverty and poverty alleviation are also among the most often used terms, indicating that zakat is vital in reducing poverty and that eradicating poverty is one of the most crucial goals of SDGs to achieve, namely SDG1. The close relationship between zakat and sustainability can be described through keyword analysis.

Table 7.2 Most Relevant Authors

No.	*Author*	*No. of Documents*
1	Saad, R.	16
2	Wahid, H.	10
3	Abdul-Jabbar, H.	9
4	Bin-Nashwan, S.	9
5	Johari, F.	8
6	Ahmad, S.	7
7	Ali, A.	7
8	Aziz, S.	7
9	Sawandi, N.	7
10	Widiastuti, T.	7

As for the word co-occurrence in the topic, there are seven clusters of co-occurrences. These clusters are associated with, among others, economic growth and poverty, social welfare, and so on. This study verifies that zakat has a close relationship with social welfare and economic development, as demonstrated by these associations.

Zakat Research on SDGs

This study conducts thematic and conceptual structural analyses to answer the third research question. The intention is to highlight the SDGs pertinent to zakat research that has been addressed and discussed. The outcomes of these analyses are detailed and discussed in the sections.

Thematic Maps

This analysis traces the development of the topic of zakat regarding sustainability. There are four main categories of themes, namely Motor themes (quadrant 1), Niche themes (quadrant 2), Emerging and Declining themes – also known as Peripheral themes – (quadrant 3) and Basic themes (quadrant 4). Motor themes represent developed themes that are most important concerning the topic, such as accountability and fairness, performance, trust, and poverty. The Niche themes also represent developed themes but are considered marginal in the field, such as education, technology, sustainability, and risk. Meanwhile, themes such as Islamic economics, technology and zakat recipients are in the Peripheral themes, which suggests these themes are either emerging or declining. Basic themes imply the general themes used in the topic area, such as poverty, welfare, institutions, and digital zakat. This thematic analysis demonstrates that zakat is a popular area of research since various key subjects have been investigated, as evidenced by prior research.

Several themes in the zakat research have addressed the SDGs agenda, as revealed by the analysis. For instance, poverty is the most discussed topic in zakat research, which indicates that zakat is very relevant to SDG 1. Likewise, the topic of zakat institution(s) relates to SDG 16, and SDG 17. Consequently, zakat institutions play a crucial role in achieving both SDGs. Moreover, welfare and education are directly tied to SDG 3 and SDG 4, respectively. Similarly, entrepreneurship, GDP, and business zakat are highly pertinent to SDG 8. Also connected to SDG 9 are topics such as technology and digital zakat. Thus, it may be argued that research on zakat has already elaborated on various sustainability agenda principles.

Thematic Evolutions

Through the analysis of the thematic evolution, the study observes a shift in themes of zakat studies in relation to sustainability principles. Although the current primary reference for sustainability is the SDGs, and it was introduced only in 2015, the researchers observe that the principles of the sustainability agenda are already well embedded in zakat and have been discussed in zakat research. Before 2019, themes such as zakat, distribution, institutions, compliance, and management were prevalent. This situation indicates that nearly all studies have concentrated on the fundamental aspects of zakat research related to SDG 1 and SDG 16. From 2019 through 2020, however, the themes have shifted, with governance, financial inclusion, economic growth, and poverty becoming more prominent. These themes are relevant to SDG 10, SDG 3, SDG 4, SDG 8, and SDG 2. More research on zakat in relation to sustainability has piqued the interest of researchers, stressing the significance of zakat concerning sustainability. As for the evolution of themes of the topic from 1991–2022, 2019 serves as the cut-off year of a significant shift in theme evolution.

Conceptual Structure Analysis

The conceptual or contextual structure analysis explains words frequently appearing in zakat and sustainability discussions. The words are split using area mapping. The mapping is based on the relationship between words that are similar to one another. The words that are frequently used in research publications are, among others, sadaqah, waqf, financial inclusion, sustainable, poverty reduction, while education, income, and social welfare are less commonly used.

Through the analysis, it is possible to conclude that research on zakat in relation to sustainability is relevant and has gained scholarly interest. Popular terms include institutions, poverty, and distribution, but compliance, accountability, and performance, to mention a few, are most frequently studied in research. In recent years, however, financial inclusion, economic growth, efficiency, health care, and income have become more prominent research terms. These terms are relevant to the SDGs agenda, including SDG 10, SDG, SDG 16, SDG 3, and SDG 1. Additionally, words such as education, social welfare, health care, and income have garnered less attention. Therefore, it is possible for academics to undertake their zakat research in SDG 4, SDG 11, and SDG 3. More research on zakat should also be conducted concerning several relevant SDGs that have yet to be addressed. Exploring these agendas concerning zakat can effectively convey the significance of zakat in relation to sustainability and explain the role of zakat in accomplishing the SDGs.

Conclusion

Through bibliometric analysis of existing literatures, this study analyses zakat research related to sustainability. In addition, the study sheds light on the essential information and intellectual structures of existing literature on zakat and sustainability. Based on its findings, the study concludes that zakat research remains robust, as demonstrated by the annual production growth. Researchers continue to investigate the subject area of zakat. Various themes have been the subject of zakat research, including governance, management, financial inclusion, economic growth, poverty, efficiency, and health care. Subsequently, these themes are closely related to sustainability as outlined in the Sustainable Development

Goals (SDGs) agenda. Several sustainability agendas, such as SDG 10 – Reduced Inequalities, SDG 8 – Decent Work and Economic Growth, SDG 16 – Peace, Justice, and Strong Institutions, SDG 3 – Good Health and Well-Being, SDG 4 – Quality Education, and SDG 1 – No Poverty, are widely covered in zakat study. This notion suggests that zakat plays an essential and substantial role in addressing the potential of achieving sustainability. The study carries several implications. This study is essential for academics to comprehend the significance of zakat in achieving the SDGs' sustainability targets. Additionally, this study can provide information regarding future research directions in zakat and sustainability. In addition, zakat policymakers might use the findings to re-evaluate their strategy for improving services to zakat recipients. Zakat governing entities or institutions responsible for zakat might improve their operations and strategies to cater to sustainable development. In addition, the implementation and outcomes of the zakat mechanism can be used to demonstrate the efforts made by zakat institutions to fulfil the sustainable development objectives. The results can be utilized to clarify the significance of zakat in relation to the SDGs. Additionally, it can highlight the SDG achievements of zakat institutions and the government. The significance of this study lies in its explanation of the critical relationship between zakat and sustainability, as well as zakat's contributions to achieving SDGs. To the researchers' best knowledge, this study is the first to investigate zakat and sustainability via a bibliometric approach. A thorough analysis of existing research provides profound insights into the necessity of achieving SDGs through the zakat mechanism. Nonetheless, this study has limitations. As a result of the insufficiency of the information returned by a search for the exact terms 'zakat' and 'sustainability,' the research included several keywords relating to sustainability concepts. Therefore, more future research is recommended and required on zakat and sustainability. Themes such as education, health care, and income remain underexplored, presenting the potential for future research. Additionally, more studies should be performed on zakat concerning various important SDGs that have yet to be addressed. Extensive research on zakat and sustainability will demonstrate that zakat is an efficient instrument for eradicating poverty, boosting economic growth, and enhancing its recipients' social welfare, as stipulated in the SDGs.

References

Adebayo, R. I. (2020). Utilizing Zakat or Attaining Sustainable Development Goals (SDGs) in Nigeria. *Proceeding, 4th International Conference of Zakat (ICONZ)* (pp. 231–242).

Alshater, M. M., Saad, R. A. M., Wahab, N. A., & Saba, I. (2021). What Do We Know about Zakat Literature? A Bibliometric Review. *Journal of Islamic Accounting and Business Research*, 12(4), 544–563.

Anam, M. S., Wicaksono, P. N., & Rosia, R. (2021). Bibliometric Analysis of the Term 'Zakat'. In *Proceedings of Annual International Conference on Islamic Economics and Business, 2021* (pp. 194–201).

Apriliyah, R. P., & Fianto, B. A. (2022). Evaluation of Zakat Literature: A Bibliometric Analysis and Systematic Literature Review. *Review of Islamic Social Finance and Entrepreneurship (RISFE)*, 1(1), 50–62.

Bahri, E. S., Ali, J., & Aslam, M. M. M. (2022). A Bibliometric Analysis of the Conceptual Model of Asnaf Entrepreneur Success. *International Journal of Economics, Management and Accounting*, 30(1), 225–251.

Fitriyanti, E., Putri, A. K., & Valeriani, D. (2019). Zakat and Economic Development Analysis of Bangka Belitung Towards Sustainable Development Goals 2030. *Asy Syar'iyyah: Jurnal Ilmu Syari'ah dan Perbankan Islam*, 4(2), 180–207.

Handoko, L. H., Bayinah, A. N., & Firmansyah, F. (2022). A Bibliometric Analysis of Research on Zakat: Past Trends and Future Directions. *Al-Uqud: Journal of Islamic Economics*, 6(2), 160–176.

Harahap, L. R. (2018). Zakat Fund as the Starting Point of Entrepreneurship in Order to Alleviate Poverty (SDGs Issue). *Global Review of Islamic Economics and Business*, 6(1), 63–74.

Harianto, S. (2018). Zakat on Sustainable Development Goals (SDGs 2016–2030). In *Proceedings of the 1st Workshop on Multidisciplinary and Its Applications Part 1, WMA-01 2018, 19–20 January 2018, Aceh, Indonesia.*

Hudaefi, F. A., Saoqi, A. A. Y., Farchatunnisa, H., & Junari, U. L. (2020). Zakat and SDG 6: A Case Study of BAZNAS, Indonesia. *Journal of Islamic Monetary Economics and Finance*, 6(4), 919–934.

Islamic Development Bank. (2022). *Sustainable Development Goals*. Retrieved November 16, 2022, from www.isdb.org/what-we-do/sustainable-development-goals

Rahman, S. M. A., Wahid, K. A., Nafi, M. N. A., Awang, S., & Setapa, M. (2021). Bibliometric Analysis of Zakat Research in Scopus Database. *International Journal of Zakat*, 6(1), 13–24.

Rusydiana, A. S., & Nailah. (2020). Zakat and Technology: A Bibliometric R Analysis. *International Journal of Zakat*, 5(3), 88–107.

Shaikh, S. A., & Ismail, A. G. (2017). Role of Zakat in Sustainable Development Goals. *International Journal of Zakat*, 2(2), 1–9.

Suprayitno, E. (2018). Zakat and SDGs: The Impact of Zakat on Economic Growth, Consumption and Investment in Malaysia. *Advances in Economics, Business and Management Research*, 101, 202–209.

Suriani, S., Nurdin, R., & Riyaldi, M. H. (2020). Optimization of Zakat for Sustainable Development Goals: Evidence from Baitul Mal Aceh. *Proceedings of the 4th International Conference of Zakat (ICONZ), 7–8 October 2020, Surabaya, Indonesia* (pp. 339–354).

Taqi, M., Sabarudinsah, & Rusydiana, A. S. (2022). Audit Zakat Research: A Bibliometric Analysis. *Amwaluna: Jurnal Ekonomi dan Keuangan Shari'ah*, 6(1), 15–28.

United Nations. (2022). *Sustainable Development Goals (SDGs)*. Retrieved November 12, 2022, from https://sdgs.un.org/goals

Uyob, R. B. (2020). Current Research in Zakat Accounting Research. *Journal on Technical and Vocational Education (JTVE)*, 5(1), 41–51.

Wahyudi, M., Ahmi, A., & Herianingrum, S. (2022). Examining Trends, Themes and Social Structure of Zakat Literature: A Bibliometric Analysis. *Global Journal Al-Thaqafah*, 12(1), 40–67.

World Bank. (2022). *Poverty and Shared Prosperity 2022*. Retrieved November 22, 2022, from www.worldbank.org/en/publication/poverty-and-shared-prosperity

Zainal, H., Mustaffa, M. F., & Othman, Z. (2019). Zero Hunger and Sustainable Development Goals: Model of Food Bank Centre by Lembaga Zakat Negeri Kedah. *UMRAN – International Journal of Islamic and Civilizational Studies*, 2(2), 85–90.

8 Role of Zakāt in Building up a Sustainable Investment

Hichem Hamza

Introduction

Zakāt (alms) is among the five pillars of Islam. Literally it means purity, growth, rent, increase, barakah[1] and righteousness. Al-Isfahani (1986) said, "The origin of Zakāt is the growth that results from Al-baraka of Allāh." Zakāt is charitable spending based on the Qurān: "O you who have believed, spend from the good things which you have earned" (Al-Baqarah (2):267). Allāh the Almighty gave wealth to humans in order to spend it and use it to protect religion as one of Maqasid *Shari'ah* (*Shari'ah* purposes). Zakāh is a debt established for Allāh, and for the needy, the poor, the debtors and all those whom Allāh has imposed on them in the text of the Quran (Ibn Hazm, 2003).[2] Zakāt means spending periodically (*Al-Hawl*) a known part (*Makadir*) of Zakāt wealth if it reaches the quorum (*Nisab*) to certain categories of society (*Masaref*). The basic conditions of Zakāt are full ownership, growth, Nisab and *Al-Hawl*. By virtue of the *Shari'ah* terminology, Zakāt (the Zakāt of wealth) is the financial obligation estimated by the Shari'ah on the wealth of the rich, for the poor and others indicated in verse 60 of Surah Al-Tawba (Al-Masri, 1997). In the authentic hadith (Qudsi), Muhammad Allāh's Messenger (saw) said: "We sent down wealth to establish prayer and pay Zakāt".[3] Qurān encourages Muslims to spend in order to succeed in life and hereafter:

> The example of those who spend their wealth in the way of Allāh is like a seed [of grain] which grows seven spikes; in each spike is a hundred grains. And Allāh multiplies [His reward] for whom He wills. And Allāh is all-Encompassing and Knowing.
>
> (Al-Bakarah (2):61)

Zakāt means continual spending of Zakāh wealth to certain categories of society (*Masaref*). The spending through Zakāt is beneficial for Zakāt payers and multiplies their wealth: "And whatever you give for interest to increase within the wealth of people will not increase with Allāh. But what you give in Zakāt, desiring the countenance of Allāh – those are the multipliers" (Al-Rum (30):39).

Economically, Zakāt is the charitable spending by redistributing wealth and spending it in the economy. In addition, Zakāt has a crucial economic role,

DOI: 10.4324/9781003468653-11

essentially through its impact on investment defined as the allocation of wealth in economic activity to realize a profit and benefit for society. Zakāt gives new thought to the investment concept through which the payers of Zakāt are determined to succeed in their investment to pay Zakāt. This thought makes worship the objective of the investors, and the investment as the driver to realize this objective. Moreover, this thought sustains the investment where the religious motivation of charitable spending is the engine of sustainable investment. Sustainable investment is one of the wealth functions and is an important means to achieve the principle of succession (*Al-Istikhlef*) and earth prosperity, which is one of the necessities of worship. The principle of succession in wealth has an impact on economic behavior through the impact of the blessing of Zakāt on investment. Therefore, investing wealth under the Zakāt approach leads to achieving the purpose of protecting and developing wealth. Allāh the Almighty said, "But whatever thing you spend [in His cause] – He will compensate it; and He is the best of providers (Saba (34):39)," which means that spending and therefore Zakāt is the cause or the right way for an increase of wealth. This view points out that conceptually Zakāt is spending that contributes to the increase of wealth and investment, indicating that sustainable investment is an important purpose of Zakāt in addition to the primary purpose, which is the charitable spending or social solidarity. The wealth circulating in the economy in the form of Zakātable wealth is the origin of the impact of Zakāt on investment. It is crucial to study the role of Zakāt for the development of investment to strengthen the elements of its success economically and socially, as well as ensuring it as an economic resource. According to the conceptual framework presented here, the remainder of this chapter is the following. In the first section, it is a question about the investment sustainability dimensions of Zakāt and the sustainable Islamic investment content of all Zakāt conditions, with a focus on their impact on finance activity. The second section emphasizes the effect of Zakāh *Masaref* on Islamic sustainable investment. The third section explains the factors of success of the impact of Zakāt on Islamic investment, mainly the wealth circulation, role of the State and the Muslim faith. The last section concludes the role of Zakāt in building a sustainable Islamic investment.

Sustainability Investment and Zakātable Wealth

Zakāt is a comprehensive term with doctrinal, financial, social and economic dimensions. This term means the right of the poor towards the rich, the purification of the soul from reprehensible morals, stinginess and miserliness, and its decoration with praiseworthy morals, giving, takaful and compassion. Al-Qarafi (1994) says:

> Allāh has enjoined Zakāt as a gratitude for the blessing given to the rich and to fill the stigma of the poor and Allāh completed this wisdom by sharing it between the rich and the poor in the assets of the funds as possible so that the hearts of the poor are not broken by the specialization of the rich with those funds.[4]

The fundamental purpose of Zakāt is its fair dealing with wealth. The importance of Zakāt through the integrity of the behavior of the individuals and society is manifested by cleansing souls of hatred, rancor, malice, envy and revenge, which reduces procrastination, theft and consuming people's wealth unjustly. Therefore, Zakāt addresses miserliness, greed and increases wealth circulation. Zakāt bridges the gap between the rich and the poor, the needy and the low-income and consolidates the relationship between them. Furthermore, Zakāt refines the economic behavior of the rich to avoid monopoly, Zakāt evasion, deception and injustice. The equitable distribution of wealth means that financial justice is achieved at the community level, so that gaps between members of the same society are reduced (Banani, 2017).

Zakāt is a financial worship that seeks to promote social justice and reinforces the social relationship between rich and poor. Zakāt is a social institution for the due rights of the poor in the wealth of the rich, and Zakāt is the essence of Islamic financial policy and an important financial and economic tool (Mortan, 2004). Economically, Zakāt is the charitable spending by redistributing wealth and spending it in its eligible categories (*Masaref*). Zakāt is an institution of social solidarity, and the performance of Zakāt is aimed at reforming the conditions and imbalances in society, such as unemployment, misery, poverty, calamities, disasters and debts. The dimensions of its legitimacy are represented in ensuring the needs of individuals and guaranteeing the stability of human life among them (Ibn Al-Khouja, 2004).

Abu Huraira reported that Muhammad Allāh's Messenger (saw) said: "Charity does not decrease wealth, no one forgives another except that Allāh increases his honor, and no one humbles himself for the sake of Allāh except that Allāh raises his status."[5] Zakāt gives an ethical dimension or social responsibility to the investment, where investment is seen as socio-economic activity and not only a profit activity. This view makes a change in the investment culture, which reinforces altruism as the principal component of the investment and supports the sustainability of the investment by the motivations of Muslims to undertake an economic activity with the aim to reinforce the relationship between Zakāt payers and needy people. Therefore, Al-Baraka in the wealth is an important dimension of Zakāt and by consequence in the investment, which means its positive effect on Muslim life and society's prosperity. Through the purification of wealth by Zakāt giving, the Zakāt payers sustain the continuity and growth of their investment. Zakāt is transferred from the Zakāt payers to needy people, among them persons who need funds for a decent life as well as for entrepreneurs who have projects to finance.

Zakāt is paid from the income of investment and from wealth assets' value. In both cases, Zakāt is a transfer of wealth from the Zakāt payers to eligible persons. Zakāt helps volunteer needy people to undertake an investment activity and transform a part of hoarded wealth into invested wealth which promotes the investment. In this regard, the role of Zakāh is valuable in circulation of money and its allocation to productive entities or individuals. In the holy hadith, Muhammad Allāh's Messenger (saw) said: "It is taken from their rich and returned to their poor,"[6] which means the fair circulation of wealth where Zakāt is a financial worship and a divine duty that aims to mobilize money, resurrect businesses and finance specific needs in society (Khelifi & Amer, 2021). Without the Zakāt system, there would be an accumulation of hoarded wealth with non-value added and a discouragement of people who have the will to invest but do not have funds for their project ideas.

Zakātable wealth are funds that are generated, circulated and grow in the economy, and thus are closely related to the economic, financial and investment environment. Zakātable wealth are the funds on which Zakāt is due. One of the conditions of Zakāt is growth, which means the growth of Zakāt wealth, and this is largely in reference to the investment dimension of Zakāt since investment is the development of wealth or the growth of capital. Zakātable wealth, by its growth and circulation, means funds with economic content. It can be said that the Zakātable wealth that fulfills the growth condition is funds that can be invested, and it is mostly the funds that circulate in the economy; the circulation of these funds is an achievement of the prosperity of earth. Zakāt must be paid on growing wealth (gold, money, seeds, livestock, trade, minerals), and the growth of Zakātable wealth as a principal condition of Zakāh due supposes the expansion of the economic activity and therefore the increase of investment. The volume of Zakāt depends on the wealth and funds acquired and circulated in the economy, and therefore its impact is implicit and latent on economic behavior and investment activity. Accordingly, Zakāt plays an essential role in the contribution of funds to stimulating investment and the economy, and it is an integral part of the state's financial policy in addressing economic problems and providing a decent life for members of society.

The quorum (Al-Nisab) is the minimum amount that, if a Muslim owns it (reaches it)[7] and one year has passed, Zakāt is due on it, and the Nisab is in excess of the original necessary needs, such as clothing, food, drink and housing. According to Surah Al-Bakarah (2:219): "And they ask you what they should spend. Say, 'The excess [beyond needs].'" Therefore, Zakāt is not due on less than Nisab, and the Nisab varies according to the Zakāt wealth types. The Prophet Muhammad (saw) said, "The best charity is that which is practiced by a wealthy person and start giving first to your dependents."[8] The quorum is an investment incentive for Muslims who have the belief to consider Zakāt as a motivation for investment. The quorum represents the minimum of Zakāt wealth, which is the wealth of economic prosperity and has a strong relationship with the economic and investment environment. The quorum can be considered as a tie-breaking point for achieving *Al-Falah*, and this is another indicator of the importance of the quorum in encouraging investment.

The quorum is variable from year to year and constitutes an indicator of wealth, which means that Zakāt is applied according to the financial capacity of the rich or economy and not in all financial capacity situations like taxes. In addition, in case of weak Zakāt volume, the quorum provides an indication to the Zakāt institution and policymakers to offer economic solutions to improve the performance of the investors and economic sectors. In this regard, the Zakāt is considered an efficient economic tool for the financial and economic policy of the country. The quorum indicates wealthy groups who are obligated to pay Zakāt, and these groups are the source of Zakāt resources. The quorum evolved according to categories, time, place, and the Zakāt base, whether it was income or capital. The economic groups charged with Zakāt in terms of income, savings, investment, and their economic status are important to know the trends of Zakāt and support the elements of its economic and social success, as well as ensuring it as an economic resource and developing its collection.

The Zakātable wealth is circulating in the economy during the completed year (*Al-Hawl*). Muhammad Allāh's Messenger (saw) said: "There is no Zakāt on wealth until one completed year has passed."[9] The completion of *Al-Hawl* is required with the full possession of the Zakāt quorum for the Zakāt payers. *Al-Hawl* is required for Zakāt on money, livestock and trade offers. It is not stipulated in the crops, fruits and minerals where Zakāt is due on them at the time of harvest: "And give its due [Zakāt] on the day of its harvest" (Al-An'am (6): 141). The condition of *Al-Hawl* is to fulfill the condition of growth by indicating the growth of Zakāt wealth. *Al-Hawl* is important for the continuity of charitable spending and giving in response to the legal *Masaref* of Zakāt. The existence of more than one *Al-Hawl* of Zakāt funds (at the end of the year or at the time of its harvest) allows covering the needs of society throughout the year and forever. Therefore, *Al-Hawl* is an important time factor of Zakāt continuity, and the recurrence of Zakāt periodically supports the sustainability aspect of financing and investment.

Zakāt amounts are fixed percentages (*Makadir*) that do not change with time or place. The amounts of Zakāt (1/40, 1/20, 1/10, 1/5) are what must be extracted from the Zakāt wealth when it reaches *Nisab* and *Al-Hawl*, and it is distributed to the legitimate *Masaref* of Zakāt. There is no doubt that the amounts of Zakat in all charity expenditures increase with the increase in earnings, and this pushes economic growth and increases production (Ibn Al-Khouja, 2004). These percentages are not considered excessive compared to taxes; they are reasonable and are not considered a burden on the payers of Zakāt. The investors are assured that the percentage of Zakāt is fixed and not changeable, which gives more stability to their investment strategy.

Sustainable Investment Through Zakāt *Masaref*

According to Surah Al-Tawbah (9:60) the Zakāt is allocated to eight categories.

> Zakat expenditures are only for the poor and for the needy and for those employed to collect [Zakāt] and for bringing hearts together [for Islam] and for freeing captives [or slaves] and for those in debt and for the cause of Allāh and for the [stranded] traveler – an obligation [imposed] by Allāh. And Allāh is Knowing and Wise.

Zakāt, through its distribution to the target groups, affects their morals, behavior and contribution to achieving economic goals, mainly sufficiency and work. The economic content of Zakāt *Masaref* are numerous, principally the redistribution of income and wealth, addressing social inequality, funding social groups and economic solidarity. The redistribution of wealth through Zakāt is primarily a social mechanism based on solidarity and Takaful. Wealth redistribution has many effects on the economic and financial situation of society members. One of the most important effects is the increase of financing capacity and investment realization.

The impact of Zakāt on the beneficiaries through investment is represented by the fact that Zakāt refers many of them to investors, in the item of the poor and needy, in the item of debtors, in the item of the wayfarers and in the item of freeing slaves, by providing resources that enable them to realize their investment projects (Dunya, 2018). The payment of Zakāt to poor and needy people is naturally a social solidarity between rich and poor but also has economic effects, leading this social category to have the necessities of looking forward to undertaking an economic activity. In this regard, Zakāt is a socioeconomic support for these people and allows the prevalence of social peace, which is considered an important condition for the improvement of the investment environment. According to Al-Mawardi (2006):

> Abu Hanifa said: If the Zakāt expands, it will be paid to the poor and the needy, what will bring them out of the name of poverty and misery to the lowest levels of wealth, and this is considered according to their condition, so some of them become rich with one dinar if they are among the people of the markets who profit in it according to their sufficiency.[10]

The relationship between needy people and the rich or investors should be stable to reflect the expansion and sustainability of the investment. In addition, this relationship is also beneficial for the rich, who will gain in terms of wealth increase and Al-baraka in the satisfaction of their needs. Abu Dardaa said, "I heard the Messenger of Allāh Muhammad (saw) said: Seek for me weak persons, for you are provided means of subsistence and helped through your weaklings."[11]

The resolutions of the International Islamic Fiqh Academy related to Zakāt clarify the encouragement of investment through Zakāt. According to resolution N° 15 (3/3):

> It is permissible, in principle, to use Zakāt funds in investment projects that are eventually owned by those who are deserving of Zakāt, or which are under the control and administration of the entity that is responsible and has the jurisdiction over collecting and distributing Zakāt, provided that it is done after fulfilling the basic and immediate needs of the recipients and providing proper guarantees to avoid loss.
>
> (IIFA)[12]

This resolution encourages the use of Zakāt in investment projects with the priority of its redistribution to the beneficiaries under strict fulfilling of Zakāt conditions. Further, the objective of this resolution is to optimally invest the Zakāt funds and their ownership to Zakāt beneficiaries.

Another resolution of the IIFA N° 165 (3/18) stipulates:

> Fourth: . . . If the poor or needy can earn income through a certain handicraft or profession, he may be given the amount he needs to, for instance, purchase

his work tools, run a small commercial business or acquire a small family farm, and thus becomes able to have a continuous flow of income to cover his needs. Based on this fact, Zakāt funds can be invested in small projects such as textile units, small sewing projects, and small workshops to be directly owned by the poor and needy. Zakāt funds can also be used for establishing income-producing and services projects as stated in resolution No. 15 (3/3) of the Academy.[13]

The resolution N° 165 (3/18) is a concretization of an optimal distribution of Zakāt to micro and small projects for poor or needy entrepreneurs, allowing them to realize their own projects or small business. This resolution gives support for small investments to become important in the future, which is considered to support sustainable investment through Zakāt funds.

Zakāt resolves the problem of insolvency or bankruptcy of persons and enterprises through *Masraf* Al-Gharimine (the indebted) and therefore saves the investors from financial difficulty, which ensures the recovery and the continuity of their economic activity and sustains their investment. Fulfilling the conditions for Zakāt entitlement to pay off a debt owed to those in debt: Zakāt is not given to a debt that is committed to sin, waste or corruption. In this regard, this rule promotes ethical and sustainable investment and improves investment behavior in compliance with *Shari'ah* and law. Legal debtors are those who have lost their money due to natural disasters, or who have incurred a financial fine for the public good or who have debts that they were unable to pay, so that their production was disrupted, so they are given Zakāt to cover those disasters, and to pay off those debts that made them not have enough money to support their lives (Khelifi & Amer, 2021). Therefore, Zakāt enables individuals to increase their financial capacity and economic contribution. Abu Sa'id al-Khudri (Allāh be pleased with him) reported that in the time of Allāh's Messenger Muhammad (saw) a man suffered loss in fruits he had bought and his debt increased; so Allāh's Messenger (saw) told (the people) to give him charity and they gave him charity, but that was not enough to pay the debt in full, whereupon Allāh's Messenger (saw) said to his creditors: "Take what you find and you have only that."[14]

Zakāt emphasizes the importance of the social and takaful dimension in debt management and its risks. The effects of giving Zakāt to debtors in financial difficulties are multiple for both debtors and creditors. For debtors, it is a reduction of the impact of debt on investment with a financial rehabilitation which contributes to ensuring the continuity of the debtors' investments. For the creditors, it is a support for providing resources and reparations, reducing the risks of non-payment, and protecting the wealth. *Masraf* Al-Gharimine of Zakāt is a kind of insurance for creditors in case of insolvency of debtors, and it is important for them to manage their risk through Zakāt solution. In addition, *Masraf* Al-Gharimine allows creditors to finance debtors with less reluctance, which promotes the investment projects of debtors and the spending plan of consumers. This solution strengthens the relationship between creditors and debtors, which is beneficial for investment sustainability and economic prosperity.

The Zakāt as a social system is finally a solution for financial issues for both debtors and creditors, which means that not only are financial products solutions for insolvency but also social solidarity as a principal factor for investment and economic sustainability. In case of extreme financial difficulty or insolvency, entrepreneurs can benefit from Zakāt Al-Gharimine, which indicates that Zakāt is the optimal redistribution of wealth between those in good and bad financial situations where solidarity prevails among them with less need for financing or indebtedness. In case of not reaching Nisab due to loss or investment difficulty or other reasons, the Zakāt is not required to Zakāt payers given the non-fulfillment of the condition of Nisab or growth. This considers the conditions of investment in cases of stagnation and recession, and in this regard, Zakāt is a servant of investment and its sustainability through *Masraf* Al-Gharimine, which contributes to saving an investment and returning it to its orbit.

Key Factors of Impact of Zakāt on Investment

As a religious obligation, Zakāt must be paid on time and for all eight categories of people, avoiding Zakāt evasion which is harmful to the role of Zakāt in society. Zakāt wealth urges the preservation and investment of wealth in order to perform the rights of Allāh and the rights of people as fully as possible (Belabes, 2019). Zakāt has a great impact on advancing the wheel of the Islamic economy and its development, because the growth of the wealth of the Zakāt payers is due to the economy's strength and prosperity (Al-Ghafili, 2008). Zakāt plays the role of an incentive for investment instead of keeping wealth in a state of hoarding, given that for the investment, the Zakāt is paid generally more in return than on Zakātable assets' value. In addition, the application of Zakāt to investment does not decrease; the Zakāt payers are always encouraged to increase their capital with an increase of their reputation in the society for their human services, which consolidates their economic activity. This point of view explains the investment thought from the Zakāt perspective and the contribution of Al-baraka as a belief in the investment increase and success. Furthermore, the concept of Nisab for Zakāt eligibility is another factor that determines the ability of the investor to pay. Without reaching Nisab, Zakāt wealth needs more investment to reach Nisab as a target for paying Zakāt, which in turn will increase the development of Zakāt wealth.

Muhammad Allāh's Messenger (ﷺ) said, "If I had gold equal to the mountain of Uhud, it would not please me that it should remain with me for more than three days, except an amount which I would keep for repaying debts."[15] The hadith is a clear statement of wealth turnover encouragement and hoarding avoidance. The Qurān insists on the necessity of circulation of wealth between rich and poor: "In order that the wealth may not circulate only amongst the rich" (Surah Al-Hashr (59:7)). The spending of wealth is mentioned three times in the same verse in Surat Al-Bakarah: "And whatever good you [believers] spend is for yourselves, and you do not spend except seeking the countenance of Allāh. And whatever you spend of good – it will be fully repaid to you, and you will not be wronged" (Al-Bakarah (2):272).[16] The repetition in the same verse is an indicator of the extreme importance of spending and money circulation and exchange, beneficial for economy and social justice.

The circulation of Zakāt wealth (*Al-Rawaj*) is an essential success factor of the impact of Zakāt on the economy and investment. Hoarding is prohibited given its undesirable effects on money velocity and money exchange, while Zakāt has the opposite effect regarding investment and redistribution of wealth through the increase of money circulation. Zakāt legislation came into Islam as a civilized means that always works to reform the movement of money in the economy, as it stimulates investment, promotes business, supports production and protects producers (Khelifi & Amer, 2021). Zakāt plays a fundamental role in combating hoarding by stimulating investment, moving capital and creating an economic boom, which reflects positively on society by providing jobs and protecting the economy from fluctuations, as well as doubling the wealth of Zakāt payers; therefore, Zakāt is a cause for multiplying wealth, not for decreasing it (Banani, 2017). The economic nature of Zakāt and its impact on investment is potential under the implication of all stakeholders towards this objective, essentially the State.

The State should be involved in the implementation of Zakāt system as a condition for the success of the Zakāt role in the economy and the promotion of investment sustainability. The legal existence of the Zakāt institution with the responsibility of strict collection and optimal distribution of Zakāt is naturally the first condition for a significant effect of Zakāt on sustainable Islamic finance, beneficial for the public and society. The Zakāt institution also means the existence of Zakāt laws regarding Zakāt payers and beneficiaries for institutional collection and distribution and efficient functioning. The effect of institutional Zakāt on investment and the socioeconomic environment is supposed to be much greater than the inexistence of Zakāt institution (in most Islamic countries) where the collection and distribution are weak and not optimal.

The State has a crucial role in sensitizing the importance of Zakāt in the economy and controlling the payment of Zakāt to avoid evasion, which impedes the socio-economic effect of Zakāt. In this regard, the effect on economy and investment is more significant when the amount of Zakāt collection increases. This increase is determined by the expansion of the Zakāt wealth base and the largest possible number of people reaching Zakāt quorum. Consequently, Zakāt impacts the economy but also undergoes the state of the economic conditions, which can increase or decrease the volume of Zakāt. Further, there is a need for collaboration between the Islamic states under the umbrella of the organization of Islamic cooperation to internationalize Zakāt collection and distribution, leading to the promotion of the Zakāt effect on investments and Islamic society's need.

Zakāt provides an investment thought based on the faith and worship of Muslims. The Holy Quran dealt with the description of payers of Zakāt, and Allāh the Almighty discussed this in three verses. The first: "And they who are observant of Zakāt (Muminun (23):4)" means to pay Zakāt with satisfaction and faith. The second: "[Are] men whom neither commerce nor sale distracts from the remembrance of Allāh and performance of prayer and giving of Zakāt (An Nur (24):37)." The third: "[And they are] those who, if We give them authority in the land, establish prayer and give Zakāt and enjoin what is right and forbid what is wrong (Hajj (22):41)." These verses highlight the faith of the Zakāt payers and their strong implication in the economic and investment environment, as well as the investment thought in light of Zakāt, which relies on it as an engine to achieve profit. Zakāt payers exert their efforts and practice economic activity with the intention of paying Zakāt, and therefore Zakāt was one of the motives for a productive activity for a Muslim and the motives for development (Dunya, 2018).

Zakāt builds an investment thought that prioritizes Zakāt over profit, where profit becomes the means and Zakāt the goal, or profit is the servant and Zakāt is the served. This thought achieves the objectives of Zakāt by stimulating investment. Investing from a Zakāt perspective includes otherworldly and material incentives that contribute to establishing an investment thought that does not only dispense with profit as a legitimate target but at the same time to achieve the most important goal, which is Zakāt. Zakāt motivates owners of funds to promote the economy and trade and increase profits to achieve the ideal goal of giving Zakāt. The increase of Zakāt payers, and by consequence Zakāt impact on sustainable investment, reflects the existence of a strong relationship between worship and economy as well as the increase in wealth and economic prosperity.

Conclusion

Zakāt is a devotional and symbiotic institution. Zakāt is a financial worship, and it is one of the pillars of Islam. Zakāt achieves double principal functions in society: the first is the giving of Zakāt to needy persons, which is the essence of Zakāt worship; the second is the prohibition of hoarding and encouragement of wealth circulation and consequently the encouragement of sustainable investment. The dual important functions serve society and the economy as well. Zakāt gives a basic vision for sustainable investment, as the investor's first goal becomes to achieve profit to pay Zakāt with faith, and thus the investment becomes a servant of Zakāt. Zakāt is also a servant of certain categories of society, so it gives them a spirit of hope and a decent life and saves them from financial difficulties in a way that serves their interests and strengthens investment and the economy.

The State should be involved in the implementation of the Zakāt system as a condition for the success of the Zakāt role in the economy and the promotion of investment sustainability. Zakāt plays an important role in sustainable investment and its preservation through the economic content of Zakāt wealth, the conditions of Zakāt and the redistribution of wealth to the categories of Zakāt in need. Further, the role of Zakāt through spending is significant in the suitable circulation of wealth and its allocation to productive entities or individuals. The Zakāt system has the capacity to significantly resolve the socioeconomic issues in Muslim societies and can transform needy persons to future entrepreneurs and investors. In the end, the wisdom of Zakāt is that the increase in wealth of rich must be matched by an increase in giving and spending for needy people. The greater the wealth, the greater the spending, and thus it represents the values of justice, rational behavior, altruism, and the hadith of the Prophet Muhammed (saw) that shows that faith is conditional to altruism: "No one of you becomes a true believer until he likes for his brother what he likes for himself."[17]

Notes

1 The abundance of goodness and benefit.
2 Al-Mohalla (Ibn Hazm).
3 Source: Al-Albani. Sahih Al-Jameh (N° 1739).
4 Al-Dhakhira, volume 3, page 7.
5 Sahih Muslim 2588 (Sunnah.com).
6 Al-Bukhari 2/104, No. 1395, and Muslim 1/50, No. 19.
7 When a Muslim reaches Nisab he becomes rich.
8 Sahih al-Bukhari 1426 (Sunnah.com).
9 Al-Albani: Sahih Al-Jami. No: 7497.
10 Al-Ahkam al-Sultaniyyah. Chapter 11.
11 Sunan Abi Dawud 2594. (Sunnah.com).
12 The Council of the International Islamic Fiqh Academy of the Organization of the Islamic Conference (1986), Resolution No. 15 (3/3) Investment of Zakāt Funds in Profit-Generating Projects without Attributing Individual Ownership to Recipients.
13 The Council of the International Islamic Fiqh Academy of the Organization of the Islamic Conference (2007), Resolution No. 165 (3/18) Enhancing the Role of Zakāt in Poverty Alleviation and the Management of its Collection and Distribution based on Fiqh Interpretations (Ijtihād).
14 Sahih Muslim 1556a (sunnah.com).
15 Sahih al-Bukhari 2389 (Sunnah.com).
16 surahquran.com.
17 Narrated by Al-Bukhari [No.: 13], and Muslim [No.: 45].

References

Al-Ghafili, A. (2008). *Zakat Issues* (1st ed.). Bank Al-Bilad and Dar Al-Maymen.

Al-Isfahani, R. (1986). *Al-Mofradat Fi Gharib Al-Quran.* Istanbul, Turkey: Dar Kahraman.

Al-Masri, R. (1997). Rules of Zakāt from Contemporary Commerce. *7th Symposium of Contemporary Zakāt Issues* (pp 281–325). Kuwait.

Al-Mawardi, A. (2006). The Guardianship of Charities. Kitab: Zakāt Disbursement. Investigator. In Gad, A. (Ed.), *Al-Ahkam Al-Sultaniyyah.* Cairo, Egypt: Dar Al-Hadith.

Al-Qarafi, C. (1994). *Al-Dhakhira. Investigator: Mohammad Boukhubza* (1st ed., Vol. 3, p. 7). Beirout: Dar Al-Gharb Al-Islami.

Banani, A. (2017, November). The Economic Purposes of the Obligation of Zakat (2). *Journal of Islamic Economics.*

Belabes, A. (2019). The Indicators of Wealth and Poverty in the Light of a Systemic Approach of Zakātable Assets. *Journal of Sciences of Zakāt*, 3(5).

Council of the International Islamic Fiqh Academy of the Organization of the Islamic Conference. (1986). *Resolution No. 15 (3/3) Investment of Zakāt Funds in Profit-Generating Projects without Attributing Individual Ownership to Recipients.*

Council of the International Islamic Fiqh Academy of the Organization of the Islamic Conference. (2007). *Resolution No. 165 (3/18) Enhancing the Role of Zakāt in Poverty Alleviation and the Management of Its Collection and Distribution Based on Fiqh Interpretations (Ijtihād).*

Dunya, C. (2018). *Economic Jurisprudence Studies in Some Islamic Rituals: Zakāt, Hajj, Endowment, and Inheritance*.

Ibn Al-Khouja, M. H. (2004). *Muhammad Al-Taher Ben Ashour and His Book Maqasid of Islamic Shari'ah: Between Sciences of Fundamentals of Jurisprudence and Maqasid.* Investigator: Mohammad Al-Habib Ibn Al-Khouja. Part 2. Section 7 p. 387. Publisher: Ministry of Awqaf and Islamic Affairs, Qatar.

Ibn Hazm, A. (2003). *Al-Mohalla Bel-Athaar. Investigator: Abdelghafaar Solaimen Al-Bandari*. Volume 4, Kitab Al-Zakāt. Question 687, page 287. First edition. Dar Al-Kotob Al-ilmiyah, Beirut.

Khelifi, R. M., & Amer, S. A. (2021). *Zakati: Towards a Civilized Role for Zakāt in the World.* International Zakāh Organisation.

Mortan, S. S. (2004). *Introduction to Economic Thought in Islam* (2nd ed.). Institution Al-Resalah.

9 Zakat Governance Towards Sustainable Finance

Tika Widiastuti, Imron Mawardi, Mir'atun Nisa' & Razali Haron

Introduction

Poverty, hunger, and inequality are social problems faced by various countries, especially developing countries. Islam has financial power and answers to address inequality and promote sustainability through Islamic Social Finance (ISF) instruments. Zakat and other ISF instruments' primary goal is to distribute the wealth of the rich to the poor to achieve socio-economic justice, increase economic growth, reduce poverty and inequality, and to promote sustainability. As a Muslim-majority country, Indonesia has great potential for developing ISF instruments. According to data, the potential for zakat reaches 22.8 billion, waqf land is USD 137.9 billion, and cash waqf is USD 13 billion (Widiastuti et al., 2022a, 2022b). ISF is an integrated socio-economic empowerment system divided into traditional and contemporary financial systems (Widiastuti et al., 2022a, 2022b). There are two types of traditional ISF instruments: Philanthropy-based instruments, such as zakat, *infaq* or alms, and waqf, and cooperation-based instruments, such as *qardh* and *kafalah*. Meanwhile, contemporary ISF mechanisms are in the form of Islamic microfinance (IRTI, 2020). Each instrument has its function and role in building economic prosperity and sustainability in society. Zakat is the only ISF mandatory instrument for every Muslim to pay at a specific size (*nisab*) and time (*haul*). The characteristic of compulsory zakat makes the potential for zakat very powerful, especially in countries with a Muslim majority, such as Indonesia and Malaysia. Therefore, the development of zakat and its governance needs to be carried out and becomes the concern of policymakers. Apte (1969) initiated the first research project on zakat, which is still strong today. This situation shows the growing interest in zakat and various zakat research issues. According to Law 23 of 2011 (Indonesia), zakat management in Indonesia includes collection management distribution application and reporting. The quality of management determines the success or failure of zakat management in zakat institutions. Mahmoud et al. reported that zakat schemes fail when there is poor governance. To collect significant potential sources of zakat funds, the Indonesian zakat institution needs to find an effective and credible way to govern all business processes. Currently, the realization of zakat is still at 17 trillion rupiahs or 5.19% of the total potential. The gap between zakat potential and its realization becomes the basis for how

DOI: 10.4324/9781003468653-12

important it is to build a governance framework that encourages the completion of the collection and management of zakat.

In zakat institutions, business processes include collecting, managing, distributing, using, and reporting zakat (Figure 9.1). One of the five most discussed topics was zakat management or governance. Zakat governance has the intention to ensure that zakat is professionally and appropriately distributed to improve the recipient's quality of life (Adiwijaya & Suprianto, 2020). Countries like Indonesia already have specific institutions that regulate the standardization of zakat governance both technically and legally through BAZNAS and the Ministry of Religion. However, several countries still need to have specific institutions or agencies. In addition, several aspects regarding zakat collection and disbursement also require further improvement (Ag Omar et al., 2021).

Researchers have extensively discussed zakat governance in zakat institutions (see for example Owoyemi, 2020; Widiastuti, Cahyono et al., 2021). Additional research demonstrates the influence of zakat on the economy (Beik & Arsyianti, 2016; Herianingrum et al., 2022; Ridwan et al., 2019; Widiastuti et al., 2021a, 2021b). However, according to some studies, zakat has not been able to elevate receivers to a level of prosperity (see for example Taha et al., 2017; Umar et al., 2022). This fact highlights the importance of studying the zakat literature to enhance its managerial activities and business operations, such as the distribution and application of zakat. Another crucial component is reporting activities, where numerous prior studies have demonstrated that openness in zakat reporting can foster more institutional zakat payment fidelity (Sawmar & Mohammed, 2021). Based on this description, this study aims to 1) describe three crucial aspects of zakat governance, 2) complete literature related to zakat governance, and 3) become a reference for zakat institutions in excellent and sustainable governance.

Research Method

This research is a library study using 51 Scopus-indexed articles sorted by subject and evaluated according to several other criteria. Systematic Literature Review (SLR) was selected as the most efficient method for conducting a comprehensive literature review of business processes at the zakat institution. This study adapts the work of Sukmana (2020), Rohman et al. (2021), and Narayan and Phan (2019) as primary sources for authoring this publication, along with much advancement. Sukmana (2020) begins his study of waqf-related literature by categorizing it. He

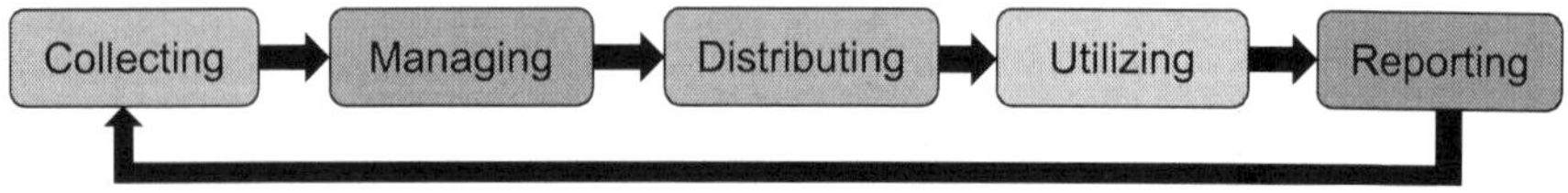

Figure 9.1 Zakat Institution's Business Process

Source: Law 21 of 2011 Indonesia Zakat Management

then draws conclusions about what can be learned, what these conclusions mean for the government, and what research can be done in the future. Rohman et al. (2021) conducted a literature review on microfinance (2021). Similarly, Narayan and Phan (2019) completed the same task by reviewing the literature in Islamic banking.

This research progressed through numerous stages (Figure 9.2). The first step is to do a general search for publications using the terms "*Zakat*," "*Zakah*," "*Al-Zakah*," "*Zaka*," "*Az-Zakat*," and "*Az-Zakah*." The next step is removing duplicates. Third, the authors established five standards for choosing review papers. According to criteria 1, publications from the Scopus database are used. Criteria 2 is eliminating predatory publishers and journals. Criteria 3 discusses the type of document used, which is a research article, and criteria 4 is choosing the research articles, which only have been published with the subject matter of economics, econometrics, business, and management. Since many zakat studies concentrate on the *fiqh* component, this study places restrictions on thoroughly evaluating the zakat governance. Criteria 5 requires that the chosen article research focus primarily on zakat. Papers that only briefly touch on zakat are eliminated at this point. After reviewing the research article, the author found 51 articles with a main concentration on three essential aspects:

- T1: Technology Optimization with a total of 33 articles.
- T2: Integration of Zakat Institutions with a total of 27 articles.
- T3: Human Resource Capacity with a total of 26 articles.

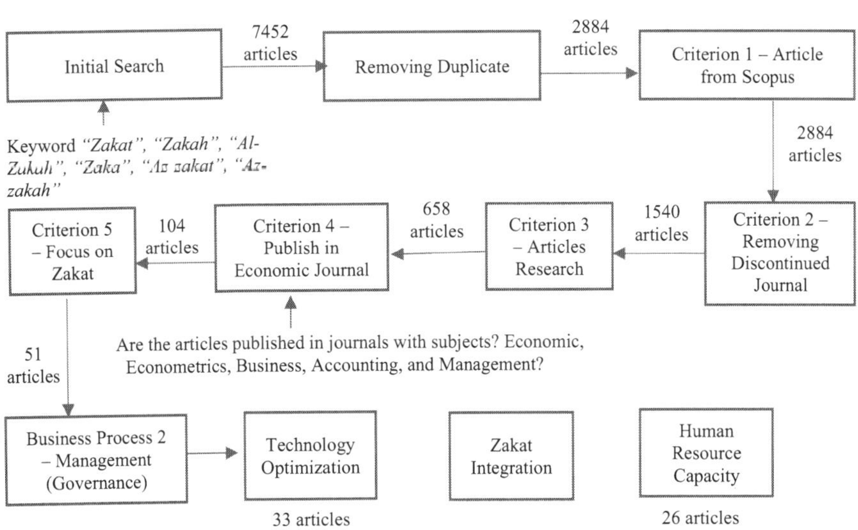

Figure 9.2 Stages of Research Progress

Source: Developed by the authors (2022)

Some publications tackle multiple topics within a single article. As an illustration, seven articles discuss technology optimization, integration of zakat institutions, and human resource capacity at once. Two articles describe technology optimization and integration between zakat institutions and other institutions, five discuss technology optimization and human resource capacity, and three mention integration between zakat institutions and other institutions and human resource capacity. Furthermore, eight articles explain technology optimization, 15 discuss the integration of zakat institutions only, and 11 describe human resource capacity.

This study builds on the previous literature by creating research that objectively evaluates the literature related to the business process in the organization of zakat. Consequently, this study provides an overview of zakat management. This study discusses detailed investigations of governmental zakat institutions and implications for future research. It is expected that this study will likely provide insights that stakeholders can apply, especially future zakat managers, policymakers, and academics.

Zakat Governance

According to Teece (2010), the governance idea of how to carry out ongoing business activities and manage its primary business is reflected in the business model. Prioritizing and tracking the management of resources and efforts to change organizational processes is called business process management (BPM). Similarities and differences in the business processes of any organization or company depend on the business type and industry (see Table 9.1). Zakat organization is one of the organizations that operate differently from other non-profit and for-profit organizations in terms of business management.

Zakat governance is a crucial component of the zakat institution's business procedures. Zakat can only be adequately handled or governed with good management. In order to optimize zakat governance, previous literature highlighted the importance of considering three aspects, which include technology optimization

Table 9.1 Comparison of Business Processes of Zakat Institutions With Other Institutions

	Zakat Institution	*Waqf Institution*	*Educational Institution*	*Trading Company*
Business Process	1. Planning 2. Collecting 3. Management 4. Distribution 5. Empowerment 6. Reporting	1. Collection of Waqf 2. Administration of waqf property 3. Management and development of waqf assets 4. Supervision and protection of waqf property 5. Reporting	1. Process Management 2. Main Process 3. Support Process	1. Planning 2. Purchasing/ Sales 3. Reporting

Source: Authors (2022)

(Al-Homaidi et al., 2021; Aziz et al., 2019; Gafoordeen et al., 2016; Hadi et al., 2021; Hasan et al., 2019; Herianingrum et al., 2022; Hossain et al., 2019; Mutamimah et al., 2021; Sawmar & Mohammed, 2021; Widiastutiet al., 2022a), integration (Amalia, 2019; Aziz et al., 2019; Gafoordeen et al., 2016; Hossain et al., 2019; Müller, 2017; Mutamimah et al., 2021), and human resources (Adiwijaya & Suprianto, 2020; Ryandono et al., 2021; Widiastuti et al., 2018, 2021a; Widiastuti et al., 2022a). The study examines them in the literature and then recommendations are made for the government and zakat institutions on how to best play their parts in zakat optimization. The study presents further research recommendations to provide researchers with essential areas that need to be explored.

Technology Optimization

Technological development is an inevitable matter in management. Technological developments certainly go hand in hand with developments in science and adapt to the needs of human life. The existence of technology aims to facilitate and support the activities carried out by humans. Likewise, regarding zakat governance, technology is essential to perform management activities more optimally. Several studies have focused on discussing technology optimization to improve zakat management. Technology is a fundamental aspect, and its use through digital zakat has enormous potential for the benefit of the people. Digital zakat will likely increase the efficiency and interest of *muzakki* in paying zakat (Herianingrum et al., 2022; Hadi et al., 2021; Sawmar et al., 2021; Al-Homaidi, 2021). Information Communication Technology (ICT) encourages collaboration between aspects of zakat management to make it more effective and efficient (Mutamimah et al., 2021). Higher levels of innovation in the industry drive the most productivity gains. Between 2003, 2006, 2008, 2009, 2011, and 2013 the sector saw enough positive technological change to push the overall pace of technological change. The comprehensive productivity variable for all zakat funds has increased significantly, primarily due to a change in technology rather than performance (Al-Homaidi et al., 2021). To raise funds in the current climate, zakat institutions must rely on digital technology to collect funds such as zakat, alms, and savings from *muzakki*, donors, savers, or *shohibul maal*, as the government has implemented a policy of restricting out-of-home activities (Herianingrum et al., 2022).

The government must fully support zakat institutions to utilize digital technology for zakat governance. In addition, through various contracts, the government must use zakat as one of the financial sources for its Islamic finance initiatives. On the other hand, to boost zakat collection, zakat distribution, and zakat reporting to the public, zakat institutions must increase their use of digital technology in zakat governance, including administration, promotion, and socialization of zakat. In order to raise funds, zakat institutions must endeavour to connect zakat with other contracts in Islamic economics. During the COVID-19 pandemic, zakat institutions should have learned that every policy enacted by the government would affect aspects of people's lives. For example, the restriction of out-of-home activities makes all aspects of activity, including zakat management and collection, rely on digital technology (Herianingrum et al., 2022). The use of digital technology, such as social media, is also an excellent tool to apply in the current era. Social media can be a place to educate and socialize Islamic Social Finance by displaying creative content as educational media. Collaboration with influential figures from each generation (baby boomers, millennials, and Gen Z) is vital to provide a different approach to each object (Widiastuti et al., 2022a, 2022b).

Government-established zakat institutions have all the resources, facilities, and technology they need to function effectively. Meanwhile, zakat institutions established by the community tend to require more support to provide facilities and technology (Ryandono et al., 2021). One example of increasing the optimization of digital zakat is the zakat collection using digital platforms. In 2022, Indonesian National *Amil* Zakat Agency (BAZNAS) collected 513.2 billion zakat, *infaq*, and alms funds, an increase of 33% from the previous year. Zakat's receipt through the BAZNAS website is optimally supported by BAZNAS' strategic plan to strengthen the digitalization of zakat. Thus, both websites and platforms for paying the zakat are increasingly in demand by *muzakki*. The government needs to support this by accelerating the integration of all private zakat institutions and centralized management of each institution through the help of digital technology. Continuous development of innovations in using digital technology for zakat governance shall be performed. Applicative research needs to be deepened, such as developing management information systems, using big data, and other related research. Empirical examples of the formation of digital ecosystems on zakat also need to be explored as lessons for digital zakat governance in other countries.

Zakat Integration

Zakat institutions have a vision of increasing the welfare of the eight *ashnaf* (Samad & Glenn, 2010). Even zakat funds with efficient management contribute to the country's welfare (Bashir, 2018). In order to launch a series of programs designed to increase social welfare, zakat institutions need to cooperate with various parties such as other ISFs, financial institutions (banks and non-banks), government, academics, and other stakeholders. Apart from integrating with external parties, zakat institutions should integrate with decency, integrity plans, loyalty, and as social institutions for better economic growth and output (Ridwan et al., 2019). Widiastuti et al. (2022a, 2022b) also believe that the active collaboration of zakat institutions with other institutions can accelerate people's welfare and maximize ISF's potential. The facts show that thanks to the integration of the zakat institution program with external parties, it can improve the living standards of the poor by 12%, more effectively than programs without integration (Widiastuti et al., 2022a, 2022b).

Integration Between Zakat and Other ISF Instrument

Even though each zakat institution has different values and codes of ethics, they have the same vision: namely, to raise the degree of the welfare of *mustahiq*. For agreement to occur between zakat institutions, Müller (2017) suggests that zakat institutions codify one legal framework that outlines the concept of collective centralization and decentralization governance (distribution) to ensure they achieve a fair and balanced zakat distribution policy. Integration between zakat institutions is one of the efforts to deal with the weaknesses of zakat institutions, namely the lack of coordination in the distribution and utilization of zakat (Widiastuti et al., 2021a, 2021b).

Zakat institutions need much interaction with waqf institutions, because waqf institutions already have programs with a high success rate in increasing the fulfilment of the basic needs of the poor (Bashir, 2018). Several previous studies offer integration models between zakat institutions and waqf institutions (Aziz et al., 2019; Hossain et al., 2019; Mutamimah et al., 2021). Hossain et al. (2019) believe combining zakat, waqf, and *sadaqah* funds can inject poverty alleviation funds into OIC countries. Zakat institutions will distribute these zakat, waqf, and *sadaqah* funds through economic activities such as financing for micro-enterprises or investments. For zakat, waqf, and *sadaqah* (ZISWAF) funds to be absorbed properly, it is highly recommended to carry out digitalization (Mutamimah et al., 2021). Widiastuti et al. (2022a, 2022b) created an integration model between zakat funds and waqf. The basis for creating this model (Integrated Model of Islamic Social Finance, refer to Widiastuti et al. (2022a, 2022b) for details) is the difference in the allocation of managed funds. Allocation of zakat funds is used for the consumptive and productive sectors, while Islamic financial institutions allocate waqf funds for the real and financial sectors. Consumptive zakat funds are directly given to *mustahiq* in cash. Productive zakat is distributed to *mustahiq* in the form of an empowerment program. The purpose of distributing productive zakat is to improve the standard of living of *mustahiq*. Meanwhile, the intention of waqf funds is for financing in the real sector for selected entrepreneurs.

Integration Between Zakat Institution and Other Parties

The existence of a fatwa institution strengthens the existence of a zakat institution. Research conducted by Zulkifli et al. (2012) stated that Mufti and Fatwa Institutions in Malaysia have also become supporting factors for increasing zakat income in Malaysia. Religious authorities also have a stake in the sustainability of zakat institutions because all matters related to religious affairs, religious education, religious law, and the management of ISF funds fall under the authority of religious authorities (Ag Omar et al., 2021). In order to strengthen the existence of zakat institutions, especially regarding the legal power of paying zakat in Indonesia, the fatwa institution, in collaboration with the zakat institution, examines the latest issues or ideas about zakat and assesses whether these issues and ideas are under Shari'ah and can be implemented in zakat management. Pati et al. explain that to implement financial technology (fintech) in zakat institution activities, the zakat institution should accommodate suggestions from various parties, including fatwa institutions, to ensure that the application of fintech complies with Shari'ah law. Involving the fatwa institution is the zakat institution's effort to improve the zakat institution's integrity in the eyes of the public so that the public has more trust in the entire management process at the zakat institution.

Müller (2017) said that zakat institutions need to cooperate with external experts, especially experts who master fields beyond the ability of zakat institutions, to create programs that are right on target and able to bring more benefits to program recipients and compete globally (Amalia, 2019). For example, the zakat institution invites business expertise to provide training to *mustahiq* who have businesses. Apart from experts, zakat forums and academics can be invited to work together, especially in developing ideas, literacy, and governance development schemes (Widiastuti et al., 2018, 2022a, 2022b). One of the roles of academics and zakat forums is to voice the importance of paying zakat collectively through zakat institution to prospective *muzakki*, because there are still *muzakki* who take the initiative to pay zakat to *mustahiq* directly (Riyanto et al., 2021). Several studies discuss the importance of paying zakat through zakat institution, such as Riyanto et al. (2021). These studies argue that zakat collected at zakat institution can significantly improve the standard of living of *mustahiq* compared to paying zakat without going through zakat institution, because zakat funds managed by zakat institution are distributed through a series of creative and sustainable programs. Research related to the impact of zakat funds managed by zakat institutions can be reviewed in Beik and Arsyianti (2016) and Ridwan et al. (2019) studies.

Zakat institutions can also use schools as springboards for an alternative to driving concern about paying zakat (Samad & Glenn, 2010). Riyanto et al. (2021) found that zakat institution often collaborates with schools to implement religious education (Ariff & Mohamad, 2017). Through this religious education, the school inserts basic knowledge related to zakat as one of the pillars of Islam. As a result, public literacy can increase regarding zakat. Literacy related to zakat needs to be improved, because the low literacy of zakat is an obstacle to achieving the potential for collecting zakat. BAZNAS revealed that Indonesia's zakat literacy level in 2020 was 66.78, indicating that zakat literacy still needs to be improved and requires more efforts to preach, socialize, and educate zakat (Puskas BAZNAS, 2022).

The mosque functions not only as a place of worship; it also functions as a means of developing people (Riyanto et al., 2021). Several mosques now also carry out zakat management activities (Omar et al., 2019). Unfortunately, only 8% of mosques are officially registered as Zakat Collection Units (UPZ) in Indonesia. Based on the Puskas BAZNAS report (2020), people still prefer to pay zakat through mosques that are not registered as UPZ. The funds collected are estimated at 61.25 trillion rupiahs. Given the potential of mosques in collecting zakat funds, integration efforts between mosques and zakat institutions need to be supported (Omar et al., 2019). The form of integration of these two institutions is by holding zakat management training for mosque management to increase the professionalism of mosque management in raising funds (Delvina et al., 2020). Ab Rahman et al. (2019) offer a model of integration between mosques and zakat institutions (Zakat Management Governance Model of Mosque). In their research, there are three central figures in the management of zakat in mosques, namely: 1) The Governance Unit of Zakat Institution; 2) The *Ashnaf* Information and Multimedia Unit; and 3) The Zakat Collection and Distribution Unit. In this model, the zakat institution can take on the role of The Governance Unit of Zakat Institution, which manages the competency of the *amil* mosque. Further investigation of zakat governance best practices in various nations is required to provide pertinent recommendations for strengthening zakat governance. Additionally, empirical research must be done on how each collaboration and integration between zakat institutions and other institutions affect zakat performance.

Developing Human Resource Capacity

The low quality and quantity of human resources or not following a work activity became a problem in the sustainability of a program. Likewise, in zakat governance, the capacity of human resources, especially managers (*'amil*), is still low (Mutamimah et al., 2021; Widiastuti et al., 2018, 2022a, 2022b). The low quality of human resources will impact service and achievement of zakat institution targets (Widiastuti et al., 2018). The results of previous research showed that the causes of low-quality *amil* include less supporting infrastructure and budget for developing *amil* competencies (Mutamimah et al., 2021). Institutions that are unable to place resources appropriately so that *amil* capabilities are not optimally explored (Wahab & Rahman, 2012), political instability within the internal institution (Sadallah & Abdul-Jabbar, 2022), and *amil's* lack of knowledge regarding zakat governance (Widiastuti et al., 2018, 2021a, 2021b) also influence the quality of *amil*. Human resource quality improves *zakāh* effectiveness and performance (Sawmar & Mohammed, 2021). Furthermore, intellectual capital or quality resources affect the performance of a zakat institution. Institutions can see this quality in experience, competence, and skills of the human resources. Establishing relationships with various parties, including zakat recipients, zakat donors, and other parties, such as the government, is crucial in increasing zakat institutions' efficiency.

There is a linear relationship between the competency level of *amil* and public trust in zakat institutions (Ahmad, 2019). Improving the quality of *amil* is one of the efforts of zakat institutions to increase public trust (Sadallah & Abdul-Jabbar, 2022). Wahab et al. have proposed a comprehensive framework for studying the service quality of zakat institutions. The framework's components include Reliability, Tangibles, Empathy, Responsiveness, and Compliance to encourage zakat institutions' sustainability and increase zakat's socioeconomic objectives. Zakat institutions need to use these five frameworks as a standard for the quality of service. The role of the heads of zakat institutions is also a reflection of how competent the institution is (Poon et al., 2021). Leaders are believed to have a high level of religiosity, and good competency can provide enlightenment and encourage people to pay zakat (Cokrohadisumarto et al., 2020). Religious leaders will also not allow fraudulent acts to tarnish the institution's good name (Bin-Nashwan et al., 2021). Leader quality contributes to improving the collection and management of zakat. The development of human resources, especially zakat managers (*'amil*) from various countries, needs to be studied continuously to find best practices. Studies related to the standardization of zakat manager competencies also need to be compared from one country to another to collect indicators of global zakat manager competency standards. The relationship between zakat manager expertise or zakat human resources with digital technology on the zakat governance results also needs further investigation.

Conclusion

This study conducts a systematic review of the literature on the management in zakat institutions, focusing on technology optimization, integration of zakat institutions with third-party institutions, and HR capabilities. This study concludes that to increase the productivity and effectiveness of zakat organizations, zakat institutions need to optimize technology, collaborate and synergize with various parties, and increase the competitiveness of human resources. However, like other studies, it has limitations. This study was only limited to zakat governance. Future research can examine the other business process, such as collection, distribution, utilization, and reporting processes in zakat institutions for other instruments of other Islamic social funds, such as waqf and Islamic microfinance.

References

Ab Rahman, A., Thaidi, A. H. A., & Ab Rahman, F. M. (2019). A Proposed Mosque Model for Zakat Governance Towards Achieving Global Peace. *Al-Shajarah*, 2019(Special Issue Shari'ah hand Law), 105–123.

Adiwijaya, Z. A., & Suprianto, E. (2020). Good Governance of Zakat Institutions: A Literature Review. *Journal of Southwest Jiaotong University*, 55(2), 1–18.

Ag Omar, P. M. F. F., Muchlis Gazali, H., Samsulbahri, M. N., Abd Razak, N. I., & Ishak, N. (2021). Establishing Zakat on Oil and Gas in Malaysia: A New Insight. *ISRA International Journal of Islamic Finance*, 13(3), 318–332.

Ahmad, M. (2019). An Empirical Study of the Challenges Facing Zakat and Waqf Institutions in Northern Nigeria. *ISRA International Journal of Islamic Finance*, 11(2), 338–356.

Al-Homaidi, E. A., Al-Matari, E. M., Anagreh, S., Tabash, M. I., & Mareai Senan, N. A. (2021). The Relationship between Zakat Disclosures and Islamic Banking Performance: Evidence from Yemen. *Banks and Bank Systems*, 16(1), 52–61.

Amalia, E. (2019). Good Governance for Zakat Institutions in Indonesia: A Confirmatory Factor Analysis. *Pertanika Journal Social Science & Humanities*, 27(3), 1–14.

Apte, M. D. (1969). The Nature and Scope of the Records from Peshwa Daftar with Reference to Zakat System. *The Indian Economic & Social History*, 6(4), 1–12. https://doi.org/10.1177/001946466900600403

Ariff, M., & Mohamad, S. (2017). Issues in Waqf and Zakat Management. In *Islamic Wealth Management: Theory and Practice* (pp. 381–390). Edward Elgar Publishing.

Aziz, M. A., Abdulsomad, K., & Din, B. H. (2019). Transaction Costs of the Zakat Institution: An Open Innovation Approach. *Institutions and Economies*, 11(2), 43–71.

Bashir, A.-H. (2018). Reducing Poverty and Income Inequalities: Current Approaches and Islamic Perspective. *JKAU: Islamic Econ*, 31(1), 93–104.

Beik, I. S., & Arsyianti, L. D. (2016). Measuring Zakat Impact on Poverty and Welfare Using CIBEST Model. *Journal of Islamic Monetary Economics and Finance*, 1(2), 141–160.

Bin-Nashwan, S. A., Abdul-Jabbar, H., & Aziz, S. A. (2021). Does Trust in Zakat Institution Enhance Entrepreneurs' Zakat Compliance? *Journal of Islamic Accounting and Business Research*, 12(5), 768–790.

Cokrohadisumarto, W. bin M., Zaenudin, Z., Santoso, B., & Sumiati, S. (2020). A Study of Indonesian Community's Behaviour in Paying Zakat. *Journal of Islamic Marketing*, 11(4), 961–976.

Delvina, A., Arifudin, O., Zulkarnaen, W., Rustandi, & Prasetyo, Y. (2020). Governance and Legal Perspectives: Problems in the Management of Zakat Funds Are Used as Collateral. *Journal of Advanced Research in Dynamical and Control Systems*, 12(6), 209–217.

Gafoordeen, N., Nayeem, M. M., & Aslam, A. M. (2016). Zakat Investment in Shari'ah. *International Business Management*, 10(12), 2398–2401.

Hadi, R., Sochimin, & Basit, A. (2021). Shari'ah Strategic Economic Model on Digital Zakat Technology in Indonesia. *Economic Annals-XXI*, 187(1–2), 82–89.

Hasan, A., Hassan, R., Engku Ali, E. R. A., Engku Ali, E. M. T., Abduh, M., & Noordin, N. H. (2019). A Proposed Human Resource Management Model for Zakat Institutions in Malaysia. *ISRA International Journal of Islamic Finance*, 11(1), 98–109.

Herianingrum, S., Widiastuti, T., Hapsari, M. I., Ratnasari, R. T., Firmansyah, F., Hassan, S. A., Febriyanti, A. R., Amalia, R. C., & Muzakki, L. A. (2022). Muzakki and Mustahik's Collaboration Model for Strengthening the Fundraising Capacity of Islamic Social Finance Institutions During COVID-19. *International Journal of Ethics and Systems*. https://doi.org/10.1108/IJOES-05-2022-0091

Hossain, I., Muhammad, A. D., Jibril, B. T., & Kaitibie, S. (2019). Support for Smallholder Farmers Through Islamic Instruments: The Case of Bangladesh and Lessons for Nigeria. *International Journal of Islamic and Middle Eastern Finance and Management*, 12(2), 154–168.

IRTI. (2020). *Islamic Social Finance Report 2020*. IsDB.

Müller, D. M. (2017). From Consultancy to Critique: The 'Success Story' of Globalized Zakat Management in Malaysia and Its Normative Ambiguities. *Globalizations*, 14(1), 81–98.

Mutamimah, M., Alifah, S., Gunawan, G., & Adnjani, M. D. (2021). ICT-Based Collaborative Framework for Improving the Performance of Zakat Management Organisations in Indonesia. *Journal of Islamic Accounting and Business Research*, 12(6), 887–903.

Omar, A. R. C., Hussin, M. Y. M., & Muhammad, F. (2019). Assessing Strategic Orientation and Mosques Performance. *Research in World Economy*, 10(5), 30–35.

Owoyemi, M. Y. (2020). Zakat Management: The Crisis of Confidence in Zakat Agencies and the Legality of Giving Zakat Directly to the Poor. *Journal of Islamic Accounting and Business Research*, 11(2), 498–510.

Poon, J. P. H., Chow, Y. W., Ewers, M., & Hamilton, T. (2021). Executives' Observance of Zakat Among Islamic Financial Institutions: Evidence from Bahrain and Malaysia. *Journal of Islamic Accounting and Business Research*, 12(4), 509–523.

Puskas BAZNAS. (2020, December 23). *BAZNAS: Zakat Masyarakat yang Tak Tercatat Rp 61,25 Triliun*. BAZNAS. https://baznas.go.id/Press_Release/baca/BAZNAS_:_Zakat_Masyarakat_yang_Tak_Tercatat_Rp_61,25_Triliun/680

Puskas BAZNAS. (2022). *Outlook Zakat Indonesia 2022*.

Ridwan, M., Asnawi, N., & Sutikno, S. (2019). Zakat Collection and Distribution System and Its Impact on the Economy of Indonesia. *Uncertain Supply Chain Management*, 7(4), 589–598.

Riyanto, S., Herningtyas, R., & Nizar, M. (2021). Muslim's Philanthropy in Singapore and the Role of Government. *Sociology and Technoscience*, 11(2), 194–214.

Rohman, P. S., Fianto, B. A., Ali Shah, S. A., Kayani, U. N., Suprayogi, N., & Supriani, I. (2021). A Review on Literature of Islamic Microfinance from 2010–2020: Lesson for Practitioners and Future Directions. *Heliyon*, 7(12), e08549.

Ryandono, M. N. H., Qulub, A. S., Cahyono, E. F., Widiastuti, T., Aisyah, B. N., & Robani, A. (2021). Efficiency Analysis of Zakat Institutions in Indonesia: Data Envelopment Analysis (DEA) and Free Disposal Hull (FDH). *Approaches. Academy of Accounting and Financial Studies Journal*, 25(6), 1–12.

Sadallah, M., & Abdul-Jabbar, H. (2022). Business Zakat Compliance in Algeria: An Ethical Perspective. *International Journal of Ethics and Systems*, 38(2), 338–355.

Samad, A., & Glenn, L. M. (2010). Development of Zakah and Zakah Coverage in Monotheistic Faiths. *International Journal of Social Economics*, 37(4), 302–315.

Sawmar, A. A., & Mohammed, M. O. (2021). How Governance Practices Influence Mandatory Zakah Payment in Saudi Arabia? *Journal of King Abdulaziz University, Islamic Economics*, 34(1), 3–24.

Sukmana, R. (2020). Critical Assessment of Islamic Endowment Funds (Waqf) Literature: Lesson for Government and Future Directions. *Heliyon*, 6(10), e05074.

Taha, R., Zulkifli, M. F., Embong, M. R., & Mohd Nor, M. N. (2017). Zakat Distribution in the East Coast: Recipients' View. *Pertanika Journal of Social Sciences and Humanities*, 27(4), 1–16.

Umar, U. H., Baita, A. J., Haron, M. H. Bin, & Kabiru, S. H. (2022). The Potential of Islamic Social Finance to Alleviate Poverty in the Era of COVID-19: The Moderating Effect of Ethical Orientation. *International Journal of Islamic and Middle Eastern Finance and Management*, 15(2), 255–270.

Wahab, N. A., & Rahman, A. R. A. (2012). Productivity Growth of Zakat Institutions in Malaysia: An Application of Data Envelopment Analysis. *Studies in Economics and Finance*, 29(3), 197–210.

Widiastuti, T., Cahyono, E. F., Zulaikha, S., Mawardi, I., & al Mustofa, M. U. (2021a). Optimizing Zakat Governance in East Java Using Analytical Network Process (ANP): The Role of Zakat Technology (ZakaTech). *Journal of Islamic Accounting and Business Research*, 12(3), 301–319.

Widiastuti, T., Cahyono, E. F., Zulaikha, S., Mawardi, I., & al Mustofa, M. U. (2021b). Optimizing Zakat Governance in East Java Using Analytical Network Process (ANP): The Role of Zakat Technology (ZakaTech). *Journal of Islamic Accounting and Business Research*, 12(3), 301–319.

Widiastuti, T., Mawardi, I., Robani, A., & Rusydiana, A. S. (2018). Optimization of Zakat Fund Management in Regional Zakat Institution. *Humanities and Social Sciences Reviews*, 6(2), 133–139.

Widiastuti, T., Ningsih, S., Prasetyo, A., Mawardi, I., Herianingrum, S., Robani, A., al Mustofa, M. U., & Hady, A. F. (2022a). Developing an Integrated Model of Islamic Social Finance: Toward an Effective Governance Framework. *Heliyon*, 8(9), e10383.

Widiastuti, T., Ningsih, S., Prasetyo, A., Mawardi, I., Herianingrum, S., Robani, A., al Mustofa, M. U., & Hady, A. F. (2022b). Developing an Integrated Model of Islamic Social Finance: Toward an Effective Governance Framework. *Heliyon*, 8(9), e10383.

Widiastuti, T., Prasetyo, A., Robani, A., Mawardi, I., Rosida, R., & al Mustofa, M. U. (2022). Toward Developing a Sustainability Index for the Islamic Social Finance Program: An Empirical Investigation. *PLoS ONE*, 17(11), e0276876.

Zulkifli, W., Hasnan, H., Sabri, M., Mohamad, Z., & Umar, A. (2012). Suitability of the Zakah Fatwa with Economics Society in Terengganu, Malaysia. *Journal of Applied Sciences Research*, 8(5), 2518–2530.

10 Effective Zakat Management Towards Sustainability

Mohamed Asmy Bin Mohd Thas Thaker, Mohamed Aslam Akbar, Mustafa Omar Mohammed & Jarita Duasa

Introduction

Islamic social finance institutions (ISFIs) have grown dramatically in recent years. ISFIs are founded based on (i) philanthropy, such as zakat, sadaqah, and waqf; (ii) collaboration, such as qard and kafalah; and (iii) Islamic microfinance institutions, which contribute significantly to poverty alleviation and socioeconomic development. According to MaRS, ISFIs invest and manage a specific fund to address societal concerns. They contribute to significant socioeconomic development outcomes such as poverty alleviation, the provision of vital infrastructures such as schools and hospitals, and the preservation of life and dignity. Thus, the ISFIs appear to be fast-spreading and developing into functional institutions, which can meet the community and stakeholders' economic and social needs. However, when the idea of IFSIs was conceptualized, Muslim scholars expected the institutions to adhere to *Maqasid al Shari'ah* once they were operationalized. In essence, ISFIs are expected to contribute to socioeconomic development, while upholding justice in their activities. Over time, ISFIs are seen as shying away from the very objective of their establishment, al-Maqasid. There are also misgivings expressed by scholars regarding the fulfilment of *Maqasid al-Shari'ah* by the activities of IFSIs. As mentioned, many scholars suggested that *Maqasid al-Shari'ah* should be the objective of IFSIs. However, Siddiqi expressed his concern regarding the failure to realize *Maqasid al-Shari'ah* by IFSIs in a changing environment. Even though the IFSIs are growing fast, many fail to fulfil the need of *Maqasid al Shari'ah*. Critics argue that the collection and distribution of funds from ISFIs are not up to the required level, and there is a lack of confidence and trust in some of the institutions.

Several attempts have been made relentlessly, especially by regulators in Malaysia, to harness the ISFIs towards *al-Maqasid*, including amending the regulations and policies. The pertinent question that arises is the extent to which these efforts are effective and how they are measured. Most of the existing studies use the conventional yardstick to measure the results of ISFIs. However, this yardstick is not suitable for measuring *Maqasid*-based performances. Therefore, the present study fills in the research gap by developing a *Maqasid*-based index to measure the performance of ISFIs in a holistic manner. This study is motivated by the apparent divergence in the practice of ISFIs from their initial objectives and aims to

DOI: 10.4324/9781003468653-13

explore the performance of ISFIs in achieving *Maqasid al-Shari'ah* goals. Most of the ISFIs' performance studies focus on measuring financial performance based on the conventional aspect of performance, without focusing on the *Maqasid* aspects. These conventional yardsticks are not adequate to measure the Maqasid-based performance that can truly measure the identity of ISFIs. Therefore, it is essential to examine the ISFIs in the Malaysian context with a proper instrument such as the *Maqasid Al-Shari'ah* Index (MSI), which was first developed by Mohammed et al. With the objective of analysing the performance of ISFIs based on *Maqasid al-Shari'ah,* this study aims to extend the analysis of the MSI employed in the literature and to determine the Maqasid accomplishment of ISFIs in their operations.

Literature Review

Overview of Lembaga Zakat Selangor (LZS)

According to Haron et al. (2010), Zakat Selangor was previously managed by a centre called Pusat Zakat Selangor (PZS), which was also called Zakat Selangor Religious Council Pte Ltd or Zakat MAIS Sdn Bhd. Before that, the name was Pusat Pungutan Zakat Selangor (PPZS), and it was first corporatized in 1994 with a paid-up capital of RM500,000 (Makhtar & Abdul Wahab, 2010). In 1996, the name changed to Pusat Zakat Selangor or PZS (MAIS). All of the entities belong to Selangor State Religious Council or Majlis Agama Islam Selangor (MAIS). It is one of the significant efforts made by the religious council to corporatize the management of Zakat to implement the corporate values to enhance the operations and activities related to Zakat collections, distributions, and management. The corporatization has tremendously increased the state Zakat collection and resulted in more efficient distribution (Haron et al., 2010). In addition, according to the Annual Report of Selangor Religious Council (MAIS) (2006), starting from 31st January 2006 or 1 Muharram 1427H, the collection of zakat is done by a new entity called Lembaga Zakat Selangor or LZS (MAIS) (Makhtar & Abdul Wahab, 2010). The move was made to re-brand the image of PZS to a new one since it already reached as high as RM100 million for the Zakat collection every year. LZS was incorporated under the Trustees (Incorporation) Act 1952 of Malaysia under the law of the Prime Minister's Office, and the management still belongs to Selangor State Religious Council (MAIS) today.

Activities of Lembaga Zakat Selangor

After 2003, PZS started to focus rigorously on entrepreneurship programs to help the *asnaf.* In 2005, PZS established Jabatan Pembangunan Asnaf to ensure the needs of *asnaf* are met through the zakat programmes. The stages of the activities were expanded by incorporating the elements of exposure, education, implementation, marketing, and monitoring. As a result, many *asnaf* have successfully gotten out of poverty and improved their living conditions (Makhtar &

Abdul Wahab, 2010). Today, under the management of Lembaga Zakat Selangor (LZS), the activities are more diverse and larger in scope, in tandem with a larger Zakat collection of more than RM900 million in 2020 (Ringkasan Prestasi Kutipan Zakat dan Agihan Zakat Lembaga Zakat Selangor, 2021). In terms of Zakat collection, LZS has managed to collect the highest amount in Malaysia, attributable to the efficient management of LZS and the high GDP value in Selangor compared to other states. Although the country recorded GDP growth of −5.6% in the year 2020 due to the Covid-19 pandemic (DOSM, 2021), LZS managed to record a 6.7% growth in its collection, from RM855.1 million to RM913 million. LZS distributed a significant amount to the rapidly rising number of *asnaf* groups due to the pandemic, which has caused many households to lose their sources of income. For the activities related to zakat distribution, LZS has managed to set up miscellaneous events that are categorized based on the corresponding 7 types of *asnaf* groups: *Faqir* (poor), *Miskiin* (needy), *Mualaf*, *Fisabilillah*, *Gharim*, *Riqab*, and *Ibnu Sabil*. For example, in the LZS 2019 annual report, the activities of fund distribution for the group of Poor and Needy are classified into four main categories: Social Development Programme, Education Development Programme, Human Development Programme, and Economic Development Programme. Each of these four categories of programmes is specified based on the kinds of activities that are run by LZS to the stated *asnaf* group. For instance, the Social Development Programme consists of 13 activities and the Education Development Programme consists of 2 activities. The Human Development Programme has 4 activities and finally, the Economic Development Programme has 3 activities.

Performance of Zakat Institutions

Studies by academic researchers on the efficiency and productivity of zakat institutions are quite limited (Jamaliah Said et al., 2012; Noor et al., 2012; Wahab & Abdul Rahman, 2012). The few studies conducted, both empirical and non-empirical, have not provided comprehensive analyses, and not many of them use *Maqasid Shari'ah* as the basis of productivity and efficiency evaluations. Jamaliah Said et al. (2012) developed a non-empirical composite performance measurement, a conceptual framework analysis that includes four indexes: the financial index, employee index, zakat recipient index, and zakat payer index. The index also includes financial and non-financial elements since Zakat is not a profit-based institution that relies on financial analysis. Using the literature review technique and interviews, the authors further developed a conceptual framework to evaluate the performance of Zakat institutions using financial performance measurements, employees' satisfaction, and customers' satisfaction, covering both the payers and the recipients. Wahab and Abdul Rahman (2012) used the application of Data Envelopment Analysis (DEA) to measure Technical Efficiency (TE), Pure Technical Efficiency (PTE), and Scale of Efficiency (SE). The data consist of the inputs and outputs from all 14 Zakat centres in Malaysia based on the annual reports for the period of 2003 until 2007. The findings show that although the technical efficiency means score was 80.6%, the technical inefficiency is moderated by the Scale Efficiency (SE), showing that the size of zakat institutions in Malaysia play a significant role in influencing the efficiency results. Saad et al. (2017) examined the framework of zakat governance that consists of the collection and distribution of zakat fund performances, zakat governance and collection, and innovation in distribution. The data were collected from zakat institutions' annual reports for the period of 2010 to 2014. The finding shows that the state of Sabah has the best zakat distribution since it recorded the lowest surplus fund. From the perspective of governance, the non-empirical data show that 6 states in Malaysia have met all the criteria of good governance, while for the analysis of the collection and distribution of the fund, Federal Territory Zakat Centre was declared as the most innovative zakat centre.

In another empirical study, Nahar (2018) analysed the perceptions of zakat stakeholders to determine the efficiency and performance of zakat organizations. Using a survey questionnaire, the sample of the study comprised 448 respondents who are the stakeholders of Lembaga Zakat Selangor, Malaysia in 2014. The questionnaire contains 4 sections: the demography, zakat collection, zakat disbursement, and the reporting. The study used a 4-point Likert scale and discarded the middle option of "neither agree nor disagree" to avoid ambiguous answers. The findings show that in general, the stakeholders believe that zakat collection has improved through time, albeit just slightly, compared to zakat disbursement and reporting. In addition, respondents from the private sector are more satisfied with the performance of zakat management compared to the respondents who work in the public sector. For the waiting period of getting zakat disbursement, the mean score shows more respondents feel no improvement has been made. Meanwhile, the finding shows that in general, the respondents have a positive perception of corporatization exercise in elevating the efficiency of zakat management. In Algeria, Djaghballou et al. (2018) examined the efficiency and productivity of Zakat institutions in the country from 2003 to 2013 using Data Envelopment Analysis (DEA) to measure Malmquist Productivity Index (MPI). The index was combined with the distance productivity function, whereby if the value is greater than 1 it means the Total Factor of Production (TFP) has positive growth and vice versa for a TFP value lower than 1. A TFP index is then developed as a geometric mean of two MPI indexes that comprise technical efficiency change (EFFCH) and technological change (TECHCH). Using the secondary data from 8 Zakat funds from different provinces as the sample of the studies, the authors found that Zakat funds of Tamanraste, Constantine, and Blida are consistently efficient under Constant Return of Scale (CRS) and Variable Return of Scale (VRS) measurements. However, the performance is generally the same for all the Zakat funds under VRS. TFP has increased by around 5.1% for all the funds in the period of the study, which indicates increasing efficiency, mainly due to technological enhancement. Based on the discussion of the literature on Malaysian zakat institutions' efficiency and performance, none of them has used *Maqasid Shari'ah* as the basis of measurement.

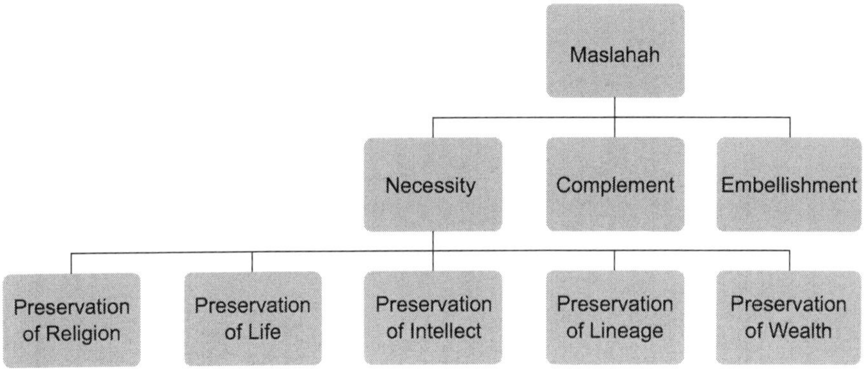

Figure 10.1 Framework of al-Ghazali's Maqasid Theory

Al-Ghazali's Theory of al-Maqasid

According to al-Ghazali, necessities are those elements without which the system of a nation will run into chaos, and they should be given priority over complements, and complements should be given priority over embellishments. Complements are things that facilitate human lives, while embellishments are elements that are related to moral and ethical conduct. Al-Ghazali further refined necessities into the preservation of 5 essential elements (*al-Dharuriyat al-Khams*), namely, religion (*al-Din*), life (*al-Nafs*), intellect (*al-Aql*), progeny (*al-Nasl*), and wealth (*al-Mal*), in descending order according to priority. For example, in case of a conflict between the preservation of human life and human intellect, priority should be given to the preservation of human life. To live up to the Shari'ah objectives, it is necessary for nations, institutions, and individuals to uphold religious principles (*al-Din*), respect human rights (*al-Nafs*), promote beneficial knowledge (*al-Aql*), promote good family institutions (*al-Nasl*), and invest their wealth (*al-Mal*). In contrast, nations, institutions, and individuals will run into chaos if they abandon religion, disrespect human lives, intoxicate their minds, destroy the family institution, and misuse their wealth. The following example explains the relationships between necessities, complements, and embellishments in al-Ghazali's theory. Let us take the example of the second element of necessity, the preservation of life. To preserve life, one needs a house, which is a complement because it facilitates life. Inside the house, one needs furniture, lighting, and other amenities. The choice of furniture and lighting is a matter of preference. If it is a moral and ethical choice, it becomes an embellishment. The framework of al-Ghazali's theory is presented in Figure 10.1.

Research Methods

The research adopts a mixed method approach that comprises an extensive literature review, Sekaran's method of operationalization, interview, focus group discussion, prioritization, and secondary data analysis. The first phase of the research focuses on an extensive literature review and Sekaran's method of operationalizing a concept

(C) by first breaking it down into dimensions (D). After that, the dimensions are further broken down into measurable items, namely elements (E). Then expert interviews were conducted to finalize the primary selected variables. After that, a focus group discussion was arranged to validate the primary selected variables. In the second phase, weights are assigned against each *Maqasid* concept's dimensions and sub-dimensions. In the last stage, an index is created to determine the score of each bank under study with respect to the achievement of *Maqasid al-Shari'ah*. These banks are ranked according to the *Maqasid* score in descending order.

Research Findings and Discussion

Computation of the Weighted Ratios

After obtaining the data and computing the 13 aforementioned ratios, the researcher utilized Hwang and Yoon's simple additive weighting method (SAW) for the weighting, aggregating, and ranking processes. According to Hwang and Yoon, the SAW method is probably the most widely used method of Multiple Attribute Decision-making Methods and Applications (MADM), and it works as follows.

The Decision Maker (DM) identifies the attributes and intra-attribute values. In this study, the attributes are the 5 Shari'ah objectives, and the intra-attributes are the 13 elements and the 13 ratios. The DM then assigns a weight to each attribute and intra-attribute identified. Accordingly, the values for the 13 ratios were derived from the annual reports of the LZS (2015 – 2019) as discussed previously. Meanwhile, the weights for the 5 Shari'ah objectives and the 13 elements have been assigned by the Shari'ah experts. The average weights for each item assigned by the 13 experts (as shown in Appendix 1, 2, 3, and 4), are reproduced in Table 10.1 to help facilitate the understanding of the way the weighted ratios are computed in the following paragraphs.

Table 10.1 Average Weight for the Shari'ah Objectives and Their Elements Assigned by the Experts

c	*Average Weight (Out of 1)*	*Elements*	*Average Weight (Out of 1)*
Religion	0.33	E1. Islamic Program	0.34
		E2. Scholarship for Islamic Education	0.33
		E3. Development of Religious Institutions	0.34
		Total	1
Life	0.22	E4. Financial Assistance	0.33
		E5. Healthcare Assistance	0.29
		E6. Debt Relief Assistance	0.20
		E7. Disaster Aid	0.18
		Total	1
Intellect	0.13	E8. Courses & Training	0.5
		E9. Education Scholarship	0.5
		Total	1

c	*Average Weight (Out of 1)*	*Elements*	*Average Weight (Out of 1)*
Lineage	0.14	E10. Family Rehabilitation Program	0.61
		E11. Family Related HIV/Drug Program	0.39
		Total	1
Wealth	0.18	E12. House Building/Maintenance	0.4
		E13. Business Capital	0.6
Total	1	Total	1

Table 10.2 The Relationship Between Shari'ah Objectives, Elements, and Ratios

Shari'ah Objectives (SO)	*Weight of Shari'ah Objectives (WSO) (a)*	*Weight of Elements (WE) (b)*	*Ratios (R) (c)*	*Weighted Ratios (WR) (axbxc)*
Religion	WSO1 (0.33)	WE1(0.34)	R1	WR1
		WE2 (0.33)	R2	WR2
		WE3 (0.34)	R3	WR3
Life	WSO2 (0.22)	WE4 (0.33)	R4	WR4
		WE5 (0.29)	R5	WR5
		WE6 (0.20)	R6	WR6
		WE7 (0.18)	R7	WR7
Intellect	WSO3 (0.13)	WE8 (0.50)	R8	WR8
		WE9 (0.50)	R9	WR9
Lineage	WSO4 (0.14)	WE10 (0.61)	R10	WR10
		WE11 (0.39)	R11	WR11
Wealth	WSO5 (0.18)	WE12 (0.40)	R12	WR12
		WE (0.60)	R13	WR13

After securing all the necessary data, the DM then obtains the weighted ratio for LZS by multiplying the scale rating for each attribute corresponding to the intra-attributes. The relationships between the 5 Shari'ah objectives and their weights, the 13 elements and their weights, and the 13 ratios are presented in Table 10.2.

Based on Table 10.2, WS01–WS05 denote weighted Shari'ah objectives 1–5, WE1–WE13 are the weighted elements 1–13, R1–R13 are the ratios calculated from the annual reports, WR1–WR13 are the weighted ratios 1–13, and the figures in the parentheses corresponding to WS01–WS05 and WE1–WE13 are the actual average weights provided by the experts. Thus in light of Table 10.2, each of the 13 ratios (R1–R13) was multiplied by the weight of the corresponding element (WE1–WE13) and the weight of the corresponding Shari'ah objective (WSO1–WSO5). For example, the first 3 Shari'ah objectives (Religion), Islamic program activities, scholarship, and development of religious institutions, are represented by the first 3 ratios R1, R2, and R3 respectively, and they correspond to the first three weighted elements WE1, WE2, and WE3. Hence, R1 is multiplied by the weight of the corresponding element WE1 and the weight of the corresponding first Shari'ah objective

WSO1, which results in the weighted ratio 1 (WR1). Similarly, R2 is multiplied by WE2 and WSO1, which gives a product WR2. In the same way, the following 4 ratios were multiplied by the weights of their corresponding four elements and then by the weight of the second Shari'ah objective. This resulted in 4 weighted ratios. The same process was applied to all ratios and Shari'ah objectives, which were multiplied by the weights of their corresponding elements and by the weight of the Shari'ah objective. Therefore, altogether 13 weighted ratios were computed. The following sub-subsection explains how the 13 weighted ratios (WR1–WR13) are used to compute the respective 5 Shari'ah objectives.

Computation of the Five Shari'ah Objectives

The sum of the first 3 weighted ratios (WR1 + WR2 + WR3) gives the measure of the first Shari'ah objective: religion. Likewise, the sum of WR4, WR5, WR6, and WR7 results in the measurement for the second objective of life. The sum of WR8 and WR9 gives the measurement for the third objective: intellect. Meanwhile, the sum of WR10 and WR11 gives the measurement for the fourth objective: lineage. Finally, the fifth objective, wealth, is measured by the sum of the last 2 weighted ratios, WR12 to WR13. Hence, mathematically, the values of the 5 Shari'ah objectives can be computed as follows. Assume the first Shari'ah objective is denoted by SO1. Therefore, the value of SO1 is computed as:

$$(SO1) = WSO1 \times WE1 \times R1 + WSO1 \times WE2 \times R2 + WSO1 \times WE3 \times R3 \text{ or } WSO1\,(WE1 \times R1 + WE2 \times R2 + WE3 \times R3) \quad (1)$$

where

(SO1) denotes the 1st Shari'ah Objective, i.e., Hifdh al-Din (Religion)
WSO1 is the weight assigned to the 1st Shari'ah Objectives (See Table 10.2)
WE1 denotes the weight assigned to the first element of the 1st Objective (Table 10.2)
WE2 denotes the weight assigned to the second element of the 1st Objective (Table 10.2)
WE3 denotes the weight assigned to the third element of the 1st Objective (Table 10.2)
R1 is the value of ratio corresponding to the first element of SO1
R2 is the value of ratio corresponding to the second element of SO1
R3 is the value of ratio corresponding to the third element of SO1

$$\text{Furthermore, } (SO1) = WR1 + WR2 + WR3 \quad (2)$$

where

$$WR1 = WSO1 \times WE1 \times R1 \quad (3)$$
$$WR2 = WSO1 \times WE2 \times R2 \quad (4)$$
$$WR3 = WSO1 \times WE3 \times R3 \quad (5)$$

Table 10.3 Maqasid Index

Maqasid Index	*2015*	*2016*	*2017*	*2018*	*2019*
	0.0548	0.0520	0.0478	0.0687	0.0630

where WR1, WR2, and WR3 denote the weighted ratios corresponding to elements 1, 2, and 3 of SO1, respectively.

Therefore, altogether 5 Shari'ah objectives of religion, life, intellect, lineage, and wealth were computed for LZS in the sample. The following sub-subsection 4.3.3 explains how the 5 Shari'ah objectives are computed to produce the Maqasid Indexes of the LZS.

Computation of the Maqasid Indexes

The total overall performance measures for the 5 Shari'ah objectives for LZS constitute its individual Maqasid Index (MI). Thus,

$$MSI = (SO1) + (SO2) + (SO3) + (SO4) + (SO5) \quad (6)$$

In other words, the Maqasid Al Shari'ah Index (MSI) for the LZS is the sum of the performance measures with respect to Shari'ah Objective 1, Shari'ah Objective 2, Shari'ah Objective 3, Shari'ah Objective 4, and Shari'ah Objective 5.

Based on the Maqasid Index as shown in Table 10.3, it indicates that MSI is improving in terms of its scores and reaffirms the importance of *Maqasid Al Shari'ah* in Islam and Islamic social finance such as Zakat institutions. It also reinforces the call by several Muslim scholars to Islamic social finance institutions to adopt Maqasid elements in their activities to achieve socio-economic justice. By having this measurement, it will be very important to determine the achievement of zakat activities. The Maqasid index is expected to assist stakeholders to measure how far the performance of Islamic social finance institutions are in line with the Maqasid al-Shari'ah.

Conclusion

The *Maqasid al-Shari'ah* framework is fundamental in Islamic banking to achieve socio-economic justice. Moreover, the GFC has highlighted the socio-economic dimensions in the banking sector and their significant implications on the distribution of wealth in society. Meanwhile, IBs market themselves on ethical and social foundations; however, they have been criticized for their deviation from accomplishing *Maqasid al-Shari'ah*. Therefore, this study explores *Maqasid al-Shari'ah* compliance by using LZS as a case study, with emphasis on disclosures related to Al-Ghazali's framework of *Maqasid al-Shari'ah*. This study applies the MSI to measure compliance with Maqasid al-Shari'ah related to religion, life, intellect, lineage, and wealth in Zakat institutions. The foremost job in the process of developing an index is the selection of appropriate, meaningful, and measurable variables. In the present research, the use of an extensive literature review and Sekaran's method of operationalization have helped select the primary variables. Expert interviews are arranged to finalize and validate the variables. The opinions from experts have improved the measurability of the selected variables with respect to performance measurement of zakat institutions based on *Maqasid al-Shari'ah*. Next, appropriate weight was assigned to each Maqasid concept, dimension, and sub-dimension through expert interviews. According to the result, a higher MSI index indicates that the zakat institutions (in this case LZS) contribute to the development of religion, life, intellect, lineage, and wealth of the Muslim and as a result, it promotes socio-economic justice in society and complies with its ethical identity. This study also put forth several recommendations for the Maqasid Index so it may be fully useful:

- The Maqasid Index can be implemented by zakat institutions at the national and local levels. It is intended that all parties in zakat can measure and improve their Zakat performance, as well as increase public understanding of zakat's contribution to the socio-economic development of the country.
- The Maqasid Index that has been developed can be evaluated annually to compare its yearly performance. Thus, the Maqasid Index can become a gauge of the underlying changes that occur in the aspects of religion, life, intellect, lineage, and life over time.
- The Maqasid Index can be authorized as a standard measurement to periodically measure the standard of national zakat performance.[1]

Note

1 The authors would like to acknowledge the International Islamic Institute of Thought (IIIT) for providing a grant (Grant ID: SPI21-054-0054) to carry out the present research activities.

References

Department of Statistics Malaysia. (2021). www.dosm.gov.my/v1_/

Djaghballou, C. E., Djaghballou, M., Larbani, M., & Mohamad, A. (2018). Efficiency and Productivity Performance of Zakat Funds in Algeria. *International Journal of Islamic and Middle Eastern Finance and Management*, 11(3), 474–494. https://doi.org/10.1108/IMEFM-07-2017-0185

Haron, N. H., Hassan, H., Jasni, N. S., & Rahman, R. A. (2010). Zakat for Asnafs' Business by Lembaga Zakat Selangor. *Malaysia Accounting Review*, 9, 123–138.

Lembaga Zakat Selangor. (2021). *Ringkasan prestasi kutipan zakat dan agihan zakat Lembaga Zakat Selangor 2021*. https://drive.google.com/file/d/1PBxByt8sRapNK3FMM9fVIfygCeqE6LG/view?usp=sharing

Makhtar, A. S., & Abdul Wahab, A. (2010). *Pengurusan zakat di negeri Selangor: Isu dan cabaran* [Conference Proceeding]. Konvensyen Kebangsaan Perancangan dan Pengurusan Harta Dalam.

Nahar, H. S. (2018). Exploring Stakeholders' Views on a Corporatized Zakat Institution's Management Performance. *International Journal of Ethics and Systems*, 34(4), 608–631. https://doi.org/10.1108/IJOES-08-2018-0115

Noor, H. M., Melaka, K., Lendu, J., Saladin, M., Rasool, A., Rahman, R. A., & Ali, S. M. (2012). Assessing Performance of Nonprofit Organization: A Framework for Zakat Institutions. *British Journal of Economics, Finance and Management Sciences*, 5(1), 12–22. www.semanticscholar.org/paper/Assessing-Performance-of-Nonprofit-Organization%3A-A-Noor-Melaka/f6d0d5318a5e8b49e86bcdedf521e965b 334280c

Saad, R. A. J., Idris, K. M., Shaari, H., Sawandi, N., & Derashid, C. (2017). Governance of Nonprofit Organizations: A Case of Zakat Institutions in Malaysia. *International Journal of Economic Research*, 14(16), 253–265. http://serialsjournals.com/articles.php?volumesno_id=1385&journals_id=41&volumes_id=1068

Said, J., Ghani, E. K., Zawawi, S. N. H., & Yusof, S. N. S. Y. (2012). Composite Performance Measurement for Zakat Organisations. *British Journal of Economics, Finance and Management Sciences*, 4(1). www.semanticscholar.org/paper/XComposite-Performance-Measurement-for-Zakat-Said-Ghani/fa2 53189922b15fafca3fce75cb96e0e28edf904

Wahab, N. A., & Abdul Rahman, A. R. (2012). Efficiency of Zakat Institutions in Malaysia: An Application of Data Envelopment Analysis. *Journal of Economic Cooperation and Development*, 33(1), 95–112.

11 Islamic Sustainable Finance

How Does Waqf Matter?

Nor Syahirah Zain, Fatimah Mohamad Noor & Rusni Hassan

Introduction

Sustainable finance is a form of finance that considers the environmental, social, and governance (ESG) impacts of investments and the long-term sustainability of the economy. It is also closely related to the UN's Sustainable Development Goals (SDGs). Sustainable finance is a rapidly growing field, with investments in sustainable projects expected to reach $30 trillion by 2030 (Lambert et al., 2020). Islamic sustainable finance further enhances sustainable finance by incorporating Islamic values and principles into the financial markets. The concept of Waqf is seen as an important part of this effort to create a sustainable source of financing for socially responsible projects. For example, a recent report by the Global Islamic Finance Forum (GIFF) noted that Waqf-based financing helps to create "an ethical, sustainable, and inclusive financial system" (GIFF, 2020). The report argued that Waqf-based financing can help to "fill the gap between traditional financing and the needs of small and medium enterprises" (GIFF, 2020). However, despite this recognition, the potential of Waqf as an instrument for ISF remains unexplored. The primary mission of this chapter is to discover and evaluate Waqf as an instrument for ISF. While looking into the potential for Waqf to create positive impact on the environment and promote sustainability, this chapter will also take a deep dive into two concepts that could potentially strengthen Waqf in meeting the Maqasid Shari'ah: the concepts of Good Governance and Accountability. In doing so, an overview of social impact measurement is also investigated as a potential tool of good governance and accountability in meeting the higher objectives of Waqf.

Waqf and Its Applications

Waqf is Arabic for "to stop," "to contain," or "to maintain." By creating an ecosystem where the wealthy help the poor achieve their basic requirements (Ali, 2019), Waqf can be viewed as charitable endowments (Zain & Sori, 2020). Waqf was initially focused on creating and overseeing religious institutions like mosques, but its responsibility was later expanded to include other socioeconomic welfare projects like creating schools and universities, healthcare facilities, cemeteries, orphanages, and other institutions (Mahamood, 2000). As things progress, more

DOI: 10.4324/9781003468653-14

innovative tools came into existence via the merging of Waqf into innovative financial tools. This section intends to discuss the current application of Waqf in some of the essential building blocks of Islamic sustainable finance, which include Islamic banking, microfinance, Takaful, and capital market.

Islamic Banking Waqf

The involvement of Islamic banks in Waqf activities may contribute to economic growth and the overall Muslim economy. This can also have a positive impact on society, particularly in terms of reducing poverty. Additionally, their involvement can reduce reliance on government funds and improve corporate accountability, good governance, and transparency in Waqf management (Ibrahim et al., 2017). Ramli and Jalil (2015) introduced a model for incorporating Cash Waqf into the modern banking system. This model was examined through the Corporate Waqf model utilised by Wakaf Selangor Muamalat, which is a partnership between Bank Muamalat Malaysia Berhad (BMMB) and the state-owned Waqf management institution Perbadanan Wakaf Selangor Berhad (PWS). The Waqf fund is based on the principle of *Wakalah bil Istithmar* and is funded through various means, such as contributions through BMMB's banking services, such as hibah from BMMB's Wadiah account, cash payments, direct debits from a savings or current account, or through the use of a cheque (Ibrahim et al., 2017). As of March 2014, Wakaf Selangor Muamalat had received approximately RM5,687,238.39 in Waqf funds, with a distribution amount of RM604,133.80 (Ibrahim et al., 2017). Additionally, the fund management company Muamalat Invest Sdn. Bhd. has been appointed to invest the funds in Shari'ah-compliant instruments to generate returns, with 25% of the returns being distributed to PWS and 75% going towards education and healthcare (Ramli & Jalil, 2015).

In the effort to meet modern needs, Kahf and Mohomed (2017) in their study examined Cash Waqf and its potential applications in a contemporary banking system. They suggested that Islamic banks could offer Cash Waqf as a personal financing option for their customers, either as an open-end fund or as a foundation. The open-end fund would operate similarly to a mutual fund, with shares that can be bought and sold at any time and administered by a fund manager. The foundation would function as a non-profit organisation that provides loans without interest and then reuses the collected funds. Additionally, they proposed that Cash Waqf could be a viable personal finance option for individuals seeking to settle debts or borrow money without interest if sufficient protections are in place to prevent exploitation. Implementing Cash Waqf-based instruments in individual personal finance by Islamic banks could improve their reputation and serve as a marketing tool (Kahf & Mohomed, 2017).

Waqf in Islamic Microfinance

An Islamic microfinance institution is one of the financial institutions that could provide funding to the poor. According to Wulandari et al. (2016), on top of incorporating Islamic values into its operations, Islamic microfinance institutions also serve as a form of social intermediation, combining financial intermediation with capacity building. Ahmad et al. (2021) found that Cash Waqf has the potential to help strengthen micro, small, and medium enterprises (MSMEs) and improve the lives of the poor through its use in Islamic microfinance. This aligns with the fundamental goal of Islamic financial institutions, which is to adhere to Allah's commands in the economic sector by providing mutual assistance and helping others. Cash Waqf funds can be used to meet a variety of needs, including funding educational infrastructure, healthcare, social and commercial programs, and creating jobs (Mohsin, 2013). The use of Cash Waqf can also contribute to social finance as a supplement to government and private sector financial institutions that may not have the resources to fund all desired initiatives (Shaikh, 2017). One example of this is the integrated Cash Waqf microenterprise investment model (ICWME-I). This model was proposed by Duasa and Thaker (2016) and provides funding for small enterprises using Cash Waqf funds and Shari'ah-compliant participation contracts between non-profit organisations and microbusinesses (Mohd Thas Thaker, 2018).

Waqf in Takaful

Waqf can be used in various ways in the Takaful industry. One opinion is that Waqf Takaful represents the way in which a Waqf fund created by a Takaful operator or company is put into action. The Waqf fund is a portion of the company's capital that is designated for those affected by a disaster, and it is used according to specific guidelines (Ahmad et al., 2022). Yayasan Waqf Malaysia (YWM) has established cooperation with several Takaful companies in Malaysia with diversified waqf methods. The Takaful companies include Takaful Ikhlas Family, Sun Life Malaysia Takaful, and AmMetLife Takaful. By adding a waqf element to the Takaful products, plan participants can choose to donate part of the contribution value or the total benefit received to YWM. Today's Takaful market features numerous Takaful models, including the Wakalah Model, Modified Wakalah Model, Mudharabah Model, Hybrid Model, Wakalah Waqf Model, and Waqf-Takaful Model (Ahmad et al., 2022). Ibrahim et al. (2016) proposed the Wakalah-Waqf Model and Waqf-Takaful Compensation Model, which focus on the use of a Waqf fund in Takaful products. These models involve the proportionate ownership of donations by participants that are not used for claim payment, but instead are transferred to a Waqf fund and invested in Shari'ah-compliant businesses to generate profit. This profit is used to assist participants in need and to donate to charities approved by the Takaful company's Shari'ah board (Al-Shami, 2015). According to Abdullah and Yaacob (2012), the Wakalah-Waqf model is an extension of the Wakalah model that employs the Tabarru' fund based on the Waqf fund. Under this model, a Cash Waqf Fund is created through the donation of a certain amount by the Takaful company shareholders and contributions from participants who purchase a policy. The Waqf fund, which is in the form of a Cash Waqf, will be used according to the provisions of the Waqf Deed. The Takaful business acts as a wakeel and Mudharib on behalf of the Waqf fund participants and will have the authority to function as a legal entity in regard to its investment, remuneration, and management of excess funds (Abdullah & Yaacob, 2012). To become a member of the Waqf fund with Takaful coverage, individuals must sign up, receive a certificate, and make an unconditional donation. The Waqf fund can provide benefits to both the participant and the Takaful company, including Qard Hassan and other Takaful benefits (Ahmad et al., 2022).

Waqf in Islamic Capital Market

Like the Waqf-banking model, Waqf in Islamic capital market (ICM) is managed by a fund management company for investment in Shari'ah-compliant securities. There have been efforts to use Waqf as an investment strategy to generate long-term returns for Waqf beneficiaries. In ICM, modern Waqf practices have led to the creation of new instruments like Waqf-sukuk, Waqf-shares, Waqf-unit trusts, and Waqf-real estate investment trusts. These instruments have found innovative ways to use Waqf as an alternative asset class for capital mobilisation in ICM (Sairally & Muhammad, 2019).

Issuance of Sukuk for the Development of Waqf Assets and Properties

Sukuk is a popular tool in Islamic capital market for financing specific economic operations that correspond to Shari'ah standards. The use of sukuk for the development of Waqf assets is not a new concept and has been implemented successfully in countries like Singapore and Saudi Arabia; The Bencoolen Waqf project in Singapore was the first fundraising project to renew a waqf property in Singapore via an issuance of Sukuk Al-Musharakah by Majlis Ugama Islam Singapore (MUIS), while a Sukuk Intifa' was issued to construct Zam Tower on a waqf land in Mekah. These sukuk issuances demonstrate how sukuk can be creatively structured to fund the improvement and revitalisation of Waqf properties into profitable businesses. These Waqf assets have been effective in fulfilling the needs of society. In 2014, the Securities Commission of Malaysia (SC) had revised the Guidelines on Sukuk to incorporate the new requirements for the issuance of SRI sukuk in Malaysia (Securities Commission Malaysia, 2014). The revision, which included waqf properties/assets as one of the eligible categories for SRI projects, inspired Zain and Sori (2020) to propose an SRI Sukuk based on Al-Musharakah contract concept for the development of waqf assets and properties in Malaysia. Their proposal is an attempt to ensure the sustainability of waqf by generating its own income to have a consistent stream of funding. In Indonesia, Ismal et al. (2015) found that local waqf can be developed via the issuance of sovereign sukuk or using the sovereign sukuk as an underlying asset of financing. This waqf-linked sukuk issuance is intended for the growth of real economic sector and can be personalised to meet commercial and social purposes.

Waqf-linked Products in ICM

The Islamic capital market offers financial products and investments that adhere to Shari'ah laws, which have the potential to generate high returns while also providing a stable and sustainable income for Waqf institutions (Securities Commission Malaysia, 2014). This involves donors giving cash or financial assets that are then professionally managed by asset managers on behalf of the Waqf institution and invested in Shari'ah-compliant financial assets to generate a sustainable return. Examples of these financial products include sukuk, Shari'ah-compliant shares, Islamic unit trust funds, Islamic real estate investment trusts, and Islamic exchange-traded funds (Securities Commission Malaysia, 2014). Permodalan Nasional Berhad (PNB), one of the largest fund management companies in Malaysia, through its wholly owned unit trust management company, Amanah Saham Nasional Berhad (ASNB), launched Wakaf ASNB in 2021. The Wakaf ASNB uses the concept of *waqf muabbad*, in which the contribution into the waqf funds is retained as the main investment to produce potential yearly income. The income will then be directed towards waqf initiatives in the areas of healthcare, education, community building, and other humanitarian efforts (Permodalan Nasional Berhad, 2021).

Methodology

This study undertakes a critical review of the literature to establish Waqf as an important instrument for ISF. In order to gain an understanding from multiple angles on emerging areas such as Waqf in ISF, an integrative review is one of the best methods to adopt (Snyder, 2019). The focus of the literature review allows the authors to further explore the relationship between good governance and accountability, with the long-term sustainability of Waqf. Drawing from the understanding of the two concepts, the study looks at the potential of Waqf in making a positive impact on the society via a social impact measurement tool.

Discussion

In attempting to relate Waqf to ISF and increase its potential impact as an ISF instrument, it is critical to explore possible approaches to improve its effectiveness. This section briefly discusses some approaches in the areas of good governance, accountability, and the fulfilment of Maqasid Shari'ah.

Good Governance of Waqf in View of Sustainable Finance

The core objective of Waqf institutions is to provide social justice through the fair and effective distribution of Waqf for the benefit of society. Waqf institutions could harness the potential of selfless charitable giving effectively for better economic impact in a targeted social segment of society. Efficient Waqf governance should help preserve valuables in either cash or non-cash fixed assets earned from the voluntary but permanent distribution of wealth in an Islamic society. Achieving this is dependent on the mutawalli (trustee) in the Waqf institution. The mutawallis must be aware of their duties and fulfil them to ensure the purpose of Waqf is achieved. This includes working collaboratively, effectively managing the Waqf properties, maintaining high integrity and accountability (Ihsan et al., 2016). The mutawalli is also in charge of shaping the Waqf institution's operational structure. He is responsible for ensuring that the Waqf's assets continue to generate income to benefit the intended recipients. In preserving the Waqf assets and revenues, the mutawalli should be creative in generating income or profit from the Waqf assets. Improving Waqf governance is crucial in gaining the trust and support of donors. Good governance practices are necessary to enhance the management and performance of Waqf institutions and safeguard the rights of those who benefit from them. This will ultimately increase trust and faith in these organisations among the public. Good Waqf governance also could act as a catalyst for achieving sustainable development (Abdul Latif et al., 2018). Waqf institutions urgently require a sound and prudent standard operating system to deal with any issues that could jeopardise the Waqf properties and the sustainability of the institution. A proper standard operating system alone is not sufficient without an effective management and regular monitoring to ensure the policies are implemented accordingly (Minhas, 2012).

Accountability in Waqf

Being accountable is taking ownership of one's choices and being able to defend them to others. It is a procedure through which people and organisations are made accountable for their deeds by reporting to a recognised authority (or authorities) (Edwards & Hulme, 1996). Ebrahim (2003) asserts that accountability involves a wide range of parties, including donors, beneficiaries, and internal stakeholders inside the organisation itself, involving members of the Board of Directors as well as staff members and volunteers at all levels. Stakeholders in Waqf specifically include the waqif (endower), Waqf board, regulators, beneficiaries, and the general public (Ihsan & Adnan, 2017). Waqf institutions are held in high regard, yet despite this, there is still plenty of room for improvement with regards to fulfilling their accountability to stakeholders (Arshad & Zain, 2017; Yaacob, 2006). The primary tenet of Islamic accountability, in contrast to conventional accountability, is that "everyone is liable to Allah in the Hereafter" (Masruki & Shafrii, 2013). The mutawalli of a Waqf organisation is responsible to the waqif and beneficiaries, and as such must work to guarantee that the intended impact on society is appropriately and sufficiently made. Accountability can generally be demonstrated in a variety of ways, including through financial and non-financial reporting. One of the strategies to improve accountability and promote transparency is by measuring impact of Waqf. Social impact measurement (SIM) is an effective tool for accountability because it gives stakeholders the chance to evaluate their contributions, engagement, and connections to the organization. Additionally, SIM can show stakeholders whether or not organisations are successful in reaching their stated aims (Helmig et al., 2014). At the end of it all, ensuring the sustainability of Waqf as an instrument of ISF is essential. Having a solid plan and effective governance are essential for meeting the expectations and obligations towards various groups, such as donors and recipients of aid (Ramli & Muhamed, 2013).

Good Waqf Governance Towards Social Impact

The government of Malaysia has given a lot of attention to the development of Waqf. The formation of the Department of Awqaf, Zakat, and Hajj under the Prime

Minister's Office in 2004 as well as many exceptional allocations made in the nation's 9th to 12th Malaysia Plans from 2006 to the present serve as evidence of this. The department's main goal is to improve the governance and service delivery systems for Waqf, Zakat, and Hajj institutions in order to promote socioeconomic growth. Nevertheless, despite the acknowledgement, Arshad and Haneef (2016) and Noordin et al. (2017) contend that the mainstream economy may still undervalue Waqf and its actual potential. On top of that, Waqf institutions are still unable to prove whether they are fulfilling their primary goal (maqasid Waqf) in accordance with the Maqasid Shari'ah. One of the potential causes of this lack of awareness could be the absence of a structured way to assess, illustrate, and convey its societal implications (Noordin et al., 2017). Waqf institutions are therefore obligated to uphold good governance and accountability to stakeholders in attaining the goals of Waqf. Good governance refers to the principles and practices that guide the decision-making and administration of an organisation. It involves transparency, accountability, participation, and rule of law, among other elements. In the context of Waqf institutions, good governance is essential for meeting the Maqasid Shari'ah, which include the protection of religion, life, intellect, property, and lineage. Accountability is a key element of good governance. In the context of Maqasid Shari'ah, accountability is important for ensuring that the principles and objectives of Islamic law are upheld, and that decisions and actions taken by leaders and administrators are in line with these principles.

Any Islamic financial institution would have a reason for their existence. Thereafter, they must put in efforts to translate the Maqasid Shari'ah into actionable and measurable results. Similarly for Waqf, the higher objectives of Waqf is founded on Maqasid Shari'ah, which is doing good deeds for the sake of Allah SWT (Mahmud & Shah, 2010). According to Ibrahim and Khan (2015), the goals of Waqf are to preserve Waqf properties, i.e. protecting them from harm and damage, unlawful activity, and corruption; promoting transparency and accountability; and meeting the requirements and terms in Waqf agreements. Besides that, Waqf must also aim to protect the permanency of Waqf by ensuring the sustainability and efficiency of its fair allocation of wealth and positive contribution to nation building. Having clarity over these higher objectives will enable Waqf organizations to be accountable in planning and establishing guidelines for their operations accordingly. Meanwhile, the specific objective of Shari'ah of good Waqf governance is to ensure Shari'ah compliance. Shari'ah-compliant governance practice in Waqf-based institutions aims to ensure that Waqf institutions always comply with the Shari'ah principles in all their operations. It also guarantees that Waqf institutions act in the best interests of the intended outcome of complying with the framework of Waqf rules and regulations is to achieve the means of preservation of wealth in Islam. Good governance does that by protecting the ownership of Waqf properties; safeguarding Waqf properties through acquisition and development; and sheltering Waqf properties from damage. These efforts are consistent with the protection of wealth, which is one of the important elements of Maqasid Shari'ah. A SIM framework, in general, is designed to assess and evaluate the impact that an organisation's or stakeholder's actions have on society (Epstein & Yuthas, 2014). It also validates an organisation's impact and helps document the "change" in a systematic way. This framework helps to prevent these instruments from their intended purpose and allows for a thorough measurement of quantitative and qualitative indicators. Specifically, for Waqf institutions, SIM can help them identify where they currently stand and how to achieve their goals of fulfilling Maqasid Shari'ah. Without a systematic tool, it can be difficult to measure the social impact of Waqf and analyse areas for improvement.

Conclusion

This chapter explores Waqf as an instrument of ISF. In doing so, it explores the current application of Waqf in several sectors including Islamic banking, microfinancing, Takaful, and ICM. Thereafter, as an effort to ensure the sustainability of Waqf, this chapter also looks into the concepts of Good Governance and Accountability. Both concepts in Waqf are necessary to ensure that the funds are used efficiently for the intended purpose and invested effectively. This requires the establishment of a governance structure, the development of a system of monitoring and accountability, and the setting up of policies and procedures for the management of Waqf funds. Additionally, it is important to ensure that the Waqf funds are managed in a transparent and accountable manner to ensure that the funds are used for the intended purpose and not diverted for other uses. Tying them all together, the authors finally proposed for a social impact measurement to be an essential tool to enhance good governance and accountability, especially in ensuring the achievement of Maqasid Shari'ah. The concept of perpetuity is an important aspect of Waqf as it allows for continuous income generation to assist the needy and address socioeconomic issues. Good governance and impact measurement are indeed crucial tools of accountability, thus ensuring the sustainability of Waqf as an ISF instrument.

References

Abdul Latif, S., Nik Din, N. M., & Mustapha, Z. (2018). The Role of Good Waqf Governance in Achieving Sustainable Development. *Environment-Behaviour Proceedings Journal*, 3(7), 113–118. https://doi.org/10.21834/e-bpj.v3i7.1292

Abdullah, A., & Yaacob, H. (2012). Legal and Shari'ah Issues in the Application of Wakalah-waqf Model in Takaful Industry: An Analysis. *Procedia – Social and Behavioral Sciences*, 65, 1040–1045. https://doi.org/10.1016/j.sbspro.2012.11.239

Ahmad, R. A., Ali, M. N., Said, R., Abu Bakar, M., Abdul Manan, F. N., & Albasri, S. H. (2022). Introduction to Waqf–Takaful Compensation Model: Adopting the Maqasid Shari'ah Concept for Socio-Economic Development in Malaysia. *International Journal of Academic Research in Business and Social Sciences*, 12(8), 1108–1122. https://doi.org/10.6007/ijarbss/v12-i8/14680

Ahmad, R. A., Mafaza, S. A., & Handayani, R. (2021). Integrated Cash Waqf and Islamic Microfinance to Poverty Alleviate. *El Barka: Journal of Islamic Economic and Business*, 4(1), 61–80.

Ali, J. (2019). *The Management of Waqf in India with a Special Reference to Delhi Waqf Board: A Critical Analysis*. International Islamic University Malaysia.

Al-Shami, A. M. (2015). Hibah, Tabarru' and Waqf Application in Takaful. In *Wief – UITM Occasional Papers* (Issue December).

Arshad, M. N. M., & Haneef, M. A. M. (2016). Third Sector Socio-Economic Models: How Waqf Fits In? *Institutions and Economies*, 8(2), 72–90.

Arshad, R., & Zain, N. M. (2017). Performance Measurement and Accountability of Waqf Institutions in Malaysia. *SHS Web of Conferences*, 36(5). https://doi.org/10.1051/shsconf/2017360000

Duasa, J., & Mohd Thas Thaker, M. A. (2016). A Cash Waqf Investment Model: An Alternative Model for Financing Micro-Enterprises in Malaysia. *Journal of Islamic Monetary Economics and Finance,* 1(2).

Ebrahim, A. (2003). Accountability in Practice: Mechanisms for NGOs. *World Development*, 31(5), 813–829.

Edwards, M., & Hulme, D. (1996). Too Close for Comfort? The Impact of Official Aid on Non-Governmental Organizations. *World Development*, 24(6), 961–973.

Epstein, M. J., & Yuthas, K. (2014). *Measuring and Improving Social Impacts: A Guide for Nonprofits, Companies, and Impact Investors*. Berrett-Koehier Publishers, Inc.

Global Islamic Finance Forum (GIFF). (2020). *Waqf-Based Financing: A New Pathway for Sustainable Finance*. www.giff.com/wp-content/uploads/2020/05/GIFF-Waqf-Financing-White-Paper.pdf

Helmig, B., Ingerfurth, S., & Pinz, A. (2014). Success and Failure of Nonprofit Organizations: Theoretical Foundations, Empirical Evidence, and Future Research. *Voluntas (Manchester, England)*, 25(6), 1509–1538.

Ibrahim, A. A. M., & Khan, S. H. (2015). Waqf Management in Bangladesh: An Analysis from Maqasid Al-Shar'ah Perspective. *Paper Presented at the International Conference on Maqasid Al-Shari'ah in Public Policy and Governance*. Kuala Lumpur.

Ibrahim, S. N., Shahrina, N., & Rafien, M. (2017). *The Involvement of Islamic Banking in Waqf Activities*. Contemporary Issues and Development in Islamic Social Finance, October, 172.

Ibrahim, S. S. B., Noor, A. H. B. M., Shariff, S. B. M., & Rusli, N. A. B. M. (2016). Analysis of Corporate Waqf Model in Malaysia: An Instrument Towards Muslim's Economic Development. *International Journal of Applied Business and Economic Research*, 14(5), 2931–2944.

Ihsan, H., & Adnan, M. (2017). Waqf Accounting and the Construction of Accountability. In Rashid, S. K. (Eds.), *Waqf Laws and Management* (pp. 57–84). IIUM Press.

Ihsan, H., Eliyanora, & Septriani, Y. (2016). Accountability Mechanisms for Awqaf Institutions: Lessons Learned from The History. *Journal of King Abdul Aziz University, Islamic Economics*, 29(1), 41–54. https://doi.org/10.4197/Islec.29-1.3

Ismal, R. I. R., Muljawan, D., Chalid, M. R., Muljawan, D., Chalid, M. R., Sastrosuwito, J. K. S., & Sastrosuwito, J. K. S. (2015). *Occasional Paper Awqaf Linked Sukuk to Support the Economic Development Awqaf Linked Sukuk to Support the Economic Development.*

Kahf, M., & Mohomed, A. N. (2017). Cash Waqf: An Innovative Instrument of Personal Finance in Islamic Banking. *Journal of Islamic Economics, Banking and Finance*, 13(3), 13–29.

Lambert, S. J., Asare, C., Boucher, N., & Spalding-Fecher, R. (2020). *Unlocking the Potential of Sustainable Finance*. McKinsey & Company.

Mahamood, S. M. (2000). *The Administration of Waqf, Pious Endowment in Islam: A Critical Study of the Role of the State Islamic Religious Councils as the Sole Trustees of a Wqaf Assets and the Implementation of Istibdal in Malaysia with Special Reference to the Federal Territory of Kuala Lumpur* (PhD). Birmingham, UK: Birmingham University.

Mahmud, M. W., & Shah, S. S. (2010). Optimization of Philanthropic Waqf: The Need for Maqasid-based Legislative Strategies. *Shari'ah Law Report*, 2.

Masruki, R., & Shafrii, Z. (2013). The Development of Waqf Accounting in Enhancing Accountability. *Middle-East Journal of Scientific Research*, 13(13), 1–16. https://doi.org/10.5829/idosi.mejsr.2013.13.1873

Minhas, I. H. (2012). Shari'ah Governance Model (SGM) and Its Four Pillars. *Journal of Islamic Banking and Finance*.

Mohd Thas Thaker, M. A. Bin. (2018). A Qualitative Inquiry into Cash Waqf Model as a Source of Financing for Micro Enterprises. *ISRA International Journal of Islamic Finance*, 10(1), 19–35. https://doi.org/10.1108/IJIF-07-2017-0013

Mohsin, M. I. A. (2013). Financing Through Cash-Waqf: A Revitalization to Finance Different Needs. *International Journal of Islamic and Middle Eastern Finance and Management*, 6(4), 304–321.

Noordin, N. H., Haron, S. N., & Kassim, S. (2017). Developing a Comprehensive Performance Measurement System for Waqf Institutions. *International Journal of Social Economics*, 44(7), 921–936. http://doi.org/10.1108/IJSE-09-2015-0257

Permodalan Nasional Berhad. (2021, October 25). PNB Launches Wakaf ASNB: Enabling Unit Holders to Invest and Donate. *Press Release*. www.pnb.com.my/pdf/mediarelease/2021/Wakaf/PR_ASNB%20WAKAF.pdf

Ramli, A. M., & Jalil, A. (2015). Banking Model of Corporate Waqf: An Analysis of Wakaf Selangor Muamalat. *Jurnal Pengurusan*, 159–167.

Ramli, N. M., & Muhamed, N. A. (2013). Good Governance Framework for Corporate Waqf: Towards Accountability Enhancement. *Paper Presented at the World Universities' Islamic Philanthropy Conference 2013*, Kuala Lumpur, Malaysia.

Sairally, S., & Muhammad, M. (2019). Exploring New Trends of Waqf in the Islamic Capital Market. In *Challenges and Impacts of Religious Endowments on Global Economics and Finance* (pp. 192–222). https://doi.org/10.4018/978-1-7998-1245-6.ch010

Securities Commission Malaysia. (2014). *Waqf Assets: Development, Governance and the Role of Islamic Capital Market*. Kuala Lumpur: Securities Commission Malaysia.

Shaikh, S. A. (2017). Application of Waqf for Social and Development Finance. *ISRA International Journal of Islamic Finance*, 9(1), 5–14.

Snyder, H. (2019). Literature Review as a Research Methodology: An Overview and Guidelines. *Journal of Business Research*, 104, 333–339. https://doi.org/10.1016/j.jbusres.2019.07.039

Wulandari, P., & Kassim, S. (2016). Issues and Challenges in Financing the Poor: Case of Baitul Maal Wa Tamwil in Indonesia. *International Journal of Bank Marketing*, 34(2)

Yaacob, H. (2006). *Waqf Accounting in Malaysian State Islamic Religious Institutions: The Case of Federal Territory SIRC* (Master's Degree). International Islamic University Malaysia, Kuala Lumpur.

Zain, N. S., & Sori, Z. M. (2020). An Exploratory Study on Al-Musharakah SRI Sukuk for the Development of Waqf Properties/Assets in Malaysia. *Qualitative Research in Financial Market*, 12, 301–314.

12 Al-Rahnu-Led Islamic Sustainable Finance

Nor Razinah Mohd Zain, Aznan Hasan & Siti Ainatul Mardhiah binti Yusof

Introduction

The emergence of intellectual discourse relating to Islamic sustainable finance is newly established in recent years, triggered by the introduction of sustainable development goals (SDGs) and the increasing interest in incorporating environmental, social, and governance (ESG) components in making impactful investments. It is considered timely to look at the Islamic financial practices, their innovative products, and the possible potentials. Al-Rahnu or Islamic pawnbroking is one Sharīʿah-compliance mechanism that can be used to improve efforts to address pressing issues related to social, economic, and environment components. It is noted here that there is an absence of a clear report on the global achievement of Al-Rahnu. Based on the available data, the revenue generated from the application of Al-Rahnu in Malaysia is recorded as reaching up to RM5.02 billion in 2018 to RM5.5 billion in 2019 (Azman et al., 2022). The number of Islamic financial services providers that offer Al-Rahnu as their products in Indonesia is also increasing and has reached up to 91 different companies (Buana et al., 2021). Al-Rahnu is accepted as one of the popular microcredit financing options in the Southeast Asia, especially in Malaysia, Indonesia, Brunei, and Thailand (Hsni et al., 2020). The application of Al-Rahnu is also gaining interest among microentrepreneurs. Al-Rahnu has the advantages of speedy generated income (fast money), simple procedures, and simple formulation of contracts (Bhatt & Sinnakkannu, 2008; Muhamat et al., 2011; Hassan et al., 2015; Nik Hadiyan et al., 2016). Generally, the process of completing an Al-Rahnu contract can easily be done over the counter with a minimum of time for its approval.

In order to understand the financial operation which takes place in the application of Al-Rahnu, it is important to understand its definition from lexical and technical-standpoints. The term "Al-Rahnu" originates from an Arabic word, i.e., "ra-ha-na," which can be understood as "constancy and continuity or holding and binding" (Mohd. Zain & Hasan, 2021; Bahari et al., 2021). In its technical sense, Al-Rahnu can be accepted as "pawning, mortgage, collateral, charge, lien, and pledge, refers to taking property as security against a debt, whereby the secured property can be utilized to repay the debt in the case of non-payment" (Bahari et al., 2021). The legality of Al-Rahnu can be traced back from the main sources of Islamic law, namely, Al-Quran and Sunnah of the Prophet Muhammad (PBUH). By following the Quranic verse,

DOI: 10.4324/9781003468653-15

the simple mode of Al-Rahnu mechanism can be traced, where it is mentioned: "if you are on a journey (and then you wish to have a contract of debt with one another) and cannot find a scribe, the let a pledge taken in hand (by the one who provides the debt" (Al-Quran, 2:283). Instead of having a mere contract of debt, pawning can be used in securing the payment (Mohd. Zain & Hasan, 2021; Bahari et al., 2021). Differing from conventional pawnbroking, there is no interest (riba) attached to the debt. It is also reported that the application of Al-Rahnu is allowed by the practice of the Prophet Muhammad (PBUH). It is narrated by his wife, Aishah, that he pawned his iron shield to a Jew to buy some food (Sahih Bukhari, Hadth No. 21 from Bukhari, 1966). Al-Rahnu is also accepted as permissible financing mechanism by the majority of Muslim scholars (Al-Zuhayli, 2003). In completing the contract of Al-Rahnu, it is important to fulfil its required pillars which are: (i) the contracting parties, (ii) the expression of contract that consists of offer and acceptance, (iii) the existence of a pawning object, and (iv) the liability or debt. This study focuses on the implementation of Al-Rahnu as one of the relevant Islamic sustainable finance tools. By adopting qualitative and legal doctrinal analysis, most of the evidence and literature indicates that Al-Rahnu is utilized extensively to provide emergency funding to individuals in need or businesses. This is especially significant during and in the aftermath of the COVID-19 pandemic that adversely impacted the global economy.

Operational Models of Al-Rahnu

Originally, Al-Rahnu is not a financing contract; rather it is a form of guaranteed contract (*Tawsiqat*) which aims to guarantee debt that is formed due to some reason of indebtedness. In Malaysia, Al-Rahnu is used as microcredit financing in the short term. According to Thaker et al. (2020), there has been an increase in demand for Al-Rahnu-based products in Malaysia. This is due to several interesting factors such as low deposit charges, Islamic awareness in Islamic mortgage selection, and positive changes in community attitudes (Mohd. Zain & Hasan, 2021). Al-Rahnu has a unique nature in comparison to other microcredit products. The reality is that the existing regulations are not capturing their true essence. Based on the evaluation of Al-Rahnu practices from the Southeast Asian countries, to avoid any existence of conflict between the existing pawnbroking laws (which are conventional in nature) with the practice of Al-Rahnu, other principles of Sharīʿah are innovatively used in structuring the operational models of Al-Rahnu products. The applications of these other principles of Sharīʿah are considered valid since they are still fulfilling the requirements of Al-Rahnu products. It is identified that there are five different operational models in the application of Al-Rahnu products, which are: (i) the original principles of Al-Rahnu; (ii) Qardhul Hasan (benevolent loan); (iii) Wadiah Yad al-Dhamanah (safe custody of deposit); (iv) Al-Ujrah (wage or fee); and (v) Tawarruq (a type of sale contract).

Original Principles of Al-Rahnu

According to the scholars from the Shāfi'ī school of legal thought (such as Al-Shirbīnī and Al-Sharqawi) (Al-Zuhayli, 2003, pp. 85–86), they consider that

Table 12.1 The Operation Based on the Original Principles of Al-Rahnu

Step 1	The customer approaches the institution for Al-Rahnu product by pawning a gold bar that he owns.
Step 2	After the valuation of the gold bar, the institution offers the customer with a 'X' price. With the conclusion of the contract, the customer is in debt with the institution for the 'X' price for a certain agreed period of time.
Step 3	If the customer is able to pay the debt, he is eligible to get back his gold bar. If he fails to do so, the institution has the right to sell off/auction said valuable item.

Source: Authors' own

Table 12.2 The Operation Based on Qardhul Hasan (benevolent loan)

Step 1	The customer approaches the institution for Al-Rahnu product by pawning a gold bar that he owns.
Step 2	After the valuation of the gold bar's value, the institution gives a benevolent loan to the customer with a 'X' price. The customer is in debt with the institution for the 'X' price for a certain agreed period of time.
Step 3	If the customer is able to pay the debt, he is eligible to get back his gold bar. If he fails to do so, the institution has the right to sell off/auction said valuable item to gain payment for the benevolent loan. Any surplus from the sale will be given back to the customer.

Source: Authors' own

Al-Rahnu contract as taking a property as security for a debt where the settlement of the debt can be settled from the value of the property held if the debt fails to be paid. They reject the use (usufruct) of a property as something that can be mortgaged. Meanwhile, the scholars from the Ḥanafī school of legal thought, which includes Al-Maydānī, Ibn 'Ābidīn, and Al-Sarakhsī (Al-Zuhayli, 2003, pp. 85–86), accept the application of Al-Rahnu as holding something in exchange for a right that can be settled by the thing. According to their opinions, the thing that is placed for the pawning must be something of value and without any defects. By following these opinions from Muslim scholars, the original principles of Al-Rahnu can be simplified as provided in Table 12.1.

Qardhul Hasan (Benevolent Loan)

Under this principle, the Islamic financial services provider will provide benevolent loans to their customers who want to pawn their valuables. This is done without any elements prohibited by the Sharī'ah (such as ribā (interest), gharar (speculation), and maysir (gambling)). A customer must pay back the loan given by the Islamic financial services provider. This can be done at the maturity of the loan as agreed between the Islamic financial services provider and their customers. The operation of Al-Rahnu by using Qardhul Hasan is simplified as provided in Table 12.2.

Table 12.3 The Operation Based on Wadiah Yad al-Dhamanah

Step 1	The customer approaches the institution for Al-Rahnu product by pawning a gold bar that he owns. After the valuation of the gold bar, the institution offers the customer with an 'X' price. With the completion of the contract, the customer is in debt to the institution for the 'X' price for certain agreed period.
Step 2	The gold bar will be deposited to the institution under the principles of Wadiah Yad al-Dhamanah or safe custody of deposit. The institution is accountable for the safety of the valuable item.
Step 3	If the customer is able to pay the debt, he is eligible to get back his gold bar. In the event of default, the institution has the right to sell off/auction said valuable item.

Source: Authors' own

Wadiah Yad al-Dhamanah (Safe Custody of Deposit)

In general, this contract operates when a person places his goods in the care of someone that he trusts. Originally, a Wadiah's contract was based on trust. If the goods are damaged or lost without any negligence or fault from the individual who takes care of the goods, then he is not responsible for replacing them. A person who takes care of the Wadiah goods only becomes responsible (Yad al-Dhamanah) when he has committed an offense against the goods, such as using or damaging them. When the concept of Wadiah Yad al-Dhamanah is used, this means that if something happens to the valuable goods that were pledged by the original owner, then the individual who receives the goods is accountable. The individual who receives the item must also be responsible for ensuring the safety of the item, regardless of its condition. If the valuables are damaged or lost while in his care, then he is responsible for replacing the valuables for the original owner, either by paying the item's price or by replacing it with the same type of item. The operation of Al-Rahnu by using Wadiah Yad al-Dhamanah is simplified as provided in Table 12.3.

Al-Ujrah (Wage or Fee)

This principle occurs when the goods that are pawned are kept by the creditor. The creditor will charge a reasonable fee for keeping the pawned valuables in a safe and sound condition. In Malaysia, the pawned valuables can be kept by the Islamic financial services provider. The receipt and storage of the goods are said to be based on the concept of Wadiah. In reality, the receipt of the pawned valuables is part of the Al-Rahnu application and must be returned to the borrower when the loan is fully repaid. Al-Ujrah, which is imposed by the Islamic financial services provider, is based on security and protection services to ensure the safety of the pawned valuables. Al-Ujrah will last until the item is returned to its owner, i.e., when his debt is settled.

Tawarruq (Sale Contract by SPV)

Based on this contract, the Islamic financial services provider that offers Al-Rahnu products will sell commodities to their customers at the sale price. The customer

Table 12.4 The Operation Based on Tawarruq

Step 1	The customer approaches the institution to apply for Al-Rahnu financing with gold as collateral.
Step 2	The institution will appraise the value of the gold to determine the financing amount that the customer can apply.
Step 3	Tawarruq is performed: a) the institution purchases commodity from the commodity supplier through the commodity trading platform provider; b) the institution then sells the commodity to the customer based on the approved financing amount plus the profit amount as determined by the institution on a deferred payment term. The institution as an agent will accept the sale of the commodity on behalf of the customer; and, c) The customer then sells the commodity to the commodity trading platform provider on a cash basis. In practice, the institution as an agent will sell the commodity on behalf of the customer.
Step 4	The proceeds from the sales are disbursed to the customer after the Tawarruq arrangement is completed.
Step 5	The customer will pay the profit to the institution every 6 months and the principal amount will be paid at the maturity of the financing. In the event of default, the IFI has the right to auction the collateral to settle the financing amount.

Source: Adopted and modified from the Shari'ah Advisory Council of Bank Negara Malaysia (SAC)'s ruling on Al-Rahnu product proposal based on Tawarruq (2019).

will then be asked to place the valuables that he wants to pawn as Al-Rahnu. The Islamic financial services provider can take the actual cost of taking care of the pawned goods. This kind of structuring of Al-Rahnu products that is based on Tawarruq is popular in Malaysia. It is accepted as valid and permissible based on the Shari'ah Advisory Council of Bank Negara Malaysia (SAC)'s ruling on the Al-Rahnu product proposal based on Tawarruq, which was issued during the 198th and 199th SAC meetings on 29th October 2019 and 26th November 2019 (Kasmon & Abas, 2020). The operation of Al-Rahnu by using Tawarruq is shown in Table 12.4.

The main motivation for the introduction of Tawarruq principles in structuring Al-Rahnu products is to achieve Sharīʿah-compliance, and it is intended to be the main structure while replacing the existing Al-Rahnu products that depend on Qard and Rahn as their underlying contracts. Even though such changes happen among the providers from the Islamic banking and finance industry in Malaysia, the Al-Rahnu products that are based on Qardhul Hasan and Wadiah Yad al-Dhamanah are still applicable through independent microfinance institutions and cooperative bodies. From Al-Rahnu practices in Indonesia (such as Aceh) (Fajri et al., 2019) and Thailand (especially their southern region, i.e., Pattani) (Mulazid, 2016), Al-Rahnu is also applied to assets such as lands and buildings. However, such practices are done between individuals, instead of between the customer and the Islamic financial services providers. Based on the observation made by Fajri et al. (2019), this practice of Al-Rahnu can be considered as traditional pawning activity that becomes a part of the local culture. They reported that:

> The recognition of Gala or traditional pawn as a part of business activities leads to its continuous practice in the midst of Aceh society and prevents its disappearance. Gala has become a source of economy and a need among the lower and middle class of the rural society in Aceh. It is used in solving a variety of micro-economic problems, regardless at the village, district or sub-district levels. In fulfilling the needs of lower and middle class of the society, Gala as a traditional financing model is very easy to be found in practice among the society of Aceh starting from the 18th century to the present. The practice of Gala as an alternative solution to poverty alleviation through microfinance products from Islamic financial institutions should be accommodated by the government. This is either at the level of provinces or districts/municipalities by the involvement of local Islamic financial institutions that operate in those territories. Since Gala is derived from local practice and based on Shari'ah, the lower and middle class of society can easily attract to do business transaction with Gala.
>
> (Fajri et al., 2019)

Without a proper legislation to be followed for this kind of Al-Rahnu practice, the involved parties are faced with legal risks and uncertainty. Nevertheless, this kind of Al-Rahnu practice seems to be successful and accepted with the existence of strong trust and the sense of accountability between the involved parties. In the case of a breach, they can still refer to the court system by following the implementation of contract laws.

Al-Rahnu as an Instrument for Financial Stability

The Central Bank of Malaysia defines financial stability as an environment in which important financial institutions and markets have a high level of confidence and in which there is fluidity in the process of intermediation (BNM, 2021; Azman et al., 2022). Financial security and stability are the primary aims for the application of Al-Rahnu in the society. Its application has significant potential and contributions in bringing a balance between the aspects of society or individual, economy, and their surroundings. The application of Al-Rahnu is accepted by those who are from the medium to low-income backgrounds, and the funding generated from Al-Rahnu can be used as capital in starting or continuing microentrepreneurs' business. Thus, it can directly or indirectly assist a more equitable distribution of income or wealth in the society (Azman et al., 2022). Simultaneously, it also has the ability to alleviate people from facing poverty (Chapra, 2008). In order to reach financial stability and security, it is essential to have an awareness of the application of Al-Rahnu, which admittedly is still low among the public. If the original principles of Al-Rahnu are properly appreciated, any types of valuables or assets can be utilized under Al-Rahnu to reinstate the status quo of a person who is facing any financial crisis. Not only limited to an individual, the application of Al Rahnu is also important for the continuation of businesses. Based on a study conducted by Meera (2009), the application of Al-Rahnu assists in the process of wealth acquisition, where it is found that the customers approached the Islamic financial services providers not only to expand their businesses by generating more capital, but it is also used to own new assets. The positive acceptance among customers can be tracked by the increasing demands on Al-Rahnu products due to its expedient potential in providing financial stability by pawning valuable items (Azila, 2011; Nik Hadiyan & Salina, 2017; Azman et al., 2022). It is noted that the application of Al-Rahnu is important in generating a source of income for female microentrepreneurs. Al-Rahnu is preferred over other instruments since it enables them to obtain immediate cash and can be completed easily. These elements are necessary for the continuous success of their businesses and their stable financial positions.

Based on findings made by Bahari et al. (2021), the success of the Al-Rahnu application can be observed significantly in ensuring financial stability and security during and in the aftermath of the COVID-19 pandemic that occurred from the beginning of 2020 to the middle of 2022. On the adverse impacts of the global pandemic on social and economic components, they report that:

> This pandemic is not only related to a health crisis, but it is also affecting societies and the economy of the country. Recently, whole sectors worldwide, including Malaysia, were jeopardized by the crisis. Many sectors were unable to operate as usual due to the implementation of the movement control orders (MCO) by governments. This action increased the unemployment of Malaysia's to 3.9 per cent, which is the highest rate since June 2010. Jobs were lost, and small entrepreneurs were badly affected. For some individuals, employers stopped paying their employees' salaries and did not provide any financial support to their employees. For small businesses, they were forced to stop business operations which led to declining profit.
>
> (Bahari et al., 2021)

While references to other financial products may lead to increasing burdens of debt, Al-Rahnu provides an ample opportunity for customers to stabilize their financial situation by pawning their valuable items. In a situation where they fail to pay, their worries can be eliminated by the Islamic financial services providers' right to sell off these valuable items. In facing a financial crisis or economic meltdown, any legal hassle with the financial institutions should be avoided, especially when it brings the customer to the brink of bankruptcy. It is detected by Bahari et al. (2021) that Al-Rahnu provides an immediate relief as a source of income, where they acknowledge that:

> They had to find solutions to survive, and one of the actions taken was to turn to the pawnbroking system. Several local newspapers reported long queues at pawnshops. Several customers started to visit conventional pawnshops and Al-Rahnu as immediate sources of quick cash for several purposes, such as to support their daily needs, pay for medical expenses, for their festival season, and reserves for any unforeseen consequences in the future. Some customers

> went to the pawnshops to extend the financing period as they could not repay their debt. Besides that, some of the customers took advantage of the rising gold price in the global market. They utilized the pawnbroking services to gain profit. They started to pawn their assets, mostly jewelry, to get a higher amount of financing and invested in gold to gain profit.
>
> (Bahari et al., 2021)

At the same time, Al-Rahnu strengthens the position of Islamic financial services providers as financial intermediaries where they are fulfilling its social commitment by assisting the locals in meeting their financial obligations. It is identified that the funds generated from Al-Rahnu application are used in many areas, such as education, healthcare, agriculture, real estate, small business development, etc. (Mohd. Zain & Hasan, 2021; Bahari et al., 2021; Azman et al., 2022).

Al-Rahnu in Modern Practice

In the early practices of Al-Rahnu, the establishment of offices by the Islamic financial services providers that offered Al-Rahnu products was more focused on the rural areas. They obtained the majority of their customers from rural communities that may have faced issues in getting funding in small amounts. Due to this, many academicians or researchers classify Al-Rahnu as a microfinance or microcredit instrument. The application of Al-Rahnu captures the interests of microentrepreneurs, women or housewives, middle and low-income customers, small farmers, and those new beginning to do business (Razak, 2007; Ismail & Ahmad, 1997; Mokhtar & Zambahari, 2013; Mohd. Zain & Hasan, 2021; Bahari et al., 2021; Azman et al., 2022). Subsequently, with the continuously increasing demands from society, the application of Al-Rahnu started to capture interest among those living in the urban areas. As identified by the early research on Al-Rahnu, its application is gaining popularity among the urban population due to the existence of low-income members of the society and those facing financial issues to meet their end-of-month expenses. Al-Rahnu is considered advantageous due to its approval only requiring a low burden of credit evaluation and its expedience in providing emergency expenses. Al-Rahnu is also found to be effective as a source of financing for social, economy, and environment-related activities (Skully, 1992; Othman et al., 2012; Shukor & Sabri, 2013; Hilaluddin et al., 2022). Al-Rahnu is flexible in providing financing relief for nature-related disasters, such as floods (Saharan et al., 2022). Based on the latest findings made by Hilaluddin et al. (2022), they report that:

> Over the past two decades, the establishment of Al-Rahnu has managed to reduce its influence on conventional pawnbroking services. Customers are more focused on Al-Rahnu due to its zero-usury concept and cheap service. This scheme is not only fast but also facilitating low-income communities, even now accepted by small and medium entrepreneurs (SMEs) in helping businesses them as immediate fundamental when pawning gold or jewellery. The establishment of an Islamic pawn scheme is seen to have the potential

> in changing the perception or image of this scheme in a more positive and fair direction which in turn has a favourable influence on the socio-economic development of community.
>
> (Hilaluddin et al., 2022)

Looking further into its prospects in the future, Amin and Hassan (2022) report that the involvement of millennials in the application of Al-Rahnu is crucial and needs to be considered by the Islamic financial services providers. Based on their survey, conducted among millennials in Malaysia for Tawarruq-based operational models of Al-Rahnu, they found that:

> Due to their information technology savvy and having access to massive information about tawarruq-based Al-Rahnu given their online presence, Muslim millennials are set to determine the success of the Al-Rahnu industry for improved business performance. As the majority and most influential segment in most Muslim majority countries, Muslim millennials not only drive and shape their Muslim communities, but they are also set to shape the Al-Rahnu industry.
>
> (Amin & Hassan, 2022)

It is pertinent to ensure the acceptance of the millennials in using Al-Rahnu products since they are the generation that will replace this current generation. Their acceptance of Al-Rahnu products may influence the widespread practice of Al-Rahnu in subsequent generations. Amin and Hassan (2022) indicate that Islamic religiosity, Islamic altruism, and Islamic debt collection policies are the significant factors in influencing the acceptability of Al-Rahnu that uses Tawarruq-based operational models.

Conclusion

Al-Rahnu has its potential in meeting social, economic, and environment components. The application of Al-Rahnu has proven to be compatible with the socio-economic conditions, especially among the plural society of the Southeast Asian countries. Due to the lack of data and literature from other parts of the world on the application of Al-Rahnu, it is safe to say that it is applied as one microfinance instrument, either in traditional or modern practices. Thus, it is important to have more research relating to Al-Rahnu from other countries. In order to ensure the success of the application of Al-Rahnu, it is essential to have stronger legislation and governance in its operation. It is common to have the involvement of gold in the application of Al-Rahnu products. Nevertheless, it should not be limited to this type of precious metal per se. The expansion of Al-Rahnu practices should be allowed for other kinds of assets, such as buildings and lands.

References

Al-Zuhayli, W. (2003). *Financial Transactions in Islamic Jurisprudence* (Vol. 2). Damascus: Dar al Fikr.

Amin, H., & Hassan, M. K. (2022). Millennials' Acceptability of Tawarruq-Based Al-Rahnu in Malaysia. *International Journal of Ethics and Systems*, 38(3).

Azila, A. R. (2011). *Economic and Religious Significance of the Islamic and Conventional Pawnbroking in Malaysia: Behavioural and Perception Analysis* (Doctoral Dissertation). Durham, UK: Durham University.

Azman, N. H. N., Rashid, M. R. A., Shaarani, A. F. A., Safian, J. S., Arshad, A., & Mokthar, N. A. I. (2022). The Effectiveness of Al-Rahnu Cooperative Financial Performance in Malaysia. *International Journal of Academic Research in Economics and Managment and Sciences*, 11(2), 176–194.

Bahari, N. F., Hanefah, M. M., & Shafii, Z. (2021). Islamic Social Finance During Economic Uncertainty: Special Roles of Al-Rahnu. In *COVID-19 and Islamic Social Finance* (pp. 214–224). London, Malaysia: Routledge.

Bank Negara Malaysia (BNM). (2021). *Financial Stability*. www.bnm.gov.my/the-importance-of-financial-stability

Bhatt, P., & Sinnakkannu, J. (2008). Al-Rahnu (Islamic Pawning Broking) Opportunities and Challengers in Malaysia. *The 6th International Islamic Finance Conference*.

Buana, M. T. L., Dali, N. R. S. M., Halim, S., & Abdul Qadir, A. H. M. (2021). Gadai Shari'ah Al-Rahnu Contract at Pawnbroking Industry in Indonesia and Malaysia. In *E-Prosiding Seminar Antarabangsa Islam and Sains 2021: Wawasan Kemakmuran Bersama 2030*. www.researchgate.net/publication/354460082_GADAI_SHARI'AH_AL-RAHNU_CONTRACT_AT_PAWNBROKING_INDUSTRY_IN_INDONESIA_AND_MALAYSIA

Bukhari, M. I. I. (1966). *Sahih Bukhari*. Karachi: Muhammad Sarid.

Chapra, M. U. (2008). The Islamic Vision of Development, Thoughts on Economics. *Q. J. Islamic Economics Research Bureau (Bangladesh)*, 18(3), 7–38.

Fajri, I., Gunawan, E., & Kesuma, T. M. (2019). Gala (Al-Rahnu) as Micro Financing Instruments in Islamic Financial Institution in Aceh. *Journal of Islamic Finance*, 8(2), 43–49.

Hassan, F. S., Ahmad, S., & Wahab, H. (2015). Penerimaan Masyarakat Terhadap Skim Gadaian Islam di Kota Bharu Kelantan. In *The Proceeding of Current Fiqh (SeFIS)*.

Hilaluddin, N., Abdullah, A., & Osman, A. A. (2022). The Role of Al-Rahnu as an Alternative in Reviving Micro-Enterprises Through Pandemic Crisis. In *International Conference on Business and Technology* (pp. 413–426). Cham: Springer.

Hsni, E. N. B. T., Samsurijan, M. S., Hamat, Z., Hanapi, M. S., & Ehigiamusoe, K. U. (2020). Micro-Credit Financing (Al-Rahnu) in South East Asia: A Review. *Solid State Technology*, 63(1s), 1781–1795.

Ismail, A. G., & Ahmad, N. Z. (1997). Pawnshop as an Instrument of Microenterprise Credit in Malaysia. *International Journal of Social Economics*, 24(11), 1343–1352. https://doi.org/10.1108/03068299710193633

Kasmon, S. A., & Abas, N. R. (2020). An Analysis on the Shari'ah and Operational of Al-Rahnu: Post-Announcement of BNM Rahn Policy Document. *Journal of Islamic Economics and Law (JIEL)*, 1(2).

Meera, M. A. K. (2009). Integrating Al-Rahn with the Gold Dinar: The Initial Building-Blocks Towards a Gold-Based Economy. In *Real Money: Money and Payment Systems from an Islamic Perspective*. Kuala Lumpur: IIUM Press.

Mohd. Zain, N. R., & Hasan, A. (2021). Al-Rahnu: Isu Dan Penyelesaian Semasa. *Malaysian Journal of Shari'ah and Law*, 9(1), 47–60. https://doi.org/10.33102/mjsl.vol9no1.239

Mokhtar, I., & Zambahari, S. R. (2013, September). Ar Rahnu: A Short-Term Financing Alternative. *5th Islamic Economics System Conference (IECONS 2013)* (pp. 863–871).

Muhamat, A. A., Rosly, H. E., & Jaafar, M. N. (2011). The Non-Muslims Response Towards Al-Rahnu (Islamic Pawn Broking) Services: An Empirical Study on the Ar Rahnu Clients of Klang Valley, Malaysia. In *The IEEE Colloquium on Humanities, Science and Engineering*.

Mulazid, A. S. (2016). *Kedudukan Sistem Pegadaian Shari'ah*. Jakarta, Indonesia: Prenada Media.

Nik Hadiyan, N. A., & Salina, H. K. (2017). Al-Rahnu as a Source of Financial Sustainability for Women Micro-Entrepreneurs in Malaysia. *Journal of Islamic Monetary Economics and Finance*, 2(2), 221–250.

Nik Hadiyan, N. A., Salina, H. K., & Adawale, A. A. (2016). Role of Al-Rahnu as Micro-credit Instrument in Achieving Financial Self-sufficiency Among Women Micro-entrepreneurs. *Intellect. Discourse*, 24, 365–385.

Othman, A., Hashim, N., & Abdullah, S. (2012). *Customer Satisfaction Levels of Service Quality at Al-Rahnu, Kelantan*. www.semanticscholar.org/paper/CUSTOMER-SATISFACTION-LEVELS-OF-SERVICE-QU ALITY-AT-Othman-Hashim/061b56a2315b4da9d51ea8c0911502bd989f5514

Razak, A. A. (2007). *Malaysian Practice of Al-Rahnu Scheme. Trends and Development*. www.assaif.org/ara/content/download/1490/16172/file/Islamic%20Pawnbroking.pdf

Saharan, M. S., Jamaludin, M. F., & Adzahar, K. A. (2022). Leveraging Al-Rahnu Micro Financing for Flood Victims. *FBM Insights*, 5(15), 41–42.

Shari'ah Advisory Council (SAC). (2019). *SAC's Ruling on Al-Rahnu Product Proposal Based on Tawarruq*. www.bnm.gov.my/documents/20124/914558/01_SAC198_Draft+SAC+Statement_Rahnu_en.pdf/eae8e754-030d-6e8c-79c6-f1ec4583bfe2?t=1590716851435#:~:text=As%20such%2C%20the%20SAC%20ruled,in%20the%20event%20of%20default

Shukor, S. A., & Sabri, H. (2013). Customer Satisfaction Towards Islamic Pawnbroking (Al-Rahnu): Antecedents and Consequences. *Global Journal of Commerce and Management Perspectives*, 2(6), 29–36.

Skully, M. T. (1992). The Development of the Pawnshop Industry in East Asia. *East Asia*, 357–374.

Thaker, H. M. T., Khaliq, A., Thaker, M. A. B. M. T., Pitchay, A. B. A., & Sakaran, K. C. (2020). Drivers of Al-Rahnu (Pawn) Acceptance: Malaysian Evidence. *Journal of Islamic Marketing,* 12(7).

13 Bay' al-Salam-Based Islamic Sustainable Finance

Azman bin Mohd Noor & Musthafa Mu'az bin Mohammad Masruh

Introduction

Islamic banking is distinguished from conventional banking since all business banking transactions must adhere to Shari'ah rules. The bank cannot recognize the income it receives if it does not adhere to Shari'ah. Different Shari'ah contracts have different Shari'ah requirements and effects even though they may fall under the same category, such as a sale-based contract. ***Bay' al Salam*** is one of the sale contracts with a future delivery feature. In some Muslim countries, like Sudan, some Islamic financial institutions have used ***Bay' al-Salam*** as a mode of financing product. This chapter presents a potential ***Bay' al-Salam*** financing model. The Muslim Scholars have defined ***Bai' Salam*** based on the characteristics relevant to the specified contract, taking into consideration the Prophet's hadith and their in-depth study of Shari'ah requirements. The following are some definitions of Bai' Salam:

In reference to Hanafi Scholar, "Sale of a deferred delivery (commodity) in exchange with immediate payment consideration".[1] In the view of Maliki Scholar,[2] "it is a sale of something known with prescriptions in exchange for a price paid in advance and the object of sale is deferred to a specified term". The Shafi'i School says[3], "the sale contract with a deferred delivery in exchange for a price that is received during the contract session". Hanbali Scholar[4] is of the opinion that, "A sale contract of a deferred delivery in exchange for immediate price during the contract". Bai' Salam as defined by Bank Negara Malaysia: "Sale contract based on order of certain asset with certain specifications. Full payment is made in cash at the time of conclusion of the contract whereas the delivery of the asset is deferred to a specified time".[5]

Main Pillars of Bai' Salam

Strict adherence to a transaction's pillars and conditions is required for it to be a legally binding contract. The following are the main pillars and conditions in respect to the ***Bay' al-Salam***, where any divergence from its requirements may render the transaction null and void.

- Contracting Party i.e. the buyer (*muslim*) and the seller (*muslam Ilaihi*). The buyer is a party that purchases goods/commodities and pays the money in advance,

DOI: 10.4324/9781003468653-16

whereas the seller is a party who sells the goods/commodities in exchange for money and agrees that the goods/commodities will be delivered on a future date.
- Contract. Offer (*ijab*) and acceptance (*qabul*).
- Capital (Price). The capital of Salam (purchase price) should be known to both parties and paid in advance. Nevertheless, ***Bay' al-Salam*** capital shall not be in the form of debt, such as the buyer's future receivable.
- Salam Goods (*muslam fihi*).

The goods/commodity must be distinguishable by kind, quality, quantity, and specification. Once the *akad* is signed, the contracted goods/commodity will become a debt, i.e. a seller's responsibility (*zimmah*), until it is delivered to the buyer according to the agreed-upon terms. During the *akad*, it is necessary to determine the delivery date and location. For *salam* commodities that are appropriate for Islamic financial institution financing activities, in order to mitigate the risk of price volatility, they are supposed to be regulated. This also mitigates the risk of potential default by the bank's customer, who is the seller of *Bay' al Salam*, to find and deliver the ordered commodities at the delivery date because of their scarcity.

Bay' al-Salam *Financing Model by Islamic Banks*

For *Bay' al-Salam*-based financing products, an Islamic bank can make lower-priced purchases (which is "financing" in Islamic terms or "loan" in conventional term) to clients in order to obtain higher-priced crude palm oils (CPOs) in the future through market prediction.

The Capital of Salam (bank's Purchase Price) will be based on the margin of total amount (in RM) for every metric ton of CPOs to be delivered by the customer through Bursa or an equivalent platform.

The application of ***Bay' al-Salam*** contract in this product will involve few Shari'ah concepts as follow:

- *Bay' al-Salam* (main concept).
- *Wakalah.*
- *Bay' al-Mutlaq* (normal purchase and sale).

Those Shari'ah concepts are further illustrated in the following descriptions, assuming the highest CPO price in Malaysia in December is RM 4,100. This structure is suitable for financing with the fixed payment scheduled seasonally.

Proposed Operational Model of CPO's Bai' al-Salam

Description of the Proposed Model

The steps in the proposed model can be explained as follows:

First Step

The bank will purchase amount of CPO from the customer at the discounted price of 1 metric ton (which is equal to the bank's financing amount) at the value of RM 3,500 on January 1, 2022, and the CPO will be delivered on December 1, 2022.

Second Step

In this scenario, the customer will deliver to the bank on 1 December 2022. In case the customer does not have access to the market, the bank may act as an agent of the customer to purchase the CPO and will purchase the CPO on the customer's behalf before the customer delivers the CPO over to the bank.

Third Step

Simultaneously, the bank will sell the CPO back to the trader's platform for cash at the current value where the bank gets RM 4,100 for 1 metric ton of CPO as a profit for whole year from January 2022 to December 2022.

Pertinent Requirement to Be Included in the Documentation

Based on this proposed structure, certain pertinent requirements need to be incorporated in the legal documentation, which are as follows:

i) Contract document of ***Bay' al-Salam*** contract which is to be executed on every season prior to the disbursement.
ii) Master agreement in relation to the CPO's product which provides the terms and condition of the financing facility, e.g., profit rate, conditions precedent, treatment upon occurrence of event of default, burden of proof on the negligence etc.
iii) Agency appointment (*wakalah*):
    - *Wakalah* by the customer to the bank to complete ***Bay' al-Salam*** transaction before disbursement.
    - *Wakalah* by the customer to the bank to purchase the CPO on delivery date.

Risk Exposure in Bai' Salam

Bai' Salam involves a different level of risk exposure for the bank than the *Tawarruq* concept; the major sources of this risk are the commodity that was transacted during the contract and the customer's duty to deliver the commodity in line with the provisions of the finalized contract. The following are a number of potential risks related to the ***Bay' al-Salam*** contract.

Default Payment

Inability or failure to deliver the agreed-upon Salam Goods to the Bank on the specified date. Theoretically, there will be three scenarios of non-delivery of Salam Goods:

- Failing to deliver the products completely.
- Failing to deliver the items in the quantity requested.
- Failing to deliver the goods in accordance with the required quality.

According to the Shari'ah principle, there are two separate Shari'ah laws for two different scenarios for failure to supply *salam* items.

First Scenario

There is no evidence of customer negligence (*non-Negligence*). For example, in the event of no Salam Goods (*muslam fihi*) can be sourced in the market by the customer at the time of delivery.

In this circumstance, a few options can be chosen by the bank:

- To terminate the contract with ***Bay' al-Salam*** and demand the principal amount (Bank Purchase Price) of the Salam Goods; OR
- To authorize an extension of the delivery date. In this case:
  - i The Bank may cancel the *Bai'Salam* contract and recover the principal amount (Bank Purchase Price) of Salam Goods if the customer is still unable to deliver on the extended date and the inability is due to non-negligence on his part.
  - ii If the client's failure to deliver is the result of his negligence, the bank may pursue payment from the client up to the current (CPO Price) of the Salam Goods on the extended delivery date (under this financing facility, the Bank may pursue payment of the outstanding Sale Price but not exceeding the current value of the CPO price); or
- To accept substituted items proposed by the customer in lieu of Salam Goods with the equivalent value of the current value (CPO price) at the time of delivery.

Second Scenario

There is evidence of the customer's negligence. For example, CPO is available in the market but the customer refuses/neglects to get the supply to deliver the Salam Goods as agreed. In this case, a few options can be chosen by the bank:

- Due to the client's failure to deliver being the result of his negligence, the bank may pursue payment from the client up to the current value (CPO Price) of the Salam Goods on the extended delivery date (under this financing facility, the bank may pursue payment of the outstanding Sale Price but not exceeding the current value of the CPO price);
- To authorize a delivery date postponement or extension of the delivery date. In the event the customer is unable to deliver on the extended delivery date, the bank may pursue payment of the outstanding sale price but not exceeding the current value of the CPO price);
- To accept substituted items proposed by the customer in lieu of Salam Goods with the equivalent value of the current values (CPO's price) at the time of delivery.

Death of Customer Before Delivery Date of Salam Goods

Upon the death of the customer, the delivery date of Salam goods will be materialized immediately on the death date of the customer, and the bank can claim directly from the Takaful Operator or his kin up to the current value (CPO price) of the

Salam goods on the extended delivery date (under this financing facility, the bank may claim the outstanding sale price (in the BDS), but not exceeding the current value of the CPO price).

Disbursement of Financing Money by Staggered, Progressive, or Deferred Disbursement

As payment of the whole *salam* price (bank purchase price) needs to be released upon conclusion of the *Bai' Salam* contract, deferred or staggered capital distribution is not permitted. The bank may decide to adopt a dual agency structure to speed up the procedure by acting on behalf of the client to complete the contract on *Bai' Salam* due to its flexibility over the payout date.

Mismatch on the Purpose of Financing

The nature of *Bai' Salam* allows the buyer to purchase CPO from the market rather than having to cultivate the palm themselves. Therefore, the mismatch in financing purposes will be considered customer negligence, and the bank may choose the aforementioned course of action.

Destruction or Calamity to the Palm Plantation

Any incidence that has an influence on the customer's palm plantation output will have no effect on the finance payment, because the customer's principal responsibility under the *Bay' al-Salam* contract is the delivery of CPO, which can be obtained from the market.

Consequences of Breach of Agreement

Determining a client's negligence can be measured from the perspective of the failure of the customer to deliver commodities according to the specified specifications, while the commodities are proven to be still available in the local market. Therefore, in principle, the customer should have bought it from the local market even at a higher price and delivered it over to the bank during the timeframe which was set in accordance with the *Bai' al-Salam* agreement. In this case, the failure to do so can be regarded as negligence from the seller's side. This is in line with Imam Nawawi's perspective in the event of non-availability of commodity:

> When Muslam fihi (commodities) are not available at all, for instance a commodity is normally produced by a country, but because of natural disaster, it becomes totally not available, this is regarded to be a real cut off. Similarly, if the muslam fihi (commodities) exists in another country but if it were carried to another country, it will be damaged, or if the commodities are owned by a group of people who are reluctant to sell them, this is also regarded to by a real cut off. However, if the traders are selling it with expensive price, and transportation is viable, then it is not regarded as a cut off.[6]

From this quotation, one can argue that in the event of total non-availability of the commodity the seller should not be held liable, as it is not his negligence.

Shari'ah Ruling on Buying and Selling of Dayn *Salam*

Shari'ah-wise, it is also suggested to adopt the opinion of the scholar who allows the sale of *salam* receivable (debt obligation) to the customer with equivalent price in the event of default because of negligence. It is permissible to sell *salam* receivable (*muslam fihi* debt) based on the opinion of Imam Ahmad in one of his narrations,[7] as well as the fatwa of Ibn Taimiyyah and his student Ibnu Qayyim,[8] with the condition to sell it at the current value in order to avoid profiting from unguaranteed items.[9] This is in reference to Shari'ah scholarly perspective:

> Ibn Taimiyyah says: "It is permissible to sell a debt liability to a debtor or others, no difference between the debt of salam and other than salam. This is one of Imam Ahmad's narrations, as this is the opinion of Ibn Abbas with the (condition) to sell it at the current value in order to avoid profiting from unguaranteed (un-owned) items . . .[10]
>
> Ibnu Taimiyyah also said: "This narration is quoted in number of places from Imam Ahmad to the extent that it is almost similar to the principle of his school of thought". He also asserted that this is also the opinion of Imam Malik. Imam Ahmad has indicated on this permissibility not at one place of his fatwas as he considers the debt of salam is similar to other sale receivables.[11]
>
> Sheikhul Islam Ibnu Taimiyyah further stated: "This is Ibnu Abbas' opinion, and there has been no record that any of the companions of the Prophet disagreed with him. Hence its (settlement) substitution is permissible similar to the payment of a loan, similar to the receivable of sale contracts. As it is one of the considerations of a sale and purchase contract, the substitution of the considerations is permissible.[12]

Notes

1 Ibn Abidin. (1836/1996). *Hasyiah Rad al-Muhtar 5/209*. Maktabah al-Babi al-Halabi.
2 Zurqani. (1687). *Syarh Zurqani ala mukhtasar Khalili 5/365*. Dar al-kutub al-ilmiyyah.
3 Abu Zakariya An-Nawawi. (1277/1991). *Raudah Talibin 4/3*. al-Maktab al-Islamiy Beirut.
4 Al-Buhuti. (1641/2008). *Kasyaaf al-Qina' an al-Iqna' 8/85*. Saudi Ministiry of Justice.
5 BNM. (2010). *Shari'ah Resolution in Islamic Finance MS 236* (2nd ed.).
6 Department of Islamic Research and Encyclopedias. (2012). *Encyclopedia of Islamic Jurisprudence "Al-Mausu'ah al-Fiqhiyyah al-Kuwaitiiyah" 25/225*. Ministry of Awqaf and Islamic Affairs of Kuwait & Abu Zakariya An-Nawawi. (1277/1991). *Raudah Talibin 12/4*. al-Maktab al-Islamiy Beirut.
7 Ibn Muflih al-Maqdisiy. (1362/2003). *al-Furu' 6/332*. Muassasah Beirut.
8 Ibn Qayyim al-Jauziyyah. (1350/1991). *I'lam al-Muwaqqi'in 2/9*. Dar Kutub al-Ilmiyyah.
9 Ibn Muflih al-Maqdisiy. (1362/2003). *al-Furu' 6/332*. Muassasah Beirut.
10 Ahmad ibn Taimiyyah. (1328/2004). *Majmoo' Al Fatawa 29/505*. Ministiry of Islamic Affairs, Da'wah and Guidance of Saudi.
11 Ahmad ibn Taimiyyah. (1328/2004). *Majmoo' Al Fatawa 29/503*. Ministiry of Islamic Affairs, Da'wah and Guidance of Saudi.
12 Ahmad ibn Taimiyyah. (1328/2004). *Majmoo' Al Fatawa 29/519*. Ministiry of Islamic Affairs, Da'wah and Guidance of Saudi.

References

Abu Zakariya An-Nawawi. (1277/1991). *Raudah Talibin*. al-Maktab al-Islamiy Beirut.
Ahmad ibn Taimiyyah. (1328/2004). *Majmoo' Al Fatawa*. Ministiry of Islamic Affairs, Da'wah and Guidance of Saudi.
Al-Buhuti. (1641/2008). *Kasyaaful Qina' an al-Iqna'*. Saudi Ministiry of Justice.
BNM. (2010). *Shari'ah Resolution in Islamic Finance* (2nd ed.).
Department of Islamic Research and Encyclopedias. (2012). *Encyclopedia of Islamic Jurisprudence "Al-Mausu'ah al-Fiqhiyyah al-Kuwaitiiyah"*. Ministiry of Awqaf and Islamic Affairs of Kuwait.
Ibn Abidin. (1836/1996). *Hasyiah Rad al-Muhtar 5/209*. Maktabah al-Babi al-Halabi.
Ibn Muflih al-Maqdisiy. (1362/2003). *al-Furu'*. Muassasah Beirut.
Ibn Qayyim al-Jauziyyah. (1350/1991). *I'lam al-Muwaqqi'in*. Dar Kutub al-Ilmiyyah.
Zurqani. (1687). *Syarh Zurqani ala mukhtasar Khalili*. Dar al-kutub al-ilmiyyah.

14 Al-Musharakah-Led Islamic Sustainable Finance

Syuhaeda Aeni Mat Ali, Rusni Hassan & Ahmad Azam Othman

Introduction

In the contemporary economic and financial environments, the tenet of Al-Musharakah plays a vital role in most circumstances. Al-Musharakah is originated from sharaka, which literally means sharing and mixing shares of two or more parties to make them interchangeable (ISRA, 2016). As one of the essential contracts in Islamic finance, the term Al-Musharakah is not being used to indicate partnership in traditional Islamic literature, although it is linguistically correct in derivation (Sadique, 2009). Al-Musharakah refers to partnership in ownership (Shirkah Al-Milk) or contractual partnership (Shirkah Al-Aqd). Shirkah Al-Milk is a type of joint ownership by two or more people of a particular property. This shirkah (partnership) is used for purchasing and owning equipment or assets jointly. On the other hand, in Shirkat Al-Aqad, the involved parties invest some capital in a commercial enterprise. Al-Musharakah is a form of partnership where two or more individuals combine their capital or labour to share the profits, enjoying similar rights and liabilities (Ahmed, 2008). Al-Musharakah has been applied to Islamic banking and Islamic capital markets across the world. Al-Musharakah is also combined with other contracts such as Al-Musharakah al-Mutanaqisah (diminishing partnership). An Al-Musharakah al-Mutanqisah contract is when the customer initially enters into a joint partnership with the view of co-owning the property with the bank. Thereafter, one of the partners is given the right to buy another partner's share based on conditions agreed upon between parties (Syuhaeda Aeni et al., 2022). However, the Islamic equity-based financing contract of Al-Musharakah, which is based on risk-sharing, is not generally friendly with financial intermediaries. Both al-Mudharabah and Al-Musharakah are rarely offered by Islamic banks (Chong & Liu, 2009; Sapuan, 2016).

It is pertinent to highlight that Islamic finance embraces sustainability when its business objectives are beyond generating profit. Value-Based Intermediation (VBI), which was introduced in 2018 by Bank Negara Malaysia, promotes a more holistic observation of Islamic principles beyond Shari'ah compliance, by delivering the intended outcomes of Shari'ah through practices that generate positive and sustainable impact to the economy, community and environment, while being consistent with shareholders' sustainable returns and long-term interests (Business Today, 2022). For instance, HSBC Amanah Bank in Malaysia has developed its sustainable framework

DOI: 10.4324/9781003468653-17

known as a **Triple Bottom Line (TBL) Framework** (Business Today, 2022). This framework assists the bank in classifying its financing and measures its impact with regard to the lens of TBL via the 3 Ps – Planet, People and Prosperity – which are guided by Bank Negara Malaysia's Value-Based Intermediation (VBI).

Rulings on Al-Musharakah Contracts

The legality of the Al-Musharakah contract is derived from the Qur'an, Sunnah of Prophet Muhammad (PBUH) and ijma' (consensus of the Muslim jurists).

Al-Quran

The following verses in Al-Qur'an indicate the legality of Al-Musharakah:

> If there be more (brothers and sisters of the same mother), they shall (equally) share the third of the estate, after payment of any bequest that may have been bequeathed or debt (incurred); the bequests made should not harm (the rights of the heirs).
>
> Surah an-Nisa', 12

And "Truly many partners (in all walks of life) are unjust to one another: but not so those who believe and do good works, and they are few." Surah as-Sod, verse 24.

As-Sunnah

The legality of Al-Musharakah is based on the narration of Abu Hurayrah (may Allah be pleased with him), who reported that: The Apostle of Allah (peace be upon him) having said: Allah s.w.t, says: "I make a third [partner] with two partners as long as one of them does not betray the other, but when one of them betrays the other, I depart from them" (Abu Daud, Sunan Abi Daud, hadith no. 2936). The narration by As-Saaib bin Abi As-Saaib, who had been a business partner of Prophet Muhammad (peace be upon him) in the early days of Islam, related that on the Day of the Muslim conquest of Makkah, the Prophet (peace be upon him) said to him, "Welcome to my brother and partner, [who] does not wrangle or dispute" (Al-Hakim, Al-Mustadrak, hadith no. 2317).

Al-Ijma'

The Muslim jurists have agreed on consensus on the permissibility of Al-Musharakah (BNM, 2015).

Literature Review

Al-Musharakah is a partnership financing whereby bank and customer cooperate in financing a project in which both parties act as capital providers and share risks and profit. Theoretical literature on Islamic banking strongly supports the notion that the adoption of profit-loss sharing (PLS) contracts would increase the value of Islamic banks and make them resilient to crisis. The PLS system in Islamic banks should be the fundamental characteristic that differentiates Islamic banks from conventional banks (Chong & Liu, 2009). The adoption of Al-Musharakah is regarded as an ideal financing contract in Islamic finance and, in the opinion of some scholars, is in the real spirit of Islam (Usmani, 2002). This is because Al-Musharakah is related to the risk-sharing between the transacting parties, a bank as a capital provider and its customer (on the asset side), and this risk can be passed on to the liability side of the Islamic banks (between depositors and investment account holders). Islamic philosophy cannot be translated into reality unless the use of Al-Musharakah is expanded by Islamic banks (Usmani, 2002). The existing literature has discussed partnership financing with credit risk management (Astrom, 2013), profitability (Hassan & Dridi, 2011; Narayan & Phan, 2019), stability and growth in an economy, and resilience in a crisis (Beck et al., 2013; Hassan & Dridi, 2011; Khan, 2015). The focus of Islamic banking on profitability and the investment rates of return in partnership financing increases the potential for directing financial resources to the most productive investments, thus increasing the efficiency of the financing process (Khoutem & Nedra, 2012). Khan (2015) is of the view that investors are expected to select relatively better projects for partnership financing, which implies efficient project financing and ultimately leads to bank efficiency.

However, Al-Musharakah is among the prime instruments in equity financing, but it is not as popular as other Islamic debt financial instruments, because most Islamic banks prefer debt financing to equity financing. Past literatures pointed out that Islamic banks are reluctant to offer PLS instruments due to credit risks, where bankers perceive PLS financing potentially generate higher credit risk than fixed return financing, principal and agent problems requires PLS financing a costly monitoring system and the discretionary power of clients (Akin et al., 2016; Mili & Abid, 2017; Fianto et al., 2018; Bello et al., 2020). Furthermore, Abdul-Rahman and Nor (2016) outlined four major impediments such as the high risk of investment, difficulty of selecting appropriate partners, creditworthiness of the partner and lack of capital security. Similarly, a few other studies concluded that because of the possibility of information asymmetry, moral hazard, adverse selection and costly monitoring, PLS financing is riskier (Beck et al., 2013; Louhichi & Boujelbene, 2016). Usmani (1998) also noted that "risk of loss, dishonesty, secrecy of business, and clients' unwillingness to share profits" have been thought to prevent wider acceptance of Al-Musharakah. Thus, the objective of this study involved an analysis of Al-Musharakah instrument in terms of its sustainability in Malaysia's financial market, which comprises three main sectors: Islamic banking, Islamic insurances (takaful) and the Islamic capital market. This study aims to provide invaluable insights into the applicability of Al-Musharakah instrument beyond generating profit, linking it with value-based intermediation (VBI) and environmental, social and governance (ESG) principles. This study also explores advantages and potential challenges of Al-Musharakah in Malaysia's financial market and consumer welfare.

Al-Musharakah in Islamic Banking

Malaysia has positioned itself as an international hub for Islamic banking and finance. In banks, Al-Musharakah is mostly used in the form of partnership. Al-Musharakah is a partnership between two or more parties, whereby all parties will share the profit and bear the loss from the partnership (BNM, 2015). The bank will receive a return according to a predetermined ratio; however, in the event of losses, the bank will also share with the entrepreneur in any losses. This contrasts with the fixed pre-determined "interest rate" to be paid by the entrepreneur in addition to the borrowed principal, regardless of the outcome of the business undertaking. Al-Musharakah is commonly used in the following Islamic banking products:

Investment Products

An investment account is defined under Section 2(1) of Islamic Financial Services Act 2013 ("IFSA 2013") as:

> an account under which money is paid and accepted for the purposes of investment, including for the provision of finance, in accordance with Shari'ah on terms that there is no express or implied obligation to repay the money in full and a) either only the profits, or both the profits or losses, thereon shall be shared between the person paying the money and the person accepting the money; or b) with or without any return.

The definition addresses the distribution of profit and loss between the contracting parties, i.e. the bank and the customer. Furthermore, both item (a) and item (b) of the definition allude to two types of Shari'ah-compliant investments, namely Al-Musharakah (where profit and loss are shared between partners) and Al-Mudharabah (where only profit is shared); the customer, in his capacity as an investor, is not guaranteed a return but is exposed to the possibility of gaining the profit or bearing the loss, depending on the performance of the investment (Tuan Soh, 2019).

There are two general types of investment accounts: al-Mudharabah investment accounts and wakalah investment accounts (Rusni et al., 2016). The investment can either be in the form of a fixed return or floating return. For a floating return, the bank will invest for instance in al-Mudharabah- or Al-Musharakah-based instruments or Shari'ah-based stocks and securities in which the profits generated are based on the investment and economic volatility. Al-Musharakah financing significantly influences economic activity; for instance, Al-Musharakah of depositors, bank and investors in the funding of project and participation in the profits and risks (Adela, 2018). Therefore, it affects savings, investment and the domestic resources gap. In contrast with the interest rate, the implementation of Al-Musharakah financing is considered more flexible than the interest rate as it includes three rates of return: a return rate of depositors' Al-Musharakah, a return rate of the bank's Al-Musharakah and a return rate of investors' Al-Musharakah (Adela, 2018).

Al-Musharakah in Investment Account Platform. Malaysia's investment account platform (IAP), which was initiated by Bank Negara Malaysia in 2016, is an internet-based multibank platform which facilitates channelling of funds from individual and institutional investors to finance viable ventures intermediated by participating Islamic banks via Restricted Investment Accounts as governed under IFSA 2013 and the Development of Financial Institution Act 2002 (IAP, 2021). At present, IAP has seven (7) partner banks: Affin Islamic, Bank Islam, RHB Islamic, Bank Muamalat, Maybank Islamic, Bank Rakyat and Bank Simpanan Nasional (IAP, 2022). The Al-Musharakah instrument becomes one of the types of contracts used in this IAP. For instance, there were five (5) successful projects known as Project Ar Rahn 1, 2, 3, 4 and 5 using an Al-Musharakah Joint venture Agreement between Muamalat Venture Sdn Bhd and Permodalan Kelantan (IAP, 2022). It is obvious that the IAP, together with the existing components of financial intermediation, will form a more complete and mutually complementary financial ecosystem.

Equity-Based Asset Financing Products

Equity-based asset financing products may be in the form of Al-Musharakah asset financing and Al-Musharakah Mutanaqisah (MM) asset financing. In practice, Al-Musharakah asset financing applies Sharikah al-'Inan (General partnership). Sharikah al-'Inan is a limited investment partnership whereby each partner may only transact with the partnership capital according to the terms of the partnership agreement and to the extent of the joint capital. Hence, their liability towards third parties is several but not joint (Ghadas & Engku, 2009). It has the following features: It does not require equality in investment, personal status, distributions of profits and liabilities; the relationship of partners is based on the notion of agency; and partners enjoy the freedom and discretion to conduct business in the area of commerce covered by their partnership (Syuhaeda et al., 2022). In other words, the liability of partners in Sharikah al-'Inan resembles that of modern-day limited liability partnerships (Abd Ghadas & Engku Ali, 2011). Therefore the bank, together with the initiator of a project, will finance the project in agreed proportions that will entitle all of them to the right to participate or waive participation in the management of the project (Bank Islam Malaysia Berhad, 1994; Alias et al., 1993). All parties will finance the project and share the profits generated from the project based on a ratio agreed by all parties. In the event of loss being incurred, they will also bear the losses according to their share of proportion in the financing (Syuhaeda et al., 2022). However, the challenges of the Al-Musharakah instrument include the existing regulatory frameworks which favour risk transfer as opposed to risk sharing under Al-Musharakah. This influences Islamic banks to strongly prefer risk transfer banking practices. For instance, in Malaysia the existing conventional regulatory framework is designed to serve the risk transfer financial system. As a result, the business model, products and services of Islamic banks closely resemble those of the conventional banks. This resemblance is evident in: (1) the pricing mechanism of products, (2) balance sheet structure and (3) preference for debt-based over equity-based contracts in Islamic bank (Said Bouheraoua et al., 2016).

Al-Musharakah Mutanaqisah (MM) Asset Financing

MM literally means diminishing partnership. MM is not found in classical fiqh literature, as it is an innovative product or hybrid product consisting of several classical contracts, namely Al-Musharakah (partnership), Ijarah (Lease) and Al-Bay (Sale) (Haneef et al., 2011). MM is clearly explained in the case of Kuwait Finance House (Malaysia) Berhad v Empee Sugar & Allied Industries Sdn Bhd, Shaji Purushothaman and Empee Sugars and Chemicals Limited, India (Unreported, Kuala Lumpur High Court (Muamalat division): D4-22A-590-2009 dated 1 July 2011), as the Court states:

> Al-Musharakah Mutanaqisah in essence means diminishing partnership agreement. It is a partnership in which one of the two partners promises to gradually buy the other partner's stake until one party owns the entire project. It is a form of credit facility for entrepreneurs who do not have much capital to begin their business and require financial assistance from a financier. Here, the financier does not act as a loan provider as in a conventional loan agreement but takes part in the equity responsibility of the business or investment. The profit derived from such partnership is supposed to be proportion to the risk that the investor is exposed to.

For acquiring completed assets, MM may be arranged whereby the partners jointly purchase an asset from a third party. Subsequently, one of the partners will lease his share of the asset ownership to the other partner based on ijarah. Simultaneously, the partner who is the lessee will purchase the share of the other partner on a gradual basis and ultimately become the sole owner of the asset (BNM, 2015). On the other hand, for the purpose of acquiring assets under construction, MM may be arranged with istisna' whereby the partners enter into an istisna' contract with a third party. Subsequently, one of the partners will lease his share of the asset ownership to the other partners based on ijarah mawsufah fi dhimmah (forward lease) until the asset is completed. Simultaneously, the partner who is the lessee will purchase the share of the other partner on a gradual basis and ultimately become the sole owner of the asset (BNM, 2015).

On the other hand, MM with the objective of venturing in profit generating business activities must be governed by the principle of shirkah al-'aqd and therefore must have the effect of shirkah al-'aqd that refers to "a contract executed between two or more partners to venture into business activities to generate profit" (BNM, 2015). Under shirkah al-'aqd, a partner is an agent for the other partners. In this regard, the conduct of one partner in the ordinary course of business represents the partnership (BNM, 2015). For examples: several Islamic banks such as Affin Bank Berhad, HSBC Amanah, Public Islamic Bank, RHB Islamic Bank and Standard Chartered Saadiq offered MM Home Financing as one of their financing products. (Nurul Iffah & Rusni Hassan, 2019). The move, taken by the Islamic banks in Malaysia to embrace MM financing products, signifies a positive development of the Islamic finance industry as it implies a departure from the heavy reliance on the debt-based products such as Al Bay Bithaman Ajil (BBA) (Tuan Soh, 2019).

However, there are several legal and Shari'ah issues faced by the Islamic banks in implementing MM, such as complicated documentation preparation, lack of lawyers who are experts in understanding the MM contract (Shahwan et al., 2013), the usage of rental rate, which is very much affected by location, tax regulations, (Meera & Abdul Razak, 2005), issues related to revaluation of property such as redemption, defaults and termination of contract (Meera & Abdul Razak, 2009). At present, most of the Islamic banks in Malaysia that offered Al-Musharakah Mutanaqisah financing have replaced it with other products such as Commodity Murabahah, Ijarah Muntahiyah bit Tamlik and Istisna' (Subky et al., 2017).

Al-Musharakah in Capital Market

Al-Musharakah plays a significant role in the Islamic Capital Market. In the sukuk market (i.e. bond market), Al-Musharakah (together with Al-Musharakah Mutanaqisah) is one of the commonly used financing contracts. Sukuk Al-Musharakah is issued for the purpose of using the funds to create a new project and to develop a financing system for transactions based on business partnership (Moriguchi et al., 2016). Sukuk holders who are involved in this partnership will be sharing profits based on an agreement with an agreed ratio while losses will be shared based on sukuk's holding (Bi, 2008). For instance, RAM rating in Malaysia has withdrawn their rating of Lingkaran Trans Kota Sdn Bhd's of RM1.15 billion Sukuk Al-Musharakah Islamic Medium Term Notes 1 Programmes and RM300 millions Sukuk Al-Musharakah Islamic Medium-Term Notes II Programme, Kesas Sdn Bhd's of RM735 million Sukuk Al-Musharakah Islamic Medium-Term Notes and Project Smart Holdings Sdn Bhd's financing facilities of RM330 million Islamic Medium-Term Notes Facility, following their full redemption on 13 October 2022 (RAM Rating Services Berhad, 2022).

Nevertheless, Shari'ah issues have some effects on Al-Musharakah's applicability in the sukuk market. Some argue that the decline in sukuk by more than 50% by the end of 2008 is due to the debates over Shari'ah principles' compliance with some Sukuk structures and the rising cost of borrowing (Hijazi et al., 2009). The decline in Sukuk issuance is also due to the credit crunch, which forced investors to step aside from the fixed income market (Khudari & Saad, 2019). Therefore, AAOIFI Shari'ah board issued a "Resolution on Sukuk" in 2008 which aims to provide some guidance in relation to Sukuk structures (Bi, 2008; Salah, 2010). Similarly, in Malaysian market practice, the Shari'ah Advisory Council of Securities Commission of Malaysia in its 251st meeting held on 13 December 2021 resolved the issue of restructuring of Sukuk Al-Musharakah i.e., on the existing sukuk Al-Musharakah as a capital contribution in new sukuk Al-Musharakah (Securities Commission of Malaysia, 2021).

Malaysia is leading in sustainability sukuk issuance in ASEAN with a 56% market share of the total ASEAN sustainability sukuk issuance as of November 2021 (Bernama, 2022). According to Capital Market Malaysia, the global Islamic finance industry, with total assets of US$3.06 trillion (US$1=RM4.63) as of 2021, has the potential to contribute significantly towards the existing funding gap in meeting the United Nations' Sustainable Development goals (SDGs) (Bernama, 2022). Malaysia has contributed in facilitating innovative sukuk structures such as the exchangeable sukuk Al-Musharakah by Khazanah Nasional Berhad and First sukuk Al-Musharakah by Al-Musharakah One Capital Berhad (RM2.5 billion) in 2005 (Bank Negara Malaysia, 2007). According to the International Islamic Financial Market Report of 2020, global Sukuk issuance posted solid growth in 2019 with 18.32% compared to 2018, an amount of USD 145.70 billion, with Malaysia continuing to be the largest Sukuk issuer with 43.16% of total issuances (IIFM, 2020).

Islamic financiers and regulatory authorities have begun to struggle with the challenge of devising a framework for green finance as businesses seek to raise capital for socially and environmentally sustainable ventures (Jaafar & Brightman, 2022). Sustainable and responsible investment SRI has been referred to as socially responsible investment (Ministry of Finance Malaysia, 2013), SRI (Securities Commission, 2014) and sustainable, responsible and impactful investment [Centre for Islamic Wealth Management (CIWM), 2015]. In other words, SRI also refers to any type of investment process which combines investors' financial objectives with concerns regarding environmental, societal and governance issues (Moghul & Safar-Aly, 2015). The presence of supporting regulatory structures such as Social and Responsible Investing (SRI) Sukuk Framework by the Securities Commission Malaysia (SC) in 2014 is valuable for the natural advancement of the sukuk market due to the rising awareness of investors and institutions towards ethically and socially responsible investment (MIFC, 2016). It raised US$59.2 million, with proceeds used to finance its large-scale solar project (Jaafar & Brightman, 2022). Significantly, Bursa Malaysia will be launching the Shari'ah-compliant Voluntary Carbon Market exchange that will enable Malaysian companies to purchase voluntary carbon credits to offset their carbon emission footprint and to support financing for projects and solutions that reduce, remove or avoid greenhouse gas emissions (Bernama, 2022).

A total of 13 SRI (Sustainable and Responsible Investment) sukuk were issued in Malaysia by April 2020, with proceeds channeled into green building and renewable energy projects as well as social initiatives (Jaafar & Brightman, 2022). This has taken place in a context of unremarkable performance in terms of achievement of the UN Sustainable Development Goals (SDGs): the UN Sustainable Development Solutions Network's 2021 Sustainable Development Report attributes to Malaysia a score of 70.88 (Jaafar & Brightman, 2022). An SRI market would allow Malaysia's capital market to promote new capital formation through innovative financing instruments. It is hoped that the global challenge of sustainability will become the catalyst for more SRI Sukuk Al-Musharakah to be offered in the future.

Al-Musharakah in Trade Finance Products

Trade finance is important to support foreign and domestic business and trade activities. It mitigates trade transaction risks such as the risk of non-payment and non-receipt of goods, especially in cross-border business and trade transactions.

Al-Musharakah is also used for funding working capital for traders/customers to purchase raw materials or goods. Additionally, Al-Musharakah can be used for financing imports and exports (Usmani, 1999). An exporter or importer can arrange for a single transaction based on Al-Musharakah and share the profit with the financier according to a pre-agreed ratio (Usmani, 1999). Al-Musharakah can also be used in a letter of credit. A letter of credit (LC) is a legal undertaking in writing by the issuing bank, given to a seller/exporter or a beneficiary at the instruction of the buyer/importer or applicant to pay at sight (cash) or at a fixed future date (usance) for a stipulated amount of money (fixed), provided that the documents presented are in full compliance with the terms and conditions of the credit (Rusni et al., 2016). Under the principle of Al-Musharakah, the customer will negotiate his LC requirements and the terms of his Al-Musharakah financing with the bank (ISRA, 2016). The customer will place a deposit with the bank for his share of the cost of goods to be purchased or imported under the principle of wadiah (Bank Islam Malaysia Berhad, 1994). Once the LC is established, the bank will use the customer's deposit and its own funds to pay the negotiating bank (Rusni et al., 2016). The bank will then release the documents to the customer, who will take possession of the goods and dispose of them in the manner agreed upon in the Al-Musharakah agreement (Alias et al., 1995). The profits generated from this transaction will be shared between the bank and the customer in accordance with the Al-Musharakah agreement (Rusni et al., 2016; Alias et al., 1995). It is obvious that the Al-Musharakah instrument could assist the customer/corporation in obtaining financing to facilitate business and trade transactions that need the bank to make payments to its counterparty and capital for managing the business.

Al-Musharakah in Islamic Social Finance

Muslim countries' financial markets, including Malaysia, are now shifting beyond their traditional function as a financial intermediary towards the creation of socially responsible objectives and ethical financial solutions for the stability and well-being of the community and society. This is reflected in various Islamic social finance activities undertaken by Islamic banks in collaboration with State Islamic Religious Councils (SIRCs) and strategic implementation partners. Nowadays, Islamic social finance may also cover modern forms of Islamic financial services such as Islamic microfinance, sukuk and takaful: for instance, iTekad microfinance, which is a blended social finance program by Islamic banks offering seed capital, microfinancing, structured training to micro-entrepreneurs in collaboration with implementation partners (BNM, 2021) and the MyZakat initiative, which pools zakat from participating financial institutions to support asnaf (groups eligible to receive zakat) microentrepreneurs in partnership with Amanah Ikhtiar Malaysia (a micro-credit organization) and Agensi Kaunseling dan Pengurusan Kredit (a credit counselling and debt management agency set up by BNM) by providing up to RM3,000 seed capital to start a business (AIBIM, 2021). However, regulatory hurdles relate to the utilization of philanthropic Islamic social finance instruments such as zakat and waqf, which are within the exclusive jurisdiction of the states.

For this reason, this collaboration is possible only if the states provide their consent. Islamic microfinance could be considered as an emerging social welfare market niche as well as an alternative form of ethical financing and investment (Bello et al., 2020). The integration of social into commercial finance will create a much larger pool of funds and at the same time pave ways for the creation of financing or projects and businesses that are not only commercially viable but also socially motivated, hence sustainable and serving a higher purpose. Thus, the profit and loss sharing approach of Islamic microfinance can be regarded as a viable and better alternative to serve the poor entrepreneurs (Islam & Ahmad, 2020). Profit sharing can substitute for interest while mutual management can be expected to enhance the profitability and growth of the business.

On the other hand, the provision that the Islamic microfinance institution share financial loss might encourage clients to undertake risky ventures or rejuvenate non-performing businesses. Besides Mudharabah, Al-Musharakah can also contribute to institutional sustainability and growth while scaling up the income of poor entrepreneurs. However, it is significant to highlight that currently, qard and kafala are largely utilized in microfinance exercises as well as banking products and services (AIBIM, 2021). In particular, the application of Al-Musharakah and Al-Mudharabah in Islamic microfinance is said to be totally absent (Rozzani et al., 2017; Usman et al., 2017).

Al-Musharakah as an Alternative Model in Takaful

Takaful is defined in Section 2 of IFSA 2013 as an arrangement based on mutual assistance in which takaful participants agree to contribute to a common fund providing for mutual financial benefits payable to the takaful participants or their beneficiaries on the occurrence of pre-agreed events. Takaful insurance is primarily based on the Islamic principles of ta'awun (cooperation) and tabarru' (donation). The principle of mutual cooperation is deduced from a verse of the Holy Quran which reads: "Help one another in al-Birr and in al-Taqwa (virtue, righteousness and piety): but do not help one another in sin and transgression." Al-Ma'idah [5]: 2. The takaful industry has experimented with various models and contracts underlying the relationship between participants and takaful operators, such as the Mudharabah Model, which was the first model employed by takaful industry in Malaysia, the Wakalah model and hybrid model, i.e. combination of Mudharabah and Wakalah and the Wakaf model.

These models were subject to criticisms such as the issue of loss of ownership of the tabarru' fund used in takaful as prescribed by rules of hibah and the issue of surplus distribution (Mahbubi, 2016). One of the suggestions to resolve this issue is introducing a new model known as Al-Musharakah Ta'awuniyyah (cooperative partnership) – that is, a contract of cooperation and shared responsibility for mutual assistance with the objective of allowing indemnification to be given when needed, while eliminating the intention of some participants to profit from others. The calculation of contributions may differ from one person to another, and the net contribution may remain unknown until ex-post dividends are paid (Ahmad,

2014). This concept of Al-Musharakah Ta'awuniyyah was first proposed at the International Islamic Fiqh Academy (IIFA) Conferences in 2010. In response, in 2014 the International Shari'ah Research Academy for Islamic Finance (ISRA) Malaysia designed a takaful model based on Al-Musharakah Ta'awuniyah scheme. The proposed Al-Musharakah Ta'awuniyyah Takaful model is intended to provide mutual benefits to the participants of the Takaful model without engaging them in a commutative contract that is more akin to commercial partnership (Ahmad, 2014). On one hand, the ta'awun concept allows participants to make donations with the intention of helping each other within the Takaful group. On the other hand, the Al-Musharakah concept allows surplus or deficit funds to be shared in accordance with the principles of Al-Musharakah (Moriguchi et al., 2016). However, the potential gap between the proposed model and the requirements of business was acknowledged (Mahbubi, 2016). Further research is imminent to examine the commercial viability and practicality of the proposed model, taking into consideration its operational and technical concerns, such as pricing, underwriting, actuary etc.

Conclusion

The Islamic financial system in Malaysia has shifted from its infancy and growth stage to a phase of maturity. The Malaysian legal regime certainly strengthens Islamic finance by reinforcing the idea of risk sharing in the Islamic banking and finance businesses. The applicability of Al-Musharakah as an equity-based financing instrument is evident in Islamic banking, Takaful and the Islamic Capital market. It is obvious that the existence of IAP, together with the existing components of financial intermediation, will form a more complete and mutually complementary financial ecosystem. This platform creates a more extensive network for Islamic financial institutions to meet the more diversified demands of investors and ventures as a fundraising avenue that would bring benefits to the economy. As a result, the implementation of Al-Musharakah is expected to grow as it promotes mutuality, sustainability, interest in the business of all parties concerned and interest in the success of the end result. Furthermore, joint efforts of governments and the private sector to build public and private partnership as part of the full Islamic ecosystem will allow for a more equitable world. The achievement of such a goal requires Islamic financial institutions to integrate both profitability and development dimensions of Islamic finance when allocating their resources. Similarly, Al-Musharakah in Islamic social finance can be a valuable tool to promote Islamic economics, which in turn can alleviate poverty.

References

Abd Ghadas, Z. A. & Ali, E. (2009). Partners's Limited-Limited Liability in Partnership Structure: An Overview of the Common Law and the Sharī'ah. *Al-Shajarah*, 24(2).

Abd Ghadas, Z. A., & Ali, E. (2011). The Development of Partnership Based Structure in Comparison to the Concept of Musherakah (Sharikah) with Special Reference to Malaysia. *Journal of Islam in Asia*, 8.

Abdul-Rahman, A., & Nor, S. M. (2016). Challenges of Profit-and-Loss Sharing Financing in Malaysian Islamic Banking. *Geografia-Malaysian Journal of Society*, 12(2).

Abu Daud, Sunan Abi Daud, hadith no. 2936.

Adela, H. (2018). The Impact of Al-Musharakah Financing on the Monetary Policy in the Islamic Economy. *Review of Economics and Political Science*, 3(3/4).

Ahmad, A. U. F. (2014). Exploring the Model of Al-Musharakah Taʿāwuniyyah in Takaful. *ISRA Research Paper, 71.*

Ahmed, G. A. (2008). The Implication of Using Profit and Loss Sharing Modes of Finance in the Banking System, with a Particular Reference to Equity Participation (Partnership) Method in Sudan. *Humanomics*, 24(3).

Akin, T., Iqbal, Z., & Mirakhor, A. (2016). The Composite Risk-Sharing Finance Index: Implications for Islamic Finance. *Review of Financial Economics*, 31.

Al-Hakim, al-Mustadrak, hadith no. 2317.

Ali, M. M. (2016). Takaful Models: Their Evolution and Future Direction. *ICR Journal*, 7(4).

Alias, A. S. H., Kamarulzaman, N. R., & Bhupalan, R. (1993). *Guide to Islamic Banking in Malaysia: An Overview*. Kuala Lumpur: Institut Bank-Bank Malaysia.

Alias, A. S. H., Kamarulzaman, N. R., & Bhupalan, R. (1995). *Guide to Islamic Banking in Malaysia: An Overview*. Malaysia: Institut Bank-Bank Malaysia.

Association of Islamic Banking and Financial Institutions Malaysia (AIBIM). (2021). *Value-Based Intermediation Full Report, 2021*. https://aibim.com/contents/pages/val e-based-intermediation/AIBIM-VBI-Full-Report-2021.pdf

Astrom, Z. H. O. (2013). Credit Risk Management Pertaining to Profit and Loss Sharing Instruments in Islamic Banking. *Journal of Financial Reporting and Accounting*, 11(1).

Bank Islam Malaysia Berhad. (1994). *Islamic Banking Practice from Practitioners' Perspective*. Kuala Lumpur: BIM Publications.

Bank Negara Malaysia (BNM). (2007). *Financial Stability and Payment Systems Report*. www.bnm.gov.my/documents/20124/856398/cp02_001_whitebox.pdf

Bank Negara Malaysia (BNM). (2015). *Musyarakah*. www.bnm.gov.my/documents/20124/938039/Musyarakah.pdf/e99baaa9-d7cda61f-8d0a-9c9f2521dd4d?t=15922 18252160

Bank Negara Malaysia. (2021). *Additional Assistance for SMEs and Individuals Under Budget 2022*. www.bnm.gov.my/-/additional-assistance-budget-2022

Beck, T., Demirgüç-Kunt, A., & Merrouche, O. (2013). Islamic vs. Conventional Banking: Business Model, Efficiency and Stability. *Journal of Banking and Finance*, 37(2).

Bello, H. S., Hassan, Y. J., & Ahmad, N. (2020). Islamic Microfinance as a Veritable Socially Responsible Investment Towards Achieving Beneficial Social and Business Goals: A Literature Review. *Studies in Indian Place Names*, 40(60).

Bernama. (2022, November 11). *COP27: CMM Highlights Islamic Finance Role in Achieving Sustainable Development Goals*. www.bernama.com/en/business/news.php?id=2137442

Bi, F. (2008). *AAOIFI Statement on Sukuk and Its Implications*. Norton Rose Fulbright. www.nortonrosefulbright.com/knowledge/publications/16852/aaoifistatement-on-sukuk-and-its-implications

Bouheraoua, S., Eskandar, M., Kasri, N., Lajis, S. M., Hassan, H. K., Shishani, A., & Alaeddi, O. (2016). Implementing the IFSA Investment Account: A Risk-Sharing Banking Model. *International Shari'ah Research Academy for Islamic Finance (ISRA) Research Paper*.

Business Today. (2022, September 28). *HSBC Amanah Develops Framework that Aligns with VBI*. www.businesstoday.com.my/2022/09/28/hsbc-amanah-develops-framework-that-aligns-with-vbi/

Centre for Islamic Wealth Management (CIWM). (2015). *SRIs and the Case for Islamic Investment Funds*. www.mifc.com/repository/0186SRIe-Book.pdf

Chong, B. S., & Liu, M. H. (2009). Islamic Banking: Interest Free or Interest Based? *Pacific-Basin Finance Journal*, 17(10).

Fianto, B. A., Gan, C., Hu, B., & Roudaki, J. (2018). Equity Financing and Debt-Based Financing: Evidence from Islamic Microfinance Institutions in Indonesia. *Pacific-Basin Finance Journal*, 52.

Haneef, R., Kunhibava, S., & Smolo, E. (2011). Al-Musharakah Mutanaqisah and Legal Issues: Case Study of Malaysia. *ISRA International Journal of Islamic Finance*, 3(1).

Hassan, M., & Dridi, J. (2011). The Effects of the Global Crisis on Islamic and Conventional Banks: A Comparative Study. *Journal of International Commerce, Economics and Policy*, 2(2).

Hassan, R., Othman, A. A., Salleh, S., & Hussain, M. A. (2016). *Islamic Banking and Takaful* (3rd ed.). Malaysia: Pearson.

Hijazi, F., Howladar, K., Lotter, P., Hassoune, A., & Gribot-Carroz, D. (2009) *Global Sukuk Issuance: 2008 Slowdown Mainly Due to Credit Crisis, But Some Impact from Shari'ah Compliance Issues*. London: Moody's Investor Service.

International Islamic Financial Market (IIFM). (2020). *Sukuk Report, a Comprehensive Study of the Global Sukuk Market* (9th ed.). www.iifm.net/frontend/generaldocuments/bb676e86bd089c016b9d937badcce1881635251491.pdf

Investment Account Platform (IAP). (2021). *Newsletter*. https://iaplatform.com/showProjectImage?name=IAP_Newsletter_2021.pdf

Investment Account Platform. (2022). https://iaplatform.com/

Islam, R., & Ahmad, R. (2020). Applicability of Al-Mudharabah and Al-Musharakah as Islamic Micro-Equity Finance to Underprivileged Women in Malaysia. *The European Journal of Development Research*, 32(1).

ISRA. (2016). *Islamic Financial System: Principles and Operations*. Kuala Lumpur: ISRA.

Jaafar, A. Z., & Brightman, M. (2022). From Structure to Purpose: Green and Social Narratives, and the Shifting Morality of Islamic Finance in Kuala Lumpur. *Sustainability*, 14.

Khan, H. (2015). Some Implications of Debt Versus Equity-Based Financing in the Backdrop of Financial Crises. *Journal of Islamic Economics*, 28(1).

Khoutem, B. J., & Nedra, B. A. (2012). Islamic Participative Financial Intermediation and Economic Growth. *Journal of Islamic Economics, Banking and Finance*, 3(8).

Khudari, M., & Saad, N. M. (2019). Sukuk Issuance in the Emerging Markets-A Relative Evaluation. *International Journal of Engineering and Advanced Technology*, 9(1).

Louhichi, A., & Boujelbene, Y. (2016). Credit Risk, Managerial Behaviour and Macroeconomic Equilibrium within Dual Banking Systems: Interest-Free vs. Interest-Based Banking Industries. *Research in International Business and Finance*, 38.

The Malaysia International Islamic Financial Centre MIFC. (2016). *SRI and Green Sukuk: Challenges and Prospects*. www.mifc.com/-/sri-green-sukuk-challenges-prospects

Mat Ali, S. A. B., Hassan, R., & Othman, A. A. (2022). *Islamic Banking in Malaysia: Laws Applicable to Al-Musharakah Mutanaqisah Home Financing*. Kuala Lumpur: Malaha Press.

Meera, A. K. M., & Abdul Razak, D. (2005). Islamic Home Financing through Al-Musharakah Mutanaqisah and Al-Bay' Bithaman Ajil Contracts: A Comparative Analysis. *Review of Islamic Economics*, 9(2).

Meera, A. K. M., & Abdul Razak, D. (2009). Home Financing Through the Al-Musharakah Mutanaqisah Contracts: Some Practical Issues. *Islamic Economics*, 22(1).

Mili, M., & Abid, S. (2017). Moral Hazard and Risk-Taking Incentives in Islamic Banks: Does Franchise Value Matter? *International Journal of Islamic and Middle Eastern Finance and Management*, 10(1).

Ministry of Finance Malaysia. (2013). www.mof.gov.my

Moghul, U. F., & Safar-Aly, S. H. (2015). Green Sukuk: The Introduction of Islam's Environmental Ethics to Contemporary Islamic Finance. *Georgetown International Environmental Law Review*, 27(1).

Moriguchi, T., Khattak, M. A., Farhan, M., Firdaus, M., Worasutr, A., Hakim, A. L., Musthafa, F., & Muneeza, A. (2016). Contemporary Practices of Al-Musharakah in Financial Transactions. *International Journal of Management and Applied Research*, 3(2).

Narayan, P. K., & Phan, D. H. B. (2019). A Survey of Islamic Banking and Finance Literature: Issues, Challenges, and Future Directions. *Pacific-Basin Finance Journal*, 53.

Nurul'iffah, M. A., & Hassan, R. (2019). Why Islamic Banks Are Reluctant to Offer Al-Musharakah Mutanaqisah for Home Financing: The Case of Maybank Islamic and Affin Islamic Bank. *Turkish Journal of Islamic Economics*, 6(1), 51–66.

RAM Rating. (2022, October 14). *Existing Financing Facilities for RAM-Rated Three Highways Fully Redeemed Following Amanat Lebuhraya's Fundraising Exercise*. www.ram.com.my/pressrelease/?prviewid=6130

Rozzani, N., Mohamed, I. S., & Syed Yusuf, S. N. (2017). Risk Management Process: Profiling of Islamic Microfinance Providers. *Research in International Business and Finance*, 41.

Sadique, M. A. (2009). *Essentials of Al-Musharakah and Al-Mudharabah: Islamic Texts on Theory of Partnership*. Kuala Lumpur: IIUM Press.

Salah, O. (2010). Islamic Finance: The Impact of the AAOIFI Resolution on Equity-Based Sukuk Structures. *Law and Financial Markets Review*, 4(5).

Sapuan, N. M. (2016). An Evolution of Al-Mudharabah Contract: A Viewpoint from Classical and Contemporary Islamic Scholars. *Procedia Economics and Finance*, 35(3).

Securities Commission. (2014). *Press Release: SC Introduces Sustainable and Responsible Investment Sukuk Framework*. www.sc.com.my/post_archive/sc-introduces-sustainable-and responsible-investment-sukuk-framework/

Securities Commission Malaysia. (2021). *Resolutions of the Shari'ah Advisory Council of the Securities Commission Malaysia*. www.sc.com.my/api/documentms/download.ashx?id=38cdfc05-7419-480a-ae40-3d38a513452e

Shahwan, S., Mohammad, M. O., & Abdul Rahman, Z. (2013). Home Financing Pricing Issues in the Bay' Bithaman Ajil (BBA) and Al-Musharakah Mutanaqisah (MMP). *Global Journal Al-Thaqafah*, 3(2).

Subky, K. H., Liu, J. Y., Abdullah, M., Farhan Mokhtar, Z., & Faizrakhman, A. (2017). The Implication of Al-Musharakah Mutanaqisah in Malaysian Islamic Banking Arena: A Perspective on Legal Documentation. *International Journal of Management and Applied Research*, 4(1).

Tuan Soh, T. B. H. (2019). *Al-Musharakah and Its Compatibility with the Malaysian Legal and Regulatory Framework: An Examination on the Implementation of Risk Sharing* (Doctoral Dissertation). Newcastle Law School. https://theses.ncl.ac.uk/jspui/handle/10443/4739

Usman, A. S., Tasmin, R., Ulum, Z. K. A. B., & Abubakar, A. A. (2017). The Role of Islamic Micro-Finance in Enhancing the Wellbeing of the Clients: Exploratory Factor Analysis. *Journal on Innovation and Sustainability RISUS*, 8(3).

Usmani, M. T. (1998). *Objection on Al-Musharakah Financing*. www.learIslamicFinance.com

Usmani, M. T. (1999). The Concept of Al-Musharakah and Its Application as an Islamic Method of Financing. *Arab Law Quarterly*, 14(3).

Usmani, M. T. (2002). *An Introduction to Islamic Finance*. The Hague: Kluwer Law International.

15 Hibah al-Ruqba and Its Contribution to Sustainable Economy

Akhtarzaite binti Abdul Aziz, Farah Herneeda binti Bahar & Nur Hafizah binti Miszairi

Introduction

Islam puts great importance on the administration of estate by Muslim families. Administration of estate can be done during the lifetime of the Muslims or after death of the Muslims. During his lifetime, a Muslim can administer his estates through various forms of tools such as *wasiyyah*, *hibah* and *waqf*, while after his death, his estate will be distributed to his heirs in accordance with the *faraid* system as set by the Shari'ah. *Hibah al-Ruqba* is a type of *hibah* that has been discussed by the Muslim jurists for decades. In a simple definition, *Hibah al-Rugba* is a type of conditional gift between two or more parties, giving rights to the surviving parties in the case of the death of any of the parties. In fact, many research papers have discussed whether *Hibah al-Ruqba* is a valid contract that conforms to Shari'ah requirements, forms of *sighah* of *Hibah al-Ruqba* and its contemporary usage as a potential tool to transfer assets to a recipient/beneficiary. According to the definition given by the Islamic Financial Services Act 2013, funds deposited by customers into a bank account with an Islamic financial institution can be categorized into two groups – one is called a deposit account; the second is called an investment account. The differentiation is made by considering the type of Shari'ah concept applied to that account. Deposit products offered by banks consist of savings accounts, current accounts and term deposit accounts. These accounts may be opened by individuals under single or joint names. Investment products have two types: restricted accounts and unrestricted accounts. This account can be opened by individuals under single name or joint names as well. Therefore, joint accounts apply to both deposit and investment accounts. Thus, the current issue could possibly occur in all types of accounts offered by Islamic banks. This research will study the concept of survivorship from a legal perspective and the *takyif fiqhi* of *Hibah al-Ruqba* for survivorship concept from the Shari'ah perspective. The research will also study whether *Hibah al-Ruqba* can apply to deposit and investment accounts under Muslim joint names as an alternative tool for the surviving party to operate the account as usual and operational requirements in operationalizing *Hibah al-Ruqba* by Islamic banks in Malaysia. While some Islamic banks already implement right of survivorship, there is room to study whether the current practice complies with Shari'ah and legal requirements on *Hibah*.

DOI: 10.4324/9781003468653-18

Joint Account and the Concept of Survivorship

Joint accounts are those accounts in the names of two or more people (known as the parties), excluding the accounts of trustees, partnerships and personal representatives of dead people.[1] The most common type encountered is that account opened by a husband and his wife.[2] Under a joint account, a mandate will normally be taken. This will render the customers jointly and severally liable for any debt owed to the bank.[3] The bank's mandate for joint accounts will specify:

- Who will sign cheques.
- Joint and severally liable of all parties for debit balances on the account.
- That if one party dies, then the remainder can authorize the release of funds.[4]

In the absence of a written mandate, the presumption will be that both or all signatures are required.[5] The choice lies with the customers, and they can authorize the bank either only to accept transactions authorized on the signatures of all parties to the account or to make payment upon the signature of only one party or two parties to the account. If a bank debits its customers' account outside the mandate, it can be liable for damages to the injured party.[6] Edelstein[7] on the right of survivorship on a bank account writes, if someone is about trying to achieve estate planning goals, he probably had prepared a will, set up a power of attorney and possibly also a living trust. He had probably taken estate planning goals into account when he had named the beneficiaries to receive his estate such as such as house, insurance and so on. This includes bank accounts. However, other than a will, there is also available a way to make sure the bank account gets passed to the person he had chosen. This is called the right of survivorship.

The right of survivorship is an account feature whereby if the primary holder of the account passes away, the named individual retains full ownership over all of the funds in the account. As with naming a beneficiary, a right of survivorship enables the assets in the underlying account to bypass the probate process after one passes away. This means that the funds in the account will not be distributed per one's will – the right of survivorship conveys ownership to the person he'd identified. It is important to understand that joint account ownership does not necessarily imply a right of survivorship; in other words, the right of survivorship is not automatic. One might have a joint account with his spouse, for example, but if that account does not include a right of survivorship provision, then the amounts in the account would go through the probate process upon the death of one of the joint account holders. However, even without such a clause, the bank may pay the whole balance to the survivor.[8] While it might not seem particularly problematic, one may wish to consider potential situations where there may be other family members (such as children from prior marriages) who might make a claim to the funds in the joint account.

A right of survivorship feature can go hand in hand with joint account ownership, but it does not necessarily need to. Joint ownership over a bank account gives each owner full rights to access the account, potentially without the consent or knowledge of the other. Therefore, one needs to be very careful when setting up a new account if he only wishes to convey a right of survivorship to someone, but not give them any current ownership rights over the account. From what Edelstein mentioned, the law permits the following:

- under the law, it is permissible to give someone one's wealth or estate without the need to go through a will – which is called the right of survivorship;
- the portion of asset which is passed to someone through the right of survivorship will not be pooled together with the deceased's other estate. In other words, the funds or wealth shall be effectively transferred to the nominee upon death of the deceased;
- however, it is important to note that the right of survivorship in a joint account is not automatic, thus clear stipulation of survivorship clause must be made;
- it is also important to understand that the right of survivorship may not necessarily be understood as joint ownership. One can pass the right to the account to someone who is not a party to the joint account through the establishment of the right of survivorship.

Practically, under normal circumstances, if the joint account is opened by a husband and his wife, upon the death of the husband, then his widow can continue to operate the former joint account, which then becomes automatically a sole account in her name.[9] This means that the surviving spouse has access to the funds immediately upon the death of his or her partner without waiting for probate to be obtained. When the certificate of death has been presented to the bank, the name of the deceased party can be deleted form the title of the account and future statement will be issued in the name of the survivor or survivors only. New arrangements should be made for any correspondence which was formerly addressed to the deceased at his own address if it was different from that of the other party or parties to the account.[10]

Concept of Hibah al-Ruqba from Fiqhi Perspective

Hibah is an alternative for Muslims to allocate benefits to beneficiaries, and *hibah* as normally practiced is given *inter vivos* during the lifetime of the parties. *Hibah* is a voluntary giving of one's wealth without the expectation of any replacement or exchange with the transferring effect on the ownership during lifetime. It means to give something to praise someone with honor because of the intention of the *hibah* provider.[11] *Hibah* in its original form must be absolute and takes effect immediately once the conditions are fulfilled. This means that the subject matter of the *hibah* automatically transfers from the donor to the beneficiary once the *hibah* is made. However, scholars have different opinions on conditional *hibah*, whereby the donor intends that his donation will only take place upon occurrence of certain events. One of the important forms of conditional *hibah* is *Hibah al-Ruqba. Ruqba* is a derivative verb from *ruqub*, *irtiqab* and *taraqqub*, which all mean waiting, because both parties wait for the death of the other, whereas death is uncertain.[12] This meaning is in line with the following saying of Allah (swt).

> So watch, [O Muhammad]; indeed, they are watching [for your end].[13]

In the context of its use in Arabic language, *ruqba* has three meanings. First, by giving the right of ownership from one person to another so if any one of the parties dies, the *hibah* asset will be owned by the surviving party. Second, it is a gift to a person where if any one of the parties dies, the *hibah* asset will be owned by the donor's heirs. Third, a gift to a person, for example a house for him to occupy, where in case the recipient dies, the house will be returned to the donor for his occupation.[14] According to Al-Kasani, *Hibah al-Ruqba* is a form of *hibah* where the ownership of the asset is suspended. In this case, there is a risk of uncertainty, i.e. whether or not the asset will be transferred to the recipient. Therefore, those ownerships that do not have the possibility of this risk are not called *hibah*; rather, they are an *'ariyah* (borrowing). This is because *ruqba* has the possibility of *muraqabah* (waiting) and possibility of *riqab*, i.e. *hibah* by way of *ruqba*. Further, he mentioned that if it carries the first meaning, then that can become an argument, whereas if it carries the second meaning, then that cannot become an argument. Notwithstanding this, there is no difference between the two in essence as both are used literally in *Hibah al-Ruqba*. Therefore, someone must have intention towards his pronunciation. If the person intends it to become *Hibah al-Ruqba*, then it is permissible without dispute among scholars, and if the persons intends to wait for the death of the other party, then it is not permissible without dispute among scholars.[15] *Hibah al-Ruqba* is a form of *hibah* traditionally practiced by the Arab people to transfer the ownership of an asset subject to condition of survivorship of the parties. In other words, it is a form of a gift that is made based on the survivorship principle, where whoever survives upon the demise of the other party will own the *hibah* asset.

Juristic Opinions on Hibah al-Ruqba

In general, the majority of Muslim jurists acknowledged that *hibah* with condition of *'Umra* and *ruqba* is valid. However, there was a minority of Muslim jurists who mentioned that *hibah* with condition of *'Umra* and *ruqba* is void. According to Al-Mawardi, Muslim scholars who held this stance are Dawud together with Zahiri groups and Ahl Hadith. Al-Tabari also claimed that there were Muslim scholars who rejected the validity of *'Umra* and *ruqba*.[16] This view is mainly based the saying of the Prophet (saw):

> Do not give (*hibah*) either by way of *'umra* or *ruqba*.

However, according to Al-Baghawi, this hadith is not meant to disallow the practice of *'Umra* and *ruqba*; rather, it is meant to provide guidance to Muslims, which means: do not give *hibah* on *'Umra* which you intend the *hibah* the asset be returned to you, for the asset will be part of inheritance of the recipient.[17] The majority of the scholars, while maintaining the validity of the *hibah*, dispute whether the condition is binding. The scholars have different views in accepting *Hibah al-Ruqba* condition as follows:

Those who viewed *Hibah al-Ruqba* as valid, but condition is nullified. Most Muslim jurists are of the opinion that *hibah* which is temporary in nature, such as

Hibah al-Ruqba and *hibah 'Umra* are permissible, but the conditions are nullified. They argued that should the conditions be applied, it will mean that it is in conflict with *muqtadha al-aqad* and the requirement of the Shari'ah rules. They were also guided by the saying of the Prophet (saw):[18]

> Look after your property and do not hibah it by way of 'umra because whoever hibah something by way of 'umra, then it becomes the possession of the person to whom it has been hibah.

On the other hand, Al-Kasani opined that *hibah* with condition of *ruqba* was not conflicting with *muqtadha al-aqad.*[19]

Those who viewed *Hibah al-Ruqba* as valid and condition is also valid. Some Muslim jurists from the Hanbali, Imam Malik, Imam Zuhri, *Mazhab* Abu Thur and others, as well as the early view (*qaul qadim*) of Imam al-Syafi'e, are of the opinion that *hibah 'Umra* is permissible, and its condition is valid provided it is not mentioned by the giver of the *hibah* that the asset which is put on *hibah* will be owned by the *hibah* receiver's next of kin after the death of the *hibah* receiver. This means that item will be returned to the *hibah* giver after the death of *hibah* receiver. There are other opinions whose approach is that being temporary in nature, in reality this is not *hibah* but *'ariyah* (lending)[20] as explained by Al-Kasani. The *mazhad* that allows *Hibah al-Ruqba* and *Hibah 'Umra* made the following saying of the Prophet (PBUH) as their argument:

> *(Hibah) 'Umra* and *Ruqba* are allowed for them.

Based on this discussion, it can be summarized that among the important issues which have brought about differing opinions among Muslim jurists on *hibah*, *'Umra* and *Hibah al-Ruqba* focus on the element of *hibah* which is temporary in nature and *hibah* that is *ta'liq* within a person's lifespan. Both issues have drawn different reactions among the Muslim jurists.

Contemporary opinions on *Hibah al-Ruqba.* The Shari'ah Advisory Council of Bank Negara Malaysia ("SAC of BNM") has allowed the application of *hibah* in takaful whereby upon the death of the takaful participants, all takaful benefits will become the rights of his nominated child and will not be distributed amongst the other legal heirs of the deceased according to *faraid*. Nevertheless, if the takaful participant is still alive when the takaful certificate matures, the benefit will be surrendered to him. SAC of BNM considers this practice as falling under the concept of *Hibah al-Ruqba*. BNM further outlines the restricted application of conditional *hibah* to takaful only in its Policy Document of *Hibah* as follows:[21]

A conditional *hibah* upon the demise of the donor must only be applied in takaful. On the other hand, the Shari'ah Advisory Council of Securities Malaysia ("SAC of SC") at its 44th meeting on January 2003 passed a resolution to accept the use of *Hibah al-Ruqba* principal as the Shari'ah basis in implementing the *Hibah* Declaration Form for transactions involving joint unit trust fund accounts, especially for Muslim account holders.[22] The resolution is based on the opinion of *mazhab* that allows *Hibah al-Ruqba* and *hibah 'Umra* whose argument based on the following *hadith* of the Prophet (saw):[23]

(Hibah) 'Umra and Ruqba are allowed for them

Despite the two rulings accepting *Hibah al-Ruqba* applications in takaful and *Hibah* Declaration in joint unit trust fund accounts in Malaysia, its application other than areas mentioned is still questionable.

Proposal for Application of *Hibah al-Ruqba* in Joint Accounts

The practice of the Islamic banks in Malaysia on the treatment of deceased joint accounts varies between banks. The study had examined the survivorship clauses (from each banks' website) for joint names in deposit and investment account products offered by 12 Islamic banks in Malaysia.

Fraction of Islamic Banks Practice Towards Credit Balance in Deceased's Joint Accounts

58% (or seven) of Islamic banks have been practicing paying the credit balance to the surviving party, 25% (or three) have been practicing that the credit balance is subject to the Shari'ah law, i.e. subject to the *faraid* system, while another 17% (or two) of Islamic banks have been practicing that the surviving parties only act as trustee of the joint accounts. From the survey, it was noted that there are three different approaches taken by the bank in the event of death of any one of the joint account holders:

- Payment of credit balance in the account to the surviving parties;
- That the credit balance is subject to Shari'ah law;
- That the surviving parties act as trustees to the account.

In other words, in all three situations, the bank will no longer be responsible for the funds, as it will now fall on the surviving party to distribute the funds according to *faraid*. From the Shari'ah point of view, the position of the surviving party is only as an administrator. In other words, the surviving parties do not enjoy the absolute right of survivorship; rather, they are exposed to the applicable law at that point of time, such as inheritance law, in case there are other claimants to the accounts from the deceased heirs. This research proposes to use *Hibah al-Ruqba* as a tool to expedite the process of transferring ownership of the funds in the joint account holders to the surviving parties, giving the ownership right to the surviving party absolutely and not subject to distribution based on *faraid*. However, clear provision must be made to indicate the intention of the parties.

During Account Opening

Under the normal modus operandi of a bank, when customers want to open an account they must fill out an account opening form. The researcher proposes to insert a *Hibah al-Ruqba* clause which all joint account holders, such as husband and wife, will sign if they agree to apply *Hibah al-Ruqba* in case of death of either party. This also protects the banks from unnecessary legal proceedings in case other parties claim the funds in the account. In addition, the clauses related to *Hibah al-Ruqba* may be inserted in the terms and conditions of the account that has been signed by both parties.

Update Signatory upon Presentation of Death Certificate by the Surviving Party

In case the mandate assigned to the account is joint signatory, the surviving party who presents the death certificate of the deceased must update the signatory condition so that he or she can legally operate the account. The bank officer also needs to ensure that the signatory condition is updated accordingly. This is to avoid dispute and the liability of the bank in the future.

Issues in *Hibah al-Ruqba* with Joint Names of Deposit and Investment Account

Legal Framework for Hibah

In order for *hibah* to become a potential alternative method of estate planning management, there must be a specific law which governs the substantive and procedural aspect of law. This is because it is widely recognized that there must be certain laws to legalize the rule. It is undoubted that the property will remain the donor's property however passionately she or he may have wished to give it away if it does not comply with the principle of law. Thus, there must be specific a law to regulate and control the implementation. In Western countries, the formalities of the law of donative transfers, including gift *inter vivos*, have a respectable historical pedigree. The requirement that a gift be delivered was discussed by Coke as early as 1675. Thus, there is an urgent need to introduce a complete legal framework of *hibah* for the implementation of this mechanism. Without the proposed framework, the implementation of *hibah* could not be brought to fruition. This complete and comprehensive legal framework must also be outlined to overcome some statutory, non-statutory and practical impediments for the implementation of *hibah*.[24]

Denial of the Right of Other Legal Heirs Over the Donor's Wealth

Hibah is a form of voluntary gift on the basis of compassion of the donor towards the one he intends to give his wealth. Notwithstanding this, *Hibah al-Ruqba* could potentially be denying the right of the other legal heirs over the donor's wealth. For example, this is true when a father of six children only opens joint accounts with the first three. Once the father passes away, funds in the joint accounts will be owned by the respective children while the father's other wealth will be distributed according to *faraid*. This may lead to dispute among the children. It is important to note that Islam does not set specific rates or limits for property for *hibah*. Since the property to be given out as a gift is owned by the donor, it is up to the donor to consider the rate at which the property is intended to be given. However, Islam encourages *hibah* to be given fairly, especially if it is given to children. Therefore, it is important for Muslim families to plan their estates accordingly and with clear and certain provisions, including those related to joint accounts.

Conclusion

Joint accounts can be operated as per mandates set by the accountholder, such as joint signatory or alternate signatory. For non-Muslim account holders, in case either one dies, the surviving party has the right of survivorship to operate the account from a legal perspective. As for Muslim account holders, currently there is no automatic right of ownership, as the funds in the account are subject to *faraid* system or *wasiyyah*. The most Shari'ah principle-mirroring right of survivorship in law is *Hibah al-Ruqba*. Muslim jurists have different opinions about the validity of *Hibah al-Ruqba*. Their differences revolve around the issue of condition attached to it, as based on its original ruling, *hibah* is a voluntary act which should not be attached to any condition. However, SAC of SC and SAC of BNM allow restricted application of *Hibah al-Ruqba*, which currently applies in takaful benefit and in *Hibah* Declaration Form for transactions involving joint unit trust fund accounts, especially for Muslim account holders. The application of *Hibah al-Ruqba* apart from the two cases allowed is still questionable. Based on the current practice of Islamic banks, the survivorship clause is inserted in the account's terms and conditions. This may potentially expose them to legal risk. The research proposed to have a *Hibah al-Ruqba* contract in the account opening form signed by both parties as under Shari'ah, *aqad* is important. In addition, in the eyes of law, once there is a written contract, it is easier to enforce *Hibah al-Ruqba*. It is proposed to extend the resolution by BNM and Securities Commission in *Hibah al-Ruqba* on the permissibility of *Hibah al-Ruqba* to the case of joint account holders to give absolute ownership to the surviving party if they so wished. However, the application of *Hibah al-Ruqba*, as it is highly disputed by scholars, entails several issues that need to be addressed. The current legal system should be enhanced where there is a need to have regulation on the issue to avoid uncertainty. The Muslims also need to understand the concept of *hibah* in terms of distribution and implementation so that there is no dispute among heirs in case of death of the Muslims concerned.

Notes

1 Keith Pond and Geoff Lipscombe, *The Business of Banking: An Introduction to the Modern Financial Services*, p 130.
2 J.E. Kelly, *Practice of Banking* 1, p 35.
3 Graham Robert, *Law Relating to Financial Services*, p 61.
4 Keith Pond and Geoff Lipscombe, *The Business of Banking: An Introduction to the Modern Financial Services*, p 130.
5 Graham Robert, *Law Relating to Financial Services*, p 61.
6 J.E. Kelly, *Practice of Banking 1*, p 36.

7 Walter Edelstein, February 14, 2014, available from 4: http://bankingadvice.com/what-is-right-of-survivorship-on-a-bank-account/. Accessed on 10 November 2019.
8 Graham Robert, *Law Relating to Financial Services*, p 61.
9 Keith Pond and Geoff Lipscombe, *The Business of Banking: An Introduction to the Modern Financial Services Industry*, p 130.
10 J.E. Kelly, *Practice of Banking 1*, p 36.
11 Muhammad Ridhwan Ab. Aziz, *Islamic Commercial Law (Fiqh Muamalat): Theory and Application of Selected Contracts*, p 30.
12 Al-Imam Alauddin Abu Bakar bin Mas'ud Al-Kasani Al-Hanafi, Bada'i al-Sana'i fi Tartib Al-Syara'i 8, p 105.
13 Surah Al-Dukhan, 44, p. 59.
14 Nasrul Hisyam Nor Muhamad, Umra dan Ruqba: Analisis Mengenai Kesannya Terhadap Kontrak Hibah dan Potensinya Sebagai Instrumen Agihan Harta, p 8.
15 Al-Kasani,
16 Nasrul Hisyam, Nor Muhamad, 'Umra dan Ruqba: Analisis Mengenai Kesannya Terhadap Kontrak Hibah dan Potensinya Sebagai Instrumen Agihan Harta, p 11.
17 Al-Baghawi, Al-Tahdhib fi Fiqh Al-Imam Al-Syafi'e, p 534.
18 Securities Commission, Resolutions of the Securities Commission Shari'ah Advisory Council, p 130.
19 Al-Kasani, Bada'i Sana'i fi Tartib al-Syara'i, p 106.
20 Securities Commission, Resolutions of the Securities Commission Shari'ah Advisory Council, p 131.
21 Bank Negara Malaysia, Hibah, p 6, available from: www.bnm.gov.my/index.php?ch=57&pg=137&ac=515&bb=file. Accessed on 2 January 2023.
22 Securities Commission, Resolutions of the Securities Commission Shari'ah Advisory Council, p 129.
23 Securities Commission, p 132.
24 Rusnadewi Abdul Rashid, Siti Aishah Hassan and Noor Inayah Yaakub, A Need for Legal Framework of Gift Inter Vivos (Hibah) in Malaysian Estate Planning, p 30.

References

Al-Imam Abu Muhammad Al-Hussain bin Mas'ud bin Muhammad bin Al-Farra' Al-Baghawi (1998). *Al-Tahdhib fi Fiqh Al-Imam Al-Syafi'e* (1st ed., Vol. 4). Beirut & Lubnan: Dar Al-Kutub Al-Ilmiyah.

Bank Negara Malaysia. *Hibah*. www.bnm.gov.my/index.php?ch=57&pg=137&ac=515&bb=file (Accessed 2 January 2023).

Kelly, J. E. (1987). *Practice of Banking 1* (2nd ed.). London: Pitman Publishing.

Muhamad, N. H. N. (2012). Umra dan Ruqba: Analisis Mengenai Kesannya Terhadap Kontrak Hibah dan Potensinya Sebagai Instrumen Agihan Harta. *Jurnal Shari'ah*, 20(1).

Pond, K., & Lipscombe, G. (1999). *The Business of Banking: An Introduction to the Modern Financial Services Industry*. UK: CIB Publishing.

Rashid, R. A., Hassan, S. A., & Yaakub, N. I. (2013). A Need for Legal Framework of Gift Inter vivos (Hibah) in Malaysian Estate Planning. *International Journal of Business, Economics and Law*, 2(3).

Roberts, G. (2009). *Law Relating to Financial Services* (7th ed.). Hawkhurst: Global Professional Publishing.

Securities Commission (2006). *Resolutions of the Securities Commission Shari'ah Advisory Council* (2nd ed.). Kuala Lumpur: Securities Commission.

Walter Edelstein. (2014, February 14). http://bankingadvice.com/what-is-right-of-survivorship-on-a-bank-account/ (Accessed 2 January 2023).

16 Islamic Sustainable Finance

How Does SRI Sukuk Matter?

Syed Marwan, Siti Saffa' Shaharuddin & Nor Syahirah Zain

Introduction

The global financial crisis (GFC) of 2008 and subsequent economic crises have highlighted the unsustainability and irresponsibility of the financial system towards society. This led to a loss of trust in traditional financial institutions and sparked a search for alternative ways to do business (Benedikter, 2011). As a result, there has been a significant rise in sustainable, social, and impact finance, which aims to address the negative impacts of traditional finance on society and the environment. This provides an alternative for people to invest their money in a way that would not only provide a financial return but also has a positive social or environmental impact. Sustainable finance (SF) looks at how finance (investing and lending) interacts with economic, environmental, social, and governance (ESG) issues (Gutterman, 2021; Schoenmaker & Schramade, 2019). Social finance refers to financial instruments that are used to fund social and environmental initiatives. It includes alternative sources of funding, such as crowdfunding, microfinance, and impact investing. Social impact investing, also known as impact investing, is a type of investment that aims to generate both financial return and positive social or environmental impact. These approaches have become more widely recognized and utilized in recent years as a means of addressing societal and environmental issues through market-based solutions (Marwan & Engku Rabiah, 2019; Social Finance, n.d.).

One of the key drivers of this shift towards social finance and impact investing was the creation of the Global Impact Investing Network (GIIN) in 2007. The GIIN is a nonprofit organization that promotes the development of the impact investing industry and provides resources and support to impact investors (GIIN, 2016). Another important development was the creation of the Principles for Investors in Inclusive Finance (PIIF). The PIIF is a set of guidelines for impact investors, which aims to provide financial services to underserved populations (PRI, 2017). At the global level, the United Nations' (UN's) 17 Sustainable Development Goals (SDGs), essentially seek to end poverty, protect the planet, provide sustainability for the future, and ensure peace and prosperity for all. The SDGs recognize that addressing social and environmental challenges requires a holistic approach that involves the financial sector. Furthermore, various frameworks and standards

DOI: 10.4324/9781003468653-19

have been developed to guide financial institutions to align their activities with the SDGs. This includes the Principles for Responsible Investment (PRI), which provide a framework for investors to consider environmental, social, and governance (ESG) factors in their investment decisions (PRI, 2017), and the Global Reporting Initiative (GRI), which offers a framework for companies to report on their sustainability performance (GRI, 2022). The Task Force on Climate-related Financial Disclosures (TCFD) has also developed recommendations for companies to report on financial risks and opportunities related to climate change.

Regulatory changes have also played a role in the emergence of sustainable and impact finance. For instance, the European Union (EU) has introduced initiatives such as the Sustainable Finance Disclosure Regulation (SFDR) and the Taxonomy Regulation to promote sustainable finance. The SFDR requires financial institutions to disclose information on how they consider sustainability risks and opportunities in their investment decision-making processes, while the Taxonomy Regulation establishes a common framework for classifying environmentally sustainable economic activities, which helps investors to identify and compare the environmental impacts of different investments. In recent years, social finance and impact investing have grown significantly, with an increasing number of investors, asset managers, and financial institutions adopting sustainable and impact investing strategies. This growth has been driven by a variety of factors, including increasing public awareness of social and environmental issues, the rise of sustainable and responsible investing, and the development of new tools and products. Thus, unsurprisingly, the progress of these sectors has coincided with the Islamic finance industry, which saw tremendous growth over the past decade. In 2020, despite the COVID-19 pandemic, the Islamic finance industry still maintained a double-digit growth of 14%, to reach $3.374 trillion in size. If the trend continues, Islamic finance assets are projected to reach $4.94 trillion in 2025 (Mohamed & Ahmed, 2022). The Islamic Finance Development Report 2021 highlights that Islamic finance assets consist of primarily Islamic banking, which contributes 70% of the assets. This is followed by sukuk, which contributes 19% or $631 billion in value. These figures highlight the potential for Islamic finance, especially due to the demand for alternative and sustainable financing tools in the global capital market.

Islamic finance aims to achieve fairness, justice, and social responsibility for society through financial transactions. However, there have been concerns raised about the extent to which Islamic financial institutions have been able to uphold these principles in practice. Some critics argue that the practices of Islamic finance are believed to fall behind in achieving its underlying social and sustainable objectives (Marwan & Haneef, 2019). In response to the perceived shortcomings, various steps such as value-based intermediation (VBI) have been developed and undertaken (Marwan & Engku Rabiah, 2019). VBI is a concept that refers to the intermediation function of Islamic financial institutions, which seeks to deliver the intended outcomes of Shari'ah through practices, conduct, and offerings that generate positive and sustainable impact on the economy, community, and environment (Bank Negara Malaysia, 2018). Such development has encouraged the Islamic finance industry to pursue sustainable and responsible investment (SRI) strategies, which include ESG, impact, and sustainability-themed investments (EY, 2022). Given the issues mentioned, the objectives of this chapter are to:

i Explore the development of SRI and impact bonds and sukuk practices in the finance industry
ii Identify the issues and challenges of developing SRI and impact sukuk
iii Propose future directions for the development of SRI sukuk

Development of SRI Finance

SRI is a generic term that some refer to as socially responsible investment (Bennet & Iqbal, 2013; Renneboog et al., 2008), sustainable and responsible investment (CIMB, 2015; Moghul & Safar-Aly, 2014), and sustainable, responsible, and impactful investments (CIWM, 2015). Moghul and Safar-Aly (2014) summarized the different interpretations of SRI and came up with the following: SRI is any investment that takes into account the (i) investors' financial goals and objectives, whilst (ii) considering some sustainable impact in terms of the environment, society, and governance (ESG) that need to be achieved as well. In short, taking up the SRI would ensure that organizations put scrutiny on their investment that helps them to achieve both profit goals and contributions to the environment, society, and governance. Generally, SRI can be defined as terminology that includes any type of investment process that combines investors' financial objectives with their concerns towards issues of environment, society, and governance (ESG).

According to OECD (2021), numerous financial institutions and policymakers all over the world have started to take steps to integrate environmental, social, and governance factors into financial frameworks. Kamil et al. (2019) highlighted some data regarding the awareness of sustainability. In 2017, the United Nations estimated that there were approximately 300 policies and regulations in place across 60 countries that were aimed at promoting sustainability. This demonstrated a significant increase in awareness compared to 2013, when the approximate number of such policies was just 140. There are distinct themes in financial instruments that vary depending on how the issue revenues are used, such as green investments, social investments, and others. Some of these themes overlap in their terms and are not mutually exclusive. For example, green investment and social investment are two different themes in investments, but they are frequently referred to as SRI.

Global Development of SRI and Impact Bonds and Sukuk

Over the past two decades, the SRI market has grown significantly, with the number of SRI mutual funds increasing from just a handful in the 1990s to over 500 today. At the start of 2020, the global value of SRI funds was estimated at $35.3tn, an increase of 15% from 2018 to 2020 (GSIA, 2021). The SRI bond market has also seen significant growth, with a range of companies and organizations issuing bonds that meet certain sustainability and social responsibility criteria. These criteria are typically established by third-party organizations, such as the Global

Reporting Initiative (GRI) or the United Nations Global Compact (UNGC), which help ensure that SRI bonds are backed by companies and organizations that are truly committed to sustainability and social responsibility (GRI, 2022). SRI bonds, also known as ESG bonds, thematic bonds, or social contribution bonds, are a type of debt instrument whose proceeds are used to finance projects that promote environmental sustainability or provide social benefits (KRX, 2022). SRI bonds are generally issued by companies and organizations that seek to demonstrate a commitment to sustainable and socially responsible practices, such as reducing their carbon footprint, promoting diversity and inclusion, and supporting local communities. SRI bonds typically offer a fixed interest rate and are designed to be more socially responsible than traditional bonds. These proceeds from the bonds are used to finance projects with social or environmental benefits, such as renewable energy projects, affordable housing projects, and conservation efforts. As SRI bonds become more common, the range of projects they can finance has also increased, with some SRI bonds now being used to fund projects related to education, health care, and poverty alleviation. Examples of SRI bonds include green bonds, social bonds, sustainability bonds, and Sustainability-Linked Bonds, while in the Islamic finance industry, the Shari'ah-compliant equivalents are green sukuk and SRI sukuk.

SRI Sukuk

The development of SRI sukuk, or socially responsible investment sukuk, is a recent phenomenon in the Islamic finance industry. SRI sukuk is a type of sukuk, or Islamic bond, that combines traditional Islamic finance principles with the principles of socially responsible investing. This combination has allowed investors to not only adhere to Islamic principles but also to make investments that align with their values and contribute to the betterment of society (Marwan et al., 2022a). Malaysia's SRI sukuk framework was introduced in 2014 as part of the Capital Market Masterplan 2, a program by the Securities Commission (SC) that encourages socially responsible financing and investment (Securities Commission Malaysia, 2014b). The framework aims to provide sophisticated investors with a wider range of investment options, creating a favorable environment for both SRI investors and issuers. The goal of this initiative is to promote sustainable and responsible investment in the country (Haneef, 2016). Securities Commission Malaysia (2014a) states that the proceeds from SRI sukuk are used to finance eligible SRI projects, which are initiatives that strive to (i) Preserve and protect the environment and natural resources; (ii) Conserve the use of energy; (iii) Promote the use of renewable energy; (iv) Reduce greenhouse gas emissions; and (v) Improve the quality of life for the society. The framework outlines eligible SRI projects in four categories: (i) Natural resources, (ii) Renewable energy and energy efficiency, (iii) Community and economic development projects, and (iv) Waqf properties/assets.

In 2015, Khazanah Malaysia Berhad, a government-linked company, launched the first SRI sukuk in Malaysia. Dubbed the "Ihsan SRI sukuk," this was the world's first ringgit-denominated SRI sukuk. The Ihsan sukuk program had a nominal value of MYR 1 billion (about USD 240 million) with a 25-year tenure (Khazanah

Nasional, 2015). The first issuance of MYR 100 million was fully subscribed on June 4, 2015, and offered a 4.3% annual return over 7 years. The second tranche of MYR 100 million was issued in 2017, with a profit rate of 4.6% or 4.3%, depending on the achievement of key performance indicators (The Star, 2015). This second issuance was also the first sukuk with a retail offering feature, which allowed individual retail investors to participate in the capital market (Eusoff, 2017). The funds raised through the Ihsan sukuk were used to finance Khazanah's Trust Schools program, which is run by the non-profit Yayasan Amir foundation. The program aims to improve the accessibility of quality education in Malaysian government schools through public-private partnerships with the Ministry of Education. It focuses on transforming schools in various ways, involving stakeholders such as school leaders, teachers, students, parents, and the community (Ghani, 2015). The Ihsan SRI sukuk is structured according to the Islamic principle of Wakalah bi Al-Istithmar, which allows the issuer to use a combination of commodities and tangible assets. This structure makes its asset efficient and suitable for use by the issuer, special purpose vehicle (SPV), and obligor (CIMB, 2015).

Green Bonds and Sukuk

One type of SRI bond/sukuk is green bonds/sukuk, which focuses on raising funds for projects to support climate-related and environmentally friendly projects. The distinction between green bonds with green sukuk primarily lies with the underlying contracts, which are Shari'ah-compliant for the sukuk (Marwan & Ali, 2016; Marwan et al., 2022a). Green sukuk is considered a subset of green bonds and may be referred to as green Islamic bonds. These green bonds are primarily issued by governments, corporations, and other organizations to raise capital for projects that are designed to have a positive impact on the environment. The funds raised through green bonds are used to finance projects that promote renewable energy, reduce greenhouse gas emissions, and protect natural resources (The World Bank, 2015). One of the main benefits of green bonds/sukuk is that they provide a way for investors to align their investment decisions with their values. By investing in green bonds, investors can support projects that promote environmental sustainability while also earning a financial return. This can be especially appealing to investors who are concerned about climate change and want to support efforts to address it (World Bank, 2019).

There are several different types of green bonds, including green infrastructure bonds, green mortgage bonds, and green energy bonds. Each of these types of bonds has a specific set of criteria that must be met to qualify as a green bond. For example, green infrastructure bonds may be used to finance projects such as public transportation systems or water treatment plants, while green mortgage bonds may be used to finance the construction of energy-efficient buildings (World Bank, 2019). The very first green bond was issued in 2007 by multilateral institutions European Investment Bank (EIB) and the World Bank (Climate Bonds Initiative, 2014). This issuance helped to establish the blueprint for future green, social, and sustainability bonds (Keenan & Russo, 2022). In recent years, the market for green bonds has grown significantly. According to a report by the Climate Bonds Initiative, the cumulative global market for green bonds reached a record $2.081 trillion at the end of September 2022 (Climate Bonds Initiative, 2022). The development of green sukuk can be traced back to the early 2000s, when Islamic finance began to gain more mainstream attention and the potential for the use of these instruments to finance environmental projects was first recognized. In 2007, the International Islamic Financial Market (IIFM) released guidelines for the issuance of green sukuk, which provided a framework for development. In 2012, funds worth USD100mln were raised through green sukuk structured in Malaysia for a 50MW photovoltaic project in Indonesia (MIFC, 2016). The issuance of Malaysia's first green sukuk in 2017 is also a note to another breakthrough in the country's Islamic financial product innovation as well as for the role of a sustainable financial center it has for the nation. Tadau Energy Sdn Bhd is the first green sukuk that was issued by a solar energy firm, a subsidiary of Kagayaki Energy Sdn Bhd and Edra Solar Sdn Bhd. The green sukuk was dubbed the "Green SRI Sukuk Tadau," with a significant issuance worth RM250 million nominally (Affin Hwang Capital & TESB, 2017; Securities Commission, 2017). As a result of the convergence between these two growing industries and the establishment of green sukuk, investors from both the Islamic and non-Islamic worlds can now contribute to the Islamic regulations, which imbues transparency and addresses this emerging challenge.

Since then, the market for green sukuk has continued to grow and evolve. In 2013, the IIFM released updated guidelines that further defined the criteria for green sukuk, including requirements for the use of proceeds and the measurement and reporting of environmental impacts. In 2015, the International Capital Market Association (ICMA) also released guidelines for the issuance of green sukuk, providing additional guidance for issuers and investors. Furthermore, the development of the Green Sukuk Index by the Malaysian Rating Corporation (MARC) and the S&P Dow Jones Indices have encouraged awareness and interest in green sukuk. Recent figures show that a total value of $2.4 billion green sukuk has been issued in H1 2022 (Altaitoon, 2022). Overall, green bonds/sukuk provide a valuable tool for financing environmentally friendly projects and driving the development of a more sustainable economy. While there are still challenges that need to be addressed to ensure that these bonds are effective, the growth of the green bond market suggests that there is strong demand for investment options that align with environmental values. The green bond market is expected to continue to grow in the coming years. As concerns about climate change and environmental sustainability continue to increase, more investors are looking for ways to support projects that have a positive impact on the planet. By offering investors a way to earn a return while also making a positive contribution to the environment, green bonds are likely to become an increasingly important tool for financing sustainability initiatives.

Social Impact Bonds

Another financial instrument that assists organizations to achieve SRI and sustainability goals is the social impact bond (SIB). The SIB is a financial mechanism designed to raise investments to address social issues such as homeless or prison support services, childcare, conservation, and others, with returns based on project outcomes. It is a novel mechanism that brings together the public, business, and independent sectors. SIB comprises the collection of a sum of money upfront from the contributions of social investors to finance a project or associated with social and environmental outcomes (Marwan et al., 2021; Marwan et al., 2022a; Marwan et al., 2022b). A distinct feature of SIB is that the returns to investors are made depending on the outcomes of the project (Marwan, 2018). The first SIB was issued in 2010 in Peterborough, UK. This SIB is to fund the rehabilitation of ex-prisoners from Peterborough's jail and reduce recidivism. This issuance of SIB is due to the high reoffending rates of 60% within a year of release for short-term prisoners. Hence, the focus is to offer support and respond to the immediate needs of an offender and family before and after their release from prison, including accommodation, medical services, family support, employment and training, as well as financial advice (Marwan & Haneef, 2019). According to the latest data, a total of 138 social impact bonds (SIBs) have been launched worldwide, raising a total of USD 441 million in capital and benefiting 1,711,902 lives through the SIB projects (Social Finance, 2022).

Issues and Challenges of Developing SRI and Impact Bonds or Sukuk

There is no doubt that the SRI bonds and sukuk have great potential in providing a social impact as well as financial returns. Their development may also help the Islamic finance industry to achieve its underlying objectives (maqasid Shari'ah) and the revival of waqf assets. Nonetheless, there are many issues and challenges that SRI finance may still face. They are summarized as follows:

Uncertain Performance and Risk for Investors

There is no question that most investors will always look for and favor investments that offer a strong return. Since the success of SRI bonds and sukuk is not guaranteed, this might not be the ideal choice for them as an investment option. As a result of the high degree of dependence on society's acceptance or the target groups, it becomes extremely challenging to predict the exact consequence that will result from the investment. In addition, there is no evidence to suggest that they are superior to regular bonds and sukuk when examining their worth (Mohd Muslimin, 2020). Therefore, it can be difficult to entice investors if they are more interested in a lucrative return on their investment. The research of Engku Ali et al. (2019) finds investors are more attracted to the expected returns, the capital guaranteed, the incentives, and the purpose of the funds. They do not take into consideration the structure of the sukuk or the Shari'ah contracts that are utilized in the model. This demonstrates that even in the realm of ethical investing, there are still investors who anticipate receiving some sort of return on their money more than anything else.

Lack of Awareness and Liquidity Constraints

SRI sukuk and bonds are still in their early stages, with a more limited secondary market than other forms of bonds or sukuk. There is an increase in demand because investors today realize the need to address the many global social and environmental challenges (Abdullah & Keshminder, 2020), Ozili, 2022). However, the secondary market for SRI and green sukuk is still very low. This is because of the relatively small percentage of SRI and green sukuk compared to the other conventional bonds (World Bank, 2020). One reason may be that most investors still lack the awareness and appetite for sustainable investing. Furthermore, it is because of the relatively new structures which lead to unfamiliarity among investors. The same is applicable for green or SRI bonds, where investors choose to hold their bonds until maturity out of concern of not being able to replace them with other SRI bonds or sukuk in the market. This makes the market less liquid and makes it more difficult for investors to diversify their portfolios into SRI sukuk or bonds. Furthermore, the financial aspect of renewable energy implementation is one of the challenges of sustainable investing. The difficulty of obtaining financing and a bank loan for a renewable energy project was attributed to the significant risk involved and the bankers' lack of technical expertise (Rahim, 2018). This demonstrates the need for additional research and knowledge, which will attract investors to sustainable and impact sukuk.

Greenwashing

Greenwashing is the practice of creating a misleading image, misunderstanding, or providing inaccurate information about how a company's products are more ecologically friendly than they actually are. Greenwashing is also defined as a firm or business making a foundationless or baseless claim to persuade clients that its products are environmentally friendly. While certain environmental claims may be valid, greenwashing businesses frequently exaggerate their benefits or claims to confuse clients. In this case, some stakeholders argue that the structure of a green sukuk is similar to that of a conventional bond, making the phrase "green sukuk structure" inaccurate (El Amri et al., 2021). The structure remains unchanged; the only difference is the type and nature of projects sponsored by green sukuk funds, which encourage ecologically friendly ventures. Furthermore, due to the relatively new reporting standards and lack of expertise on the matter, there may be a lack of governance and audit processes to check whether the funds are really used for impactful "green" purposes.

Sukuk: Shari'ah and Legal Issues

Shari'ah and legal concerns about sukuk may contribute to some extent to the obstacles and issues surrounding sustainable and impact investing. Uluyol (2021) examined the challenges faced in the sukuk sector. He suggested that concerns with sukuk stem from a lack of consistency in sukuk documentation and sukuk relevant to Shari'ah interpretation. This issue may also result in a poor sukuk secondary market, sukuk market uncertainty, and higher sukuk issuance costs. As a result, establishing a unified International Shari'ah Board is critical to avoiding the issue of "fatwa shopping" among Islamic finance practitioners. The researcher discovered that "fatwa shopping" is frequent in cross-border Islamic finance transactions, such as cross-border sukuk trades, where restrictions are less stringent.

Additional Disclosure for Issuers

Another challenge facing the SRI sukuk/bond market is the need for increased transparency and disclosure. Investors need to be able to trust that the proceeds from SRI bond issuances are being used for their intended purpose, and this requires clear and accurate reporting on the use of funds. SRI sukuk and bond issuers are obligated to undergo external or second opinion reviews prior to issuance, and they are subject to impact reporting after the issuance. This is to guarantee that they are meeting market expectations and industry best practices (World Bank, 2020). This impartial review is also critical in assisting investors in making investment decisions. While this external review is seen as a crucial assessment, it comes at an additional expense to the issuer. For example, to demonstrate the project's environmental impact, frequent audits of the operations are required. According to Rapi et al. (2021), green investments are frequently associated with high initial capital expenditures, extended payback times, and a heavy reliance on legislative restraints. Most of the time, these projects in the sphere of public infrastructure are not financially sustainable and frequently fail to achieve the projected rate of return. Furthermore, because of the standards for ecological certification, green sukuk necessitates more planning before issuance than conventional sukuk. As a result, the planning process takes longer and costs more money. This added expense raises the price of SRI sukuk and bonds. This eventually causes potential SRI issuers to lose interest in participating.

Standardization

One of the main challenges facing the green bond market is the need for clear and consistent definitions of what constitutes a green bond. In order to ensure that the proceeds from green bond issuances are used to fund projects with genuine environmental benefits, it is important to have clear guidelines for what qualifies as a green bond. Without such standardizations, it can be difficult for investors to determine which bonds are truly green and may lead to the issuance of bonds that are not as environmentally friendly as they claim to be. Despite these challenges, the SRI and green bond/sukuk market is expected to continue to grow in the coming years. As concerns about climate change and environmental sustainability continue to increase, more investors are looking for ways to support projects that have a positive impact on the planet. By offering investors a way to earn a return while also making a positive contribution to the environment, green bonds are likely to become an increasingly important tool for financing sustainability initiatives.

Challenges and the Way Forward

Despite these challenges, several steps can be taken to overcome them and promote the growth of SRI sukuk and bonds:

Firstly, it is essential to address the perceived lower returns and higher risk of SRI sukuk/bonds. This can be done through education and outreach efforts to highlight the long-term benefits of SRI bonds, as well as the development of tools and resources to help investors assess and manage the risks associated with these investments. It is not necessarily true that socially responsible investing (SRI) bonds give lower returns than traditional bonds. The performance of any investment, including SRI bonds, is dependent on a variety of factors such as the creditworthiness of the issuer, the interest rate environment, and market conditions. Some SRI bonds may have lower returns due to the additional costs associated with evaluating and monitoring the social and environmental impact of the projects they fund, but this is not necessarily the case for all SRI bonds. In fact, many studies have found that SRI bonds may offer similar or even higher returns compared to traditional bonds. For example, the study by Sjöström (2011), which performed a meta-analysis of 21 previous studies on the matter, found that 7 studies conclude that SRI has similar performance relative to their conventional peers, 5 studies report that SRI outperforms conventional investment, a mere 3 studies find that SRI generates inferior performance relative to its conventional peers and 6 studies report mixed results. Another study by Leite and Cortez (2018) found that SRI-balanced funds perform similarly to conventional funds, whereas SRI bond funds significantly outperform their peers. Therefore, it is important for investors to carefully consider the potential risks and returns of any investment, including SRI bonds, and to diversify their portfolio to minimize risk. It is also important to note that the primary goal of SRI sukuk/bonds is not necessarily to maximize financial returns, but rather to provide funding for projects that have a positive social and environmental impact.

Secondly, there needs to be greater standardization and transparency in the SRI bond market. This can be achieved through the development of industry-wide criteria and guidelines for evaluating SRI bond projects, as well as the creation of publicly available databases that provide information on the social and environmental impact of individual SRI bond offerings. Certainly, efforts are already underway where several institutions have developed guidelines and standards for green bonds, including the Green Bond Principles, the Climate Bond Standard, and the Global Reporting Initiative. Standardization and transparency can be a key tool for addressing greenwashing in the SRI and green bond market. By providing clear and accurate information about the projects being financed and the environmental impact of those projects, bond issuers can help to ensure that investors can make informed decisions about the sustainability of their investments. Better transparency can be promoted in the green bond market using third-party certification bodies. These organizations can provide independent assessments of the environmental impact of green bond projects and help to ensure that they meet certain standards and criteria. Furthermore, improved disclosure can be undertaken using publicly available reports or online databases that provide information about the projects and the environmental impact of each green bond issuer. By promoting transparency in the SRI and green sukuk/bond market, investors can be more confident that their investments are contributing to environmentally sustainable projects and that they are not being misled or deceived by greenwashing. This can help to increase the credibility and attractiveness of SRI and green sukuk/bonds as a sustainable investment option.

Finally, it is important to increase the availability of SRI bond options. This can be achieved through the development of new SRI bond offerings and the expansion of existing programs to make them more accessible to a wider range of investors. This expands the pool of market participants and helps address the issue of liquidity. This can be done through outreach and education efforts to promote the benefits of SRI bonds and encourage more investors to consider these investments as part of their portfolios. Furthermore, developing electronic trading platforms or other market infrastructure that allows for the efficient buying and selling of SRI sukuk/bonds can also help to increase liquidity. This can make it easier for investors to find counterparties and transact in the SRI sukuk/bond market. Overall, while there are challenges to be overcome in the SRI bond market, there is significant potential for these investments to play a more significant role in the financial landscape. By addressing the issues of risk, standardization, and availability, the way forward for SRI sukuk/bonds is bright, and investors can make a positive impact on the world while achieving their financial goals.

References

Abdullah, M. S., & Keshminder, J. S. (2020). What Drives Green Sukuk? A Leader's Perspective. *Journal of Sustainable Finance & Investment*, 1–21.

Affin Hwang Capital, & TESB. (2017). *Tadau Energy Sdn. Bhd.* Issues Rm250 Million Sri Sukuk; The First Green Sukuk in Malaysia [Press Release].

Altaitoon, J. (2022, October 28). *Green and Sustainability Sukuk Set New Records*. www.refinitiv.com/perspectives/market-insights/green-and-sustainability-sukuk-set-new-records/

Bank Negara Malaysia. (2018). *Value Based Intermediation: Strengthening the Roles and Impact of Islamic Finance* (BNM/RH/DP 034–2). Malaysia. Bank Negara Malaysia.

Benedikter, R. (2011). *Social Banking and Social Finance: Answers to the Economic Crisis*. New York: Springer.

Bennet, M. S., & Iqbal, Z. (2013). How Socially Responsible Investing Can Help Bridge the Gap Between Islamic and Conventional Financial Markets. *International Journal of Islamic and Middle Eastern Finance and Management*, 6(3), 211–215.

CIMB. (2015). *Ihsan Sukuk Berhad: Information Memorandum*. Kuala Lumpur, Malaysia: Commerce International Merchant Bankers Berhad.

CIWM. (2015). *SRI & The Case for Islamic Investment Funds*. www.mifc.com/repository/0186SRI%20e-Book.pdf

Climate Bonds Initiative. (2014). *Explaining Green Bonds*. www.climatebonds.net/market/explaining-green-bonds

Climate Bonds Initiative. (2022). *Sustainable Debt Market Summary Q3 2022*. www.climatebonds.net/files/reports/cbi_susdebtsum_highlq32022_final.pdf

El Amri, M. C., Mohammed, M. O., & Abdi, M. H. (2021). How Green Sukuk Structure Contributes to SDGs? In *Islamic Wealth and the SDGs* (pp. 621–637). Cham: Palgrave Macmillan.

Engku, R. A. E. A., Syed, M. M. S. A., Nor, R. M. Z., Rusni, H., & Salina, K. (2019). Potential Development of SRI Sukuk Models for Higher Learning Institutions in Malaysia

Based on Wakalah and Waqf. *IIiBF Journal of Islamic Finance* (Special Issue), 090–106. ISSN 2289-2117.

Eusoff, N. S. (2017, August 2). *Khazanah Raises RM100m from Second SRI Sukuk Tranche*. www.theedgemarkets.com/article/khazanah-raises-rm100m-second-sri-sukuk-tranche

EY. (2022). *Trending: Sustainable Responsible Investment in Malaysia and the Region*. Kuala Lampur, Malaysia: Ernst & Young Consulting Sdn Bhd.

Ghani, M. I. (2015). *The World's First Ringgit-Denominated SRI Sukuk Thomson Reuters – RFI Responsible Finance Report 2015: The Emerging Convergence of SRI, ESG and Islamic Finance*. Edinburgh: Thomson Reuters.

GIIN. (2016). *The Business Value of Impact Measurement*. https://thegiin.org/assets/GIIN_ImpactMeasurementReport_webfile.pdf

GRI. (2022). *The GRI Standards: Enabling Transparency on Organizational Impacts*. Amsterdam: GRI Standards.

GSIA. (2021). *Global Sustainable Investment Review 2020: Global Sustainable Investment Alliance*.

Gutterman, A. S. (2021). *Sustainable Finance and Impact Investing*. New York: Business Expert Press.

Haneef, R. (2016, May 17). Retail Sukuk and SRI Sukuk: The Malaysian Experience. *1st Annual Islamic Finance Conference*. www.irti.org/English/Research/Documents/Conferences/IDB-AM-41/Retail%20Sukuk%20and%20SRI%20Sukuk-The%20Malaysian%20Experience.pdf

Kamil, W. A. R., Bakhor, S. A. S. M., De Luna-Martinez, J., Zhang, W., & Aziz, A. H. A. (2019). Islamic Green Finance: Development, Ecosystem and Prospects. *Disclosure*.

Keenan, C., & Russo, Z. (2022). *The World Bank Impact Report: Sustainable Development Bonds & Green Bonds 2021*. Washington. https://treasury.worldbank.org/en/about/unit/treasury/impact/impact-report

Khazanah Nasional. (2015). *Khazanah to Issue First Ringgit-Denominated Sustainable and Responsible Investment Sukuk* [Press Release]. www.khazanah.com.my/Media-Downloads/News-Press-Releases/2015/Khazanah-to-issue-first-Ringgit-denominated-sustai

KRX. (2022). *About SRI Bonds*. https://sribond.krx.co.kr/en/01/01010000/SRI01010000.jsp

Leite, P., & Cortez, M. C. (2018). The Performance of European SRI Funds Investing in Bonds and Their Comparison to Conventional Funds. *Investment Analysts Journal*, 47(1), 65–79. https://doi.org/10.1080/10293523.2017.1414911

Marwan, S. (2018). *An Exploratory Study on Shari'ah-Compliant Social Impact Bonds in Malaysia: Stakeholders' Perspective* (Doctor of Philosophy in Islamic Banking and Finance). International Islamic University Malaysia (IIUM), Malaysia.

Marwan, S., & Ali, E. R. A. E. (2016). Sustainable and Responsible Investment (SRI): Trends and Prospects. *Jurnal Muamalat*, 9, 1–21.

Marwan, S., & Engku Rabiah, A. E. A. (2019). Islamic Social Finance and the Imperative for Social Impact Measurement. *Al-Shajarah: Journal of the International Institute of Islamic Thought and Civilization (ISTAC)*, 2019(Special Issue: Islamic Banking and Finance), 43–69.

Marwan, S., & Haneef, M. A. (2019). Does Doing Good Pay Off? – Social Impact Bonds and Lessons for Islamic Finance to Serve the Real Economy. *Islamic Economic Studies*, 27(1), 23–37.

Marwan, S., Haneef, M. A., Ali, E. R. A. E., & Ismail, S. (2021). Beyond Shari'ah Compliance: Achieving Maqasid Al-Shari'ah Through Social Impact Bonds (SIB) and Sustainable & Responsible Investment (SRI) Sukuk. *Pembinaan Tamadun Melalui Industri Patuh Shari'ah*, 1(Kewangan dan Pengurusan Patuh Shari'ah), 350–362.

Marwan, S., Ismail, S., Haneef, M. A. M., & Ali, E. R. A. E. (2022a). An Empirical Comparison of Sustainable and Responsible Investment Ṣukūk, Social Impact Bonds and Conventional Bonds. *ISRA International Journal of Islamic Finance*, 14(3). https://doi.org/10.1108/IJIF-04-2021-0074

Marwan, S., Ismail, S., Haneef, M. A. M., & Ali, E. R. A. E. (2022b). Critical Success Factors of Implementing Sustainable and Responsible Investment (SRI) Sukuk for Economic Recovery from COVID-19 Pandemic. *Journal of Economic and Administrative Sciences* (ahead-of-print).

MIFC. (2016). *SRI & Green Sukuk: Challenges & Prospects*. www.mifc.com/index.php?ch=28&pg=72&ac=162&bb=uploadpdf

Moghul, U. F., & Safar-Aly, S. H. K. (2014). Green Sukuk: The Introduction of Islam's Environmental Ethics to Contemporary Islamic Finance. *The Georgetown International Environmental Law Review*, 27(1), 1–60.

Mohamed, S., & Ahmed, T. (2022). *Islamic Finance Development Report 2021*. London. www.refinitiv.com/content/dam/marketing/en_us/documents/gated/reports/report-2021-all-color2.pdf

Mohd Muslimin, A. S. (2020). *Investinsights: Islamic Financial Planning – Socially Responsible Investing, Green Sukuk and Sukuk Prihatin: Here's What You Need to Know*. www.comparehero.my/investment/articles/sociallyresponsible-investment-sri-sukuk

OECD. (2021). *ESG Investing and Climate Transition: Market Practices, Issues and Policy Considerations*. OECD, Paris. www.oecd.org/finance/ESG-investing-and-climatetransition-Market-practices-issues-and-policy-considerations.pdf

Ozili, P. K. (2022). Green Finance Research Around the World: A Review of Literature. *International Journal of Green Economics*.

PRI, P. F. R. I. (2017). *PIIF Report on Progress 2016: Assessing the Impact of Responsible Investors in Inclusive Finance*. London: UNEP Finance Initiative and the UN Global Compact.

Rahim, S. R. (2018). Green Sukuk for Financing Renewable Project. *Turkish Journal of Islamic Economics*, 5(2), 129–144.

Rapi, K., Maisarah, S., Rambe, S. A. F., Chandra, W., & Rahmana, A. (2021). Green Finance for the Era of Post COVID-19: A Systematic Literature. In *Conference Towards ASEAN Chairmanship 2023 (TAC 23 2021)* (pp. 190–195). Malaysia: Atlantis Press.

Renneboog, L., Horst, J. T., & Zhang, C. (2008). Socially Responsible Investments: Institutional Aspects, Performance, and Investor Behavior. *Journal of Banking and Finance*, 32, 1723–1742.

Schoenmaker, D., & Schramade, W. (2019). *Principles of Sustainable Finance*. Oxford: Oxford University Press.

Securities Commission Malaysia. (2014a). *Guidelines on Sukuk*. Malaysia: Securities Commission Malaysia.

Securities Commission Malaysia. (2014b). *SC Introduces Sustainable and Responsible Investment Sukuk framework*. Retrieved September 9, 2014, from Securities Commission Malaysiawww.sc.com.my/post_archive/sc-introduces-sustainable-and-responsible-investment-sukuk-framework/

Securities Commission Malaysia. (2017). *Malaysia's First Green Sukuk under SC's Sustainable Responsible Investment Sukuk Framework* [Press Release]. www.sc.com.my/post_archive/malaysias-first-green-sukuk-under-scs-sustainable-responsible-investment-sukuk-framework/

Sjöström, E. (2011). *The Performance of Socially Responsible Investment – A Review of Scholarly Studies Published 2008–2010*. Online: SSRN.

Social Finance. (2022, February 25). *Impact Bond Global Database*. https://sibdatabase.socialfinance.org.uk/

Social Finance. (n.d.). *History: Social Finance*. www.socialfinance.org.uk/about-us/history/

The Star. (2015). *Khazanah's RM100m Sustainable Sukuk Priced at 4.3%*. www.thestar.com.my/Business/Business-News/2015/06/04/Khazanah-RM100m-sustainable-Sukuk/?style=biz

Uluyol, B. (2021). A Comprehensive Empirical and Theoretical Literature Survey of Islamic Bonds (sukuk). *Journal of Sustainable Finance & Investment*. https://doi.org/10.1080/20430795.2021.1917224

The World Bank. (2015). *What are Green Bonds?* Washington, DC: The World Bank.

World Bank. (2019). *Green Bond Impact Report*. http://pubdocs.worldbank.org/en/790081576615720375/IBRD-Green-Bond-Impact-Report-FY-2019.pdf

World Bank. (2020). *Pioneering the Green Sukuk: Three Years On*. https://openknowledge.worldbank.org/bitstream/handle/10986/34569/Pioneering-theGreen-Sukuk-Three-Years-On.pdf?sequence=1&isAllowed=y

Part III

Islamic Sustainable Finance

Challenges in Modern Practices

17 Issues and Challenges of Sustainable Finance

An Experience From the Islamic Banking Industry

Nik Anis Idayu Nik Abdullah, Nurhaiyyu Abdull Hamid & Razali Haron

Introduction

Sustainable, responsible, and impact (SRI) investing and Islamic finance share similar origins and aspirations. However, these two forms of finance have largely coexisted as distinct strategies in separate worlds. Both have an ethical foundation that prioritizes stewardship and the development of social value over other financial goals. Environmental, social, and governance (ESG) considerations are the fundamental elements around which an SRI investment approach is developed, including through screening, complete integration into security valuation and portfolio management, and thematic and impact investing. They are at the centre of any discussion of SRI investing. Islamic finance adheres to Islamic prohibitions on the purpose and design of finance. Specifically, it must avoid financing prohibited businesses and abide by the Islamic prohibitions of riba and excessive gharar, generally understood to include lending money at interest and the sale of risk, respectively (Hayat et al., 2014). Islamic finance has been gaining prominence in the global financial system, particularly since the global financial crisis of 2008 and the "Arab Spring" in 2010. Compared to conventional financing, Islamic finance is believed to offer lower systemic risks and a sustainable financing system (Dridi & Hasan, 2010). To non-Muslims, Islamic finance is a form of socially responsible or ethical finance, although ethical and Islamic finance have both similarities and differences (RFI, 2019). Specifically, Islamic finance is well-positioned to maximize social impact and achieve the United Nations Sustainable Development Goals (UN SDGs) as it adopts sustainability criteria (DinarStandard, 2019).

Islamic Banking and Sustainable Finance

The conversation about climate change and sustainability at banks and financial institutions has dramatically shifted in the last five years. It requires collaboration on an international scale to resolve numerous sustainability issues. Financial institutions must provide value to their clients and contribute to society to remain relevant. SRI investments and Islamic finance have a natural tendency to evaluate their social and environmental impact. In 2018, the UN Environment Program – Finance Initiative (UNEP FI) created the Principles for Responsible Banking, with

DOI: 10.4324/9781003468653-21

28 founding banks worldwide pledging to connect their business objectives with societal goals. More banks have joined these banks, illustrating the rapidly expanding global trend of responsible finance. The principles will define the role and responsibilities of the banking industry in creating a sustainable future. By agreeing to the new framework, banks will align their business objectives with those of the SDGs and the Paris Climate Agreement. The principles establish the global standard for being a responsible bank and ensure that banks create value for their shareholders and society.

Some providers of financial services in Organization of Islamic Cooperation (OIC) countries have committed to ESG frameworks and pursued policies consistent with current notions of sustainable banking. For instance, a study comparing Islami Bank Bangladesh Limited and Triodos Bank, based in the Netherlands, reveals that Islamic Bank is ahead of other Islamic banks in Bangladesh in terms of financial inclusion, microfinance, small and medium-sized enterprise (SME) financing, and green banking while remaining financially stable and profitable. However, it lags behind Triodos, a leading sustainable banking institution. CIMB Group, which includes CIMB Islamic, is a founding member of the UN Environment Programme Finance Initiative Principles for Responsible Banking in Malaysia. It has been ranked among the top 100 most diverse and inclusive organizations in the world by the Thomson Reuters Diversity & Inclusion Index. It asserts that it has integrated the Value-Based Intermediation principles of Bank Negara Malaysia into its core businesses and sustainability strategies. These examples demonstrate that providers of financial services can develop products that qualify as Islamic and SRI investments.

The Islamic finance industry reached about $4 trillion in 2021, a 17% increase from 2020's 14%. The global net income recorded by Islamic financial institutions (IFIs) tripled from $10.5 billion in 2020 to $32 billion in 2021, indicating more robust results for Islamic banks. Numerous businesses financed by Islamic banks are exposed to high ESG risks, and IFIs must share these risks with those they fund. While some banks demonstrate relatively good ESG performance (scoring between 50% and 75% on the social and governance dimensions), most Islamic banks ranked poorly on the environmental dimension. This is the ESG category in which Islamic banks must demonstrate substantial progress (Nik Abdullah & Haron, 2022). Islamic social finance and Islamic commercial banking are the two branches of Islamic finance. Islamic social finance is distinct but not unique from Islamic banking, as it focuses on providing social and economic benefits, which ties it closely to achieving development objectives. Investments in Islamic social finance create benefits for those in need through education, healthcare, welfare, and infrastructure. Muslims are urged to aid their immediate communities and prioritize the needs of the underprivileged. Islamic finance tries to redistribute assets across communities to ensure a fair distribution of wealth. Islamic social finance principles, such as Zakat and Waqf, are one of the religious requirements Muslims must meet to fulfil this need through continuous charitable means. As such, Islamic social finance's redistributive and social equality elements have an essential role in realizing SDG1: 'End poverty in all its forms everywhere' (DinarStandard, 2019).

However, Zakat and Waqf are not coordinated adequately to meet development objectives. They continue to be underreported in development statistics and are rarely reflected in development finance flows. Islamic social finance can ensure that more sustainable and inclusive financial resources are deployed for the SDGs. Defining a space for Islamic finance in the global development framework and narrative could mobilize Muslims globally to contribute to development and the SDGs.

As with the traditional banking industry, Islamic commercial banking, which encompasses insurance, capital markets, and asset management, seeks financial returns and is not just concerned with growth. Ijara (lease), Al-Mudharabah (capital and labor partnership), and Musharaka are some instruments used in commercial Islamic banking transactions. Murabaha, which makes up a significant portion of Islamic finance, is a cost-plus financing of a non-interest-bearing loan (profit- and loss-sharing partnership). Sukuk, an Islamic fixed-income form, has become more popular worldwide, although not all forms are used for social benefit. Sukuk and Islamic finance lending are two areas that can be utilized to provide infrastructure and extensive programs in Muslim-majority nations and beyond. Sukuk offers investors low risk and guaranteed profits. In countries where there is low financial inclusion, Islamic microfinance programs can provide solutions by lowering risk and debt levels while fostering equity, social welfare, and economic stability. These two Islamic finance instruments can be used effectively to respond to the SDGs.

There are still efforts to improve sustainability through rules and regulations in the major Islamic finance markets. For instance, to increase sustainability in its capital market, which includes more than 200 companies, Saudi Arabia's stock exchange introduced ESG disclosure guidelines in October 2021. This aligns with the Kingdom's Vision 2030, which positions sustainability as an important pillar. In Malaysia, the Securities Commission launched an SRI-linked Sukuk framework in June 2022, and the regulator released the SRI Taxonomy framework at the end of 2022. A new set of regulations permits the use of funds for general purposes if the

Table 17.1 Overview of Islamic Financial Instrument

Instruments	*Description*
Waqf	Endowment on the property is made to religious, educational, or charitable causes.
Zakat	Almsgiving in Islam is obligatory for all Muslims who meet specific wealth criteria. One of the five pillars of Islam.
Sadaqa	Voluntary almsgiving in Islam.
Sukuk	Islamic asset-based financial certificates can be compared to conventional bonds (debt- or quasi-equity-based).
Al-Mudharabah	Partnership contract where delegated authority is given to an agent to carry out trades and transactions. One party provides money and expertise/labour from the other.
Murabaha	Receivables created are trade receivables from the cost economic outcomes as a loan.
Musharaka	Joint enterprise or partnership where partners share profits and losses.

Source: Organization for Economic Co-operation and Development (OECD, 2020)

issuer agrees to achieve predetermined sustainability results by a predetermined deadline and under the supervision of performance measures.

Issues and Challenges of Islamic Sustainable Finance in the Islamic Banking Industry

Islamic finance, specifically Islamic social finance, is well positioned to offer new forms of development assistance, with opportunities for donors and beneficiaries. However, some challenges need to be addressed for IFIs to embrace the sustainability agenda. The trend toward doing good for the planet is attracting Islamic finance institutions to capitalize on the increasing demand of reaching a broader investor base – which is often the driving reason to turn to Islamic sustainable finance in the first place. The key challenges faced by the IFIs are discussed here:

Lack of Standard Definitions and Performance Measurement

The standard definition of a sustainable project or green asset is still missing (Weerasinghe & Ramachandra, 2018). The issuer's definition of a green project may differ from that of the regulator, preventing potential green financial facilities from being issued. The clash between various definitions causes the issuer to occasionally violate the authority body's regulations, not only the sustainability guidelines but also the Islamic finance guidelines, which increases the issuer's costs (Keshminder et al., 2022). As the sustainability of the Islamic finance market matures, the need for a standard taxonomy for sustainability projects to ensure consistent public demand for Islamic sustainability finance is crucial. This is in line with a previous study that agreed on the necessity of standard and clear definitions to boost green investment (Sangiorgi & Schopohl, 2021). Without a consensus definition, it is equally challenging for the prospective investor to decide. For instance, even though the green Sukuk framework has been available on the Islamic capital market since 2017, there has been no issuance for its integration. A standard definition will enable the organization to be more transparent in responding to inquiries from potential investors and most likely will give the investor the option of not proceeding with the investment in a green project if they are not satisfied with the issuer's response.

Due to the shoddy green taxonomy, issuers were frequently obliged to limit their green boundaries (Keshminder et al., 2022). It takes time to reach a consensus on understanding between all related parties, and that will eventually hold up the growth of the sustainable Islamic finance market. Furthermore, the key performance indicators for many green projects also lack standardization (Rahman et al., 2020). Due to non-standardized benchmarks, comparing green projects will be pointless and lacking in credibility. It is challenging to monitor and forecast the return for various sustainability-driven Islamic investments. Alternatively, they may opt for the conventional facilities due to the guaranteed returns and low risk.

Limited Green Asset

Solar projects and hydro companies and buildings are currently considered green projects, but the types of activities deemed sustainable projects are still lacking (Al-Shetwi, 2022). Whether it contributes directly or indirectly to greener outcomes, the public must be re-convinced if a new technology or machine is brought in, and regulators must be re-educated. As a result, insufficient standard guidelines concerning what is deemed green and what is not will affect the sort of assets and projects considered green. Tapping only certain activities to be classified as green projects can also be detrimental. In Malaysia, green Sukuk has been issued with a value of up to $250 million for a 50 MW solar plant, which is significantly less than non-solar green projects such as green buildings or rail transportation that cost billions and had greater liquidity (Keshminder et al., 2022). That's the problem with solar activity per se, not with green projects. The lack of diversity in green assets makes it more difficult for issuers to increase their supply of green Sukuk in the market.

Lack of Incentives and High Cost

Compared with non-green financial instruments, the issuance of Islamic sustainability instruments are more expensive (Liu & Lai, 2021). The complexity of establishing an SRI Sukuk increases the transaction expenses (Rahman et al., 2020). The issuer must incur additional costs in complying with Islamic finance regulations and undergo the assessment of greenness before it can be deemed green. Issuers must disclose more information, provide an additional report, and demonstrate how their project will positively impact social and environmental issues, among other things. These require significant preparation time and could make it more challenging to accomplish the organizational objectives (Kamil et al., 2019). In essence, the entire planning process is time-consuming and expensive. That's the challenge with the issuance cost alone; once it's been issued, the issuer has to address various queries from investors and prepare the progress report (Keshminder et al., 2022). The enormous number of tasks involved in preparing the reports and educating the investors on Sukuk matters hamper the members of the green project team, disrupting their work-life balance (Keshminder et al., 2022). Ultimately, it becomes additional work and a burden with no genuine pricing gain to the issuers.

Further, a lack of incentives hindered issuing of Islamic green instruments (Hassan, 2020). Currently, there are incentives offered for Islamic green financing, including tax deductions for the issuance cost of SRI Sukuk and tax and financing incentives that fall under green technology in Malaysia. Nevertheless, whether through conventional or Islamic finance, it is necessary to share these stimulants with other green initiatives. This will limit the benefits available to green Sukuk issuers and increase transaction costs. Both returns are equivalent when compared to non-green Sukuk. Therefore, from the issuer's perspective, the only advantages of issuing green Sukuk are the incentives offered. Most issuers are more experienced and familiar with the procedures of ordinary Sukuk due to a larger market and greater supplies than green Sukuk. It also has a better rate and is fluctuation-free (Keshminder et al., 2022), making it more appealing to them and discouraging the growth of green Sukuk. Issuers will only accept green Sukuk because of its green designation and government incentives (Keshminder et al., 2022).

Lack of Confidence by Investors

After the pandemic hit globally, many parties were affected, and naturally, the investors will primarily concentrate on the financial return. Those who choose to invest in such sustainable projects are often driven by factors of good cause and being morally good. With the economy struggling, financial goals take precedence over upholding morality. As a result, investors frequently choose ventures with guaranteed steady returns. They tend to be more risk-averse and selective in choosing investments to avoid unnecessary loss. Due to a lack of market data, it is difficult for investors to assess the performance of Islamic sustainable projects. In addition to the hazy definition of what constitutes green and the absence of green, Sukuk awareness also makes it difficult for stakeholders to comprehend the Sukuk business process (Abubakar & Handayani, 2020). In addition to being concerned with the financial rewards, investors who engage in Islamic sustainable assets are also held accountable if the social or environmental requirements cannot be satisfied. In comparison to the conventional market, or more precisely, the Islamic market driven by SDGs, the scale of the Islamic financial market in Malaysia is substantially smaller. The lack of a definitive standard, framework, and performance measurement in the green Islamic market causes stakeholders to lose faith in the Islamic sustainability market. There is still much work to be done before they can tap into these potential stakeholders in the market. Due to the complexity of SRI-related projects' risk evaluation, investors may not be as familiar with the risk assessment as many projects related to SRI introduce new and innovative methodologies (Rahman et al., 2020). This will hinder the support for this market's growth. Despite the constant demand for SDG Islamic instruments, these needs cannot be met due to the narrow definition of a green asset.

High-risk Profiles

As for some countries, green technology is still developing and relatively new compared with non-green technology, so investment in this field is considered high-risk for potential investors. Eventually, any ambiguity and risk associated with green projects will ultimately impact the credit standing of green Sukuk. The journey of the green Sukuk has not been entirely trouble-free up to this point because of various issues with prior issuances, such as rating downgrades that scare investors (Keshminder et al., 2022). The investors are concerned about its likelihood of success; hence, many decide not to proceed. In conclusion, investors prioritize the return aspect of green Sukuk over the green aspect itself and make a positive impact environmentally.

Shari'ah and Legal Issues

Some of the accepted procedures and regulations are dubious in that they emphasize adhering to the rules. Consequently, this diverts attention from the actual goal that led to the establishment of such an instrument in the first place. For example, the gist of SRI-driven Sukuk is merely to focus on society's well-being. However, some of the procedures adopted are questionable. Rather than looking at the social outcome, the authority might concentrate more on rule adherence and whether it is to comply with regulations. For instance, to appear more appealing to the investors, Khazanah Nasional Berhad gives their full guarantee on Ihsan SRI Sukuk's capital and return, resulting in a more risk-free Sukuk and contradicting with a "true" risk-sharing concept, one of the principles that is always known with Islamic finance tenets (Marwan & Haneef, 2019). Inherently, if the investments do not achieve the objective, they will be rewarded by the guarantor. Therefore, the risk-sharing concept is not a real risk shared between the investor and guarantor. It is problematic in that this will encourage the investor to see this as enjoying financial return without making a positive impact socially and environmentally. Unlike the Social Impact Bond, based in the UK, the investors will lose all their capital if the program is unsuccessful, applying the true concept of risk-sharing (Marwan & Haneef, 2019). Marwan and Haneef (2019) argue this is the leading example where Islamic finance focuses on rule adherence but fails to look at the Maqasid al-Shari'ah as the spirit of the investment. He also highlighted the term "formalist-deadlock" by Balz, which refers to the Islamic Finance practice that focuses on copying conventional financial products and making them Shari'ah-compliant, preventing the industry from establishing a financial system that is indeed founded on Islamic ideals.

Conclusion

Islamic financial principles encourage development-oriented, environmentally responsible, and socially inclusive initiatives. The Islamic finance sector will need to overcome several obstacles before it can play a more significant role in achieving these objectives; therefore, there is still a long way to go. With their focus on defensive and resilient sectors with minimal gearing, it is generally acknowledged that investments in Islamic finance tend to perform better during economic crises. A defensive and low-debt investment strategy is inherently appealing as the world approaches what is quite likely to be a new phase of low growth and recession in 2023. This indicates a growing possibility for Islamic banks as investors seek out conservative investment options that are low volatility and follow ESG standards. Investors must view Islamic finance as something in line with the ESG for it to become ingrained in the development agenda and be appropriately accounted for.

References

Abubakar, L., & Handayani, T. (2020). Green Sukuk: Sustainable Financing Instruments for Infrastructure Development in Indonesia. *Proceedings of the 1st Borobudur International Symposium on Humanities, Economics and Social Sciences* (pp. 983–987).

Al-Shetwi, A. Q. (2022). Sustainable Development of Renewable Energy Integrated Power Sector: Trends, Environmental Impacts, and Recent Challenges. *Science of the Total Environment*, 822, 153645. https://doi.org/10.1016/j.scitotenv.2022.153645

DinarStandard. (2019). *State of the Global Islamic Economy Report 2019/20: Driving the Islamic Economy Revolution 4.0*. https://cdn.salaamgateway.com/special-coverage/sgie19-20/fullreport.pdf

Dridi, J., & Hasan, M. (2010). *The Effects of the Global Crisis on Islamic and Conventional Banks: A Comparative Study*. USA, Washington, DC: International Monetary Fund.

Hassan. (2020, February 21). *Why So Few Green Sukuk? Sector Still Faces Longstanding Challenges, Say Practitioners | Salaam Gateway – Global Islamic Economy Gateway*. Retrieved December 30, 2022, from https://salaamgateway.com/story/why-so-few-green-sukuk-sector-still-faces-longstanding-challenges-say-practitioners

Hayat, U., & Malik, A. (2014, November). Islamic Finance: Ethics, Concepts, Practice. *CFA Institute Research Foundation L2014–3*. www.cfainstitute.org/-/media/documents/book/rf-lit-review/2014/rflr-v9-n3-1-pdf.ashx

Kamil, W. A. R., Bakhor, S. A. S. M., De Luna-Martinez, J., Zhang, W., & Aziz, A. H. A. (2019). Islamic Green Finance: Development, Ecosystem and Prospects. *Securities Commission Malaysia*.

Keshminder, J. S., Abdullah, M. S., & Mardi, M. (2022). Green Sukuk – Malaysia Surviving the Bumpy Road: Performance, Challenges and Reconciled Issuance Framework. *Qualitative Research in Financial Markets*, 14(1), 76–94.

Liu, F. H., & Lai, K. P. (2021). Ecologies of Green Finance: Green Sukuk and Development of Green Islamic Finance in Malaysia. *Environment and Planning A: Economy and Space*, 53(8), 1896–1914. https://doi.org/10.1177/0308518x211038349

Marwan, S., & Haneef, M. (2019). Does Doing Good Pay Off? Social Impact Bonds and Lessons for Islamic Finance to Serve the Real Economy. *Islamic Economic Studies*, 27(1).

Nik Abdullah, N. A. I., & Haron, R. (2022). Esg Reporting Practices Among Islamic Banks: A Global Perspective. *IIUM Law Journal*, 30(S2), 1–36. https://doi.org/10.31436/iiumlj.v30iS2.755

OECD. (2020). How Islamic Finance Can Help Achieve the Sustainable Development Goals. *OECD Development Co-operation Policy Papers*, 30 OECD Publishing, Paris.

Rahman, M., Isa, C. R., Dewandaru, G., Hanifa, M. H., Chowdhury, N. T., & Sarker, M. (2020). Socially Responsible Investment Sukuk (Islamic Bond) Development in Malaysia. *Qualitative Research in Financial Markets*, 12(4), 599–619.

RFI. (2019). *Responsible Finance Champions: CIMB, Case Study*. http://rfifoundation.org/application/uploads/RFI_CIMB_CaseStudy.pdf

Sangiorgi, I., & Schopohl, L. (2021). Why Do Institutional Investors Buy Green Bonds: Evidence from a Survey of European Asset Managers. *International Review of Financial Analysis*, 75(March), 101738.

Weerasinghe, A. S., & Ramachandra, T. (2018). Economic Sustainability of Green Buildings: A Comparative Analysis of Green vs Non-Green. *Built Environment Project and Asset Management*, 8(5), 528–543. https://doi.org/10.1108/bepam-10-2017-0105

18 Issues and Challenges of Sustainable Finance in the Islamic Capital Market

Razali Haron & Mukhtar Arif Siraj

Introduction

The discussion on sustainable finance has gained significant attention from academicians and practitioners. Sustainability becomes an important agenda because society and nature face social and environmental challenges. Preservation for sustainability is significant for the next generation due to the high concern of long-term impacts to the society and environment. There are risks due to its negligence, such as water crises, climate change, underemployment, and ecosystem collapse (Alam et al., 2022). Due to the importance of this issue, there are calls for action to reduce the effects of this problem. The emergence of sustainable finance can be traced back to the early 1990s. Oldford et al. (2021) explained that the environmental issue might be a thread to shareholder value, so companies should prioritize both pollution reduction and profitability. This concept attracted communities, mainly academicians and professionals involved in climate change mitigation projects. Khemir (2019) stated that as a principle for responsible investment, the notion of the environmental, social, and governance (ESG) investment was first launched in 2006. The terminology of ESG is used to define the corporate behaviour, and the purpose to embed it on investment is to mitigate the ESG issues.

The governments put substantial efforts into tackling socio-economic issues. At the same time, corporations are trying to adopt the concept of ESG standards in their business activities due to high demand from stakeholders. The investors and shareholders need to cooperate for sustainable projects, and they need to know how the companies run their business. Because of that, investment managers are under pressure to build social and environmental responsibility into their business activities to attract investors. Apart from that, societies are also looking for better solutions for communities (Al-Hiyari et al., 2022). Achieving the sustainability agenda, moreover, is not without the effort of the international organizations developing the frameworks to support a sustainable green economy. Some of these organizations are the International Integrated Reporting Council (IIRC), the Global Reporting Initiative (GRI), the Sustainability Accounting Standard Boards (SASB), the United Nations Global Compact, and the Carbon Disclosure Project (Ellili, 2022). To actualize this program, the idea of Socially Responsible Investment (SRI) was established. This investment motivates companies and investors to consider ESG

DOI: 10.4324/9781003468653-22

investments within their portfolios. This sort of investment exists because investors do not merely consider firms' performance but also consider social and environmental concerns. Throughout the years, there have been funds channelled for the purpose of SRI investment. In 2014, the SRI total Assets Under Management (AUM) was around $21.4 trillion and then reached $35.3 trillion in 2020, an increase of 65%. Moreover, $53 trillion is predicted to be invested in SRI by 2025 (Qoyyum et al., 2022a, 2022b). Countries also recognize the importance of sustainability investments, such as companies in the European Union (EU). Eliwa et al. (2019) elaborate that the increasing levels of ESG performance and disclosure are good for firms, because firms can get a lower cost of capital from lending institutions. Moreover, in term of the cost of debt, the ESG practices in the EU countries are shaped by the stakeholders' orientation. This ethical investment also shows a good trend in some of the ASEAN countries. In Indonesia, the government's strong support can be seen by the implementation of Green Investments (Law No.25, 2007 Article 3) to preserve the environment. Furthermore, the green investment stock indexes, namely Sri-Kehati and IDX ESG Leaders, were introduced in 2009 and include firms which are active in preserving the society and the environment and implementing good corporate governance (Trisnowati et al., 2022).

Malaysia, as an emerging country in the economy, has been encouraging firms to improve the quality of investment by paying attention to the protection of life and environment. The government also considers the related responsible investments. Reports on sustainable development in the country were introduced in 1987, and the first Corporate Social Reporting (CSR) was implemented by firms beginning in 2006. The Malaysian government established SRI funds back in 2003. The purpose is to invest in companies that are excluded from alcohol and gambling business but display good corporate governance and environmental awareness. In 2014, the FTSE4Good Bursa Malaysia Index was introduced as the market benchmark for Sustainable Development Goals (SDGs). Furthermore, starting in 2015, all companies must apply the Sustainability Framework with ESG disclosures, which was followed by establishing the Companies Act 2016 to encourage CSR disclosures (Mohamad & Wasiuzzaman, 2021). Islamic finance is not left behind in achieving sustainability. One of the purposes of this investment is to have a good impact on society and environment, which is also seen as a purpose of ESG investment. Hence, both share the same vision (Muhamad et al., 2022). There is an immense effort made for this movement. With respect to the Islamic capital market (ICM) and sustainability, green sukuk has been developed as a Shari'ah-compliant instrument to fund environmentally-friendly investments, and it has played a significant role. To boost green sukuk issuance, the World Bank in collaboration with several bodies made a huge effort to promote the instrument (Abdullah & Keshminder, 2020). In Malaysia, the very first SRI sukuk was established in 2014 by the Malaysian Securities Commission (SC), and the investment attempts to integrate the ESG principles with Shari'ah principles, creating a strong connection between sustainability and Islamic finance (Noordin et al., 2016; Foglie & Keshminder, 2022).

Charitable endowment (*waqf*), compared to other types of donations in Islamic finance, has a feature of sustainability known as perpetuity. *Waqf* can play an important role in achieving SDGs and is one of the alternatives in solving different socioeconomic issues such as poverty, lack of health care facilities, and providing shelter, food, and education. The contribution of *waqf* to Muslims' socioeconomic growth in Egypt, Turkey, Kuwait, Indonesia, Malaysia, and other countries is deemed as the most visible proof charities in Islam. The valuation of *waqf* assets globally is expected to be between $94.5 billion and $945 billion (Misbah et al., 2022). The initiative to integrate between sukuk and *waqf* for the sustainable projects and social impact has also been performed by the Indonesian Ministry of Finance with the issuance of Cash *Waqf* Linked Sukuk in 2020. Approximately $3.5 million was raised for this investment. The profit generated has been allocated to health facilities and hospitals for the poor in Serang, Indonesia (Fauziah et al., 2021).

Islamic sustainable finance has momentum, considering the initiative to establish the ethical investments that are aligned with Shari'ah principles. Through Islamic finance concepts such as zakat and *waqf*, the delivery of the SDGs might be ensured. Furthermore, the attraction of Islamic sustainable finance creates new opportunities in the market. However, this is not an easy journey since the Shari'ah-compliant sustainable finance is far from free of issues and challenges. This chapter, in general, aims to elaborate more on the issues and challenges of Islamic sustainable finance in ICM.

Islamic Finance and Sustainability

Islamic finance must be Shari'ah-compliant, and there is a general concept that Islamic finance prohibits certain practices that are commonly used in conventional finance, such as usury (*riba*), ambiguity in contracts (*gharar*), gambling (*maysir*), and any transactions that are prohibited by Shari'ah (Nomran & Haron, 2020). Shari'ah does allow trade, so the services and products of Islamic finance are based on profit and loss sharing (Al Rahahleh et al., 2019). The avoidance of the prohibited transactions for Islamic finance institutions (IFIs) is to promote justice in the society. If an institution does not comply with these restrictions, it can't be considered Islamic (Nomran & Haron, 2020). The Islamic revelation clearly states that non-Shari'ah-compliant transactions are forbidden in Islam. Allah Almighty says, "That is because they say: 'Trade is like usury'. But Allah hath permitted trade and forbidden usury" (Qur'an; 2:275). Moreover, in one of his prophetic traditions, Prophet Muhammad (PBUH) prohibits ambiguity in contracts. Abu Hurairah (RA) narrated: "The Messenger of Allah (PBUH) prohibited the *gharar* sale and the *hasah* sale" (Tirmidhi). The condemnation of gambling is also mentioned in the Qur'an. Allah SWT says: "O you who believe! Intoxicants and gambling, dedication of stones, and divination by arrows, are an abomination of Satan's handwork. Eschew such abomination, that you may prosper" (Qur'an; 5:90). From these verses and hadith, it is inferred that Shari'ah condemns that which is harmful to society and a threat to social responsibility and tries to uphold justice and prosperity for human beings.

Nowadays, Islamic finance is receiving a lot of attention from academicians, scholars, and practitioners in assessing the ethical values that should be followed by Islamic finance institutions. Moreover, Islamic finance is increasing in global popularity because it offers solutions to social and environmental problems that concern people worldwide (Kuanova et al., 2021). Islamic finance assets are projected to reach USD 4,940 billion by 2025. According to the Islamic Finance Development Report (IFDI) 2021, Islamic banking constitutes 70% of these assets, followed by sukuk with 19% of the distribution. Furthermore, Islamic funds, other IFIs, and takaful contribute 5%, 4%, and 2% of the shares, respectively. It is also reported that the global Islamic finance industry components contributed outstanding numbers in 2020. During the year, there were 1,595 IFIs, 1,008 Islamic finance education providers, 1,235 Shari'ah scholars representing IFIs, and 844 Islamic finance events recorded. Other components with significant numbers are Islamic finance research papers, CSR funds disbursed by IFIs, and news on Islamic finance (IFDI, 2021). This huge number cannot be separated from the worldwide Muslim population of 1.97 billion followers, making up about a quarter of the world population. Based on the report, the application of Islamic finance regulation has been widely used in 47 countries, and mostly is seen in the countries with a Muslim majority population. Outside the Islamic world, the popularity of Islamic finance has also grown in non-Muslim majority countries in Asia, Europe, and the US (Alam et al., 2022). Islamic finance is an alternative to its conventional counterpart due to its distinct concept. Table 18.1 shows some of the religious obligations in Islam, such as zakat, sadaqah, and waqf, that could be used in Islamic finance. Furthermore, there are some instruments used in Islamic commercial transactions such as Al-Musharakah, Murabahah, and al-Mudharabah. Islamic bond or sukuk are also Islamic investments that are utilized widely in many countries (OECD, 2020).

As a part of Islamic finance, ICM plays a significant role in economic progress. Muamalah is a key that its existence is unavailable in the conventional capital market. In the transactions, Shari'ah view is different from its counterpart. Any business activities incorporated in prohibited elements by Shari'ah law are clearly banned; hence the ICM needs to satisfy Islamic principles (Yusfiarto et al., 2022). Investors use the term "ESG" to evaluate the companies and determine their financial performance. This covers the areas considered to be sustainable, responsible, and ethical investments and is divided into two schools of thought. The first idea is that ESG practices might create a negative impact on firms' financial performance,

Table 18.1 Overview of Islamic Finance Concepts

Concept/Instrument	*Definition*
Zakat	Compulsory alms giving
Sadaqah	Voluntary alms
Waqf	Charitable endowment
Sukuk	Islamic asset-based financial certificate
Al-Musharakah	Profit- and loss-sharing partnership
Murabahah	Cost-plus financing of a non-interest-bearing loan
Al-Mudharabah	Capital and labour partnership

Source: OECD Publishing (2020)

and this is based on the agency theory. By contrast, the stakeholder theory argues that the ESG might have a positive impact on the companies' performance. However, based on the second idea, many companies have recently engaged in ESG practices in their business activities and policies due to concerns for social and environment issues. It means that ESG investments are a good alternative for investors. This is because some non-environmental assets are excluded from the investments, such as alcohol, tobacco, weapons, and gambling, whereby it can create a good reputation for the companies (Lee & Isa, 2022). The CSR concept encourages the establishment of ESG investment. This benchmark is utilized to create a strategic way to achieve Sustainable Development Goals (SDGs) for the global financial services (Chin, 2022).

According to Hardiningsih et al. (2019), ESG practices in companies might boost profits, so it is suitable for all kind of investors. The integration with the ESG might assist the companies to cut costs and improve their revenues and profits. The study shows that firms with ESG implementation have larger net profits and outperformed the non-ESG firms. Hence, this investment needs to be applied innovatively and creatively. Islamic finance is advancing in achieving the sustainability agenda. ESG and Islamic finance share the same principles and fundamental ideas. Aligned with ESG principles, the prohibited elements in Islam, such as alcohol, gambling, weapons, and tobacco, are not exclusive in Islamic business activities. The integration of Islamic finance with the social purpose will make a huge step in achieving sustainability. The sustainability agenda can be smoothly connected to Shari'ah principles due to the existence of the Maqasid al-Shari'ah. To fulfil the objectives or the maqasid, Islam puts these aspects above anything, such as preserving life (nafs), lineage (nasl), intellect ('aql), wealth (maal), and religion or belief (deen). In Islamic finance, this system is seen as a balance between economic, social, and environmental (Musari, 2022; Muhamad et al., 2022).

BAZNAS depicts the relationship between SDGs and Shari'ah objectives as shown in Table 18.2. It is argued that the implementation of maqasid Shari'ah could lead to achieving socioeconomic justice because it prioritizes the preservation of the five elements from any harms. Some common features of SDGs provide a close relation with maqasid Shari'ah, namely healthy life, poverty eradication, equality, and social position (Jan et al., 2021). Though both investments are principally the same, there are certain areas where they might differ. Table 18.3 illustrates their similarities and differences.

Sustainable Investment in ICM

One of the innovations of sustainable finance in ICM is Shari'ah-compliant green sukuk. It focuses on renewable energy and other environmental assets. This investment can attract all types of investors (conventional, Shari'ah-compliant, and conventional green investors). The fund of the investment will be channelled to ESG projects. The issuance of this breakthrough is to encourage investors in considering green and sustainable sukuk investments and fulfilling Islamic principles. (World Bank Group, 2020; Liu & Lai, 2021). In collaboration with the Central

Table 18.2 The Connection Between SDGs and *Maqasid Shari'ah*

No	*SDGs*	*The Principles of Maqasid Shari'ah*
1	No poverty	Preserve wealth
2	Zero hunger	Preserve life and wealth
3	Good health and well-being	Preserve life and wealth
4	Quality education	Preserve intellect
5	Gender equality	Preserve wealth, intellect, life, and lineage
6	Clean water and sanitation	Preserve life and lineage
7	Affordable and clean energy	Preserve lineage
8	Decent work and economic growth	Preserve wealth
9	Industry, innovation, and infrastructure	Preserve wealth
10	Reduced inequalities	Preserve wealth
11	Sustainable cities and communities	Preserve lineage, life, and wealth
12	Responsible consumption and production	Preserve lineage and life
13	Climate action	Preserve lineage and intellect
14	Life below water	Preserve lineage, wealth, and intellect
15	Life on land ecosystem	Preserve lineage
16	Peace, justice and strong institutions	Preserve life, wealth, and lineage
17	Partnership for the goals	Preserve wealth and intellect

Source: BAZNAS (2017)

Table 18.3 Similarities and Differences Between Shari'ah and ESG Investment

Items	*Shari'ah Investment*	*Sustainable Investment*
Similarities	• Both investments encourage sustainability in the form of social responsibility and ethical investment. • Both investments align with *maqasid* Shari'ah where benefit should be obtained and harm should be eliminated in the investment.	
Screening	Shari'ah-compliant screening	ESG screening
Focus on environmental and social issues	Indirect	Direct
Focus on sustainability	Indirect	Direct
Investors	Muslim and conventional investors	Conventional investors

Source: Principal (2022)

Bank of Malaysia and the World Bank to achieve the sustainability agenda, Securities Commission (SC) Malaysia launched its very first green sukuk in 2017. The massive support from the Malaysian government encouraged the establishment of rules, frameworks, and policies for this investment. The existence of Sustainable and Responsible Investment (SRI) sukuk back in 2014 fully supported the development of green sukuk (Rozman & Azmi, 2022). A year after its first issuance of green sukuk in Malaysia, Indonesia's Global Sovereign Green Sukuk was introduced in 2018 with the value of $1.25 billion. A huge response from the market made the Indonesian government consider reissuing the sukuk in the following years (Septiana & Dewi, 2022).

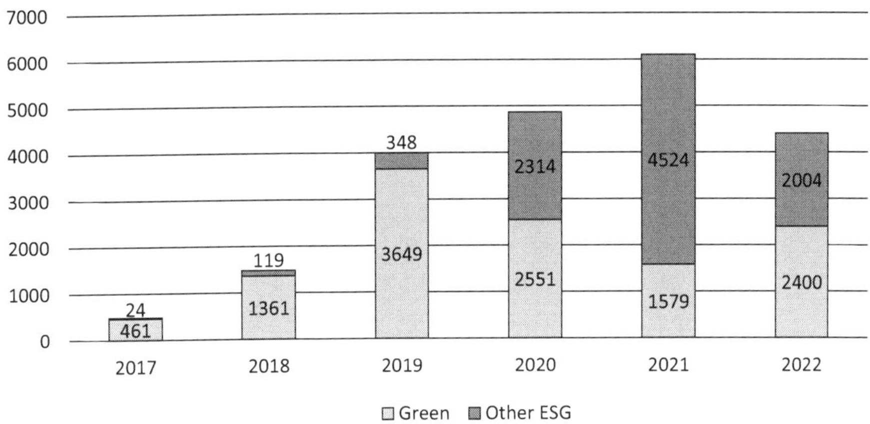

Figure 18.1 Green and Sustainability Sukuk Issuance

Note: The data is represented in US$ Million

Source: Refinitiv (2021)

The application of waqf and sukuk together as an innovation of ESG investment in the ICM has been illustrated by Bank Indonesia and the Indonesian Ministry of Finance with the issuance of Cash Waqf Linked Sukuk. This investment refers to Indonesian Fatwa Ulama No. 131/DSN-MUI/X/2019 about Sukuk Waqf, and it is done under a wakalah contract (Yunita, 2020). Since its first launch, green and sustainability sukuk has seen good growth. The data issued by Refinitv (as shown in Figure 18.1) tells us that in 2019 immense growth was recorded compared to the previous year. Though the trend decreased during the pandemic, it returned to gradual growth in 2022.

ESG Shari'ah equity is another form of Islamic sustainable investment in ICM. The constituents must follow Shari'ah rulings and ESG principles. The screening of ESG investments is related to the issues about environmental, social, and governance. The environment portion covers environmental issues such as pollution, climate change, global warming, and greenhouse gas emissions. The social portion covers health, education, work and occupation, and human rights. The governance portion concerns the area of management, shareholders' interest and welfare, and corporate social responsibility (CSR) (Lee & Isa, 2022). The Shari'ah requirement is divided into business screening and financial screening. Referring to the Shari'ah screening by Ratings Intelligence Partners (RI) standards, certain business activities are excluded if its revenue is more than 5%, such as advertising related to non-Islamic activities, media entertainment, alcohol, conventional financial services, gambling, pork related, pornography, tobacco, and trading of gold and silver as cash on a deferred basis. Moreover, from accounting-based screening, the equity is considered compliant if its non-compliant debt over market value of equity is less than 33%, the account receivable over market value of equity is less than 49%, and cash plus interest-bearing securities over market value of equity is less than 33% (S&P Dow Jones Indices, 2022).

Issues and Challenges

Non-Compliance

To be Shari'ah-compliant, an investment needs to pass certain qualitative and quantitative tests. If the investment fails to meet certain criteria, it is not considered Shari'ah-compliant. Similarly, ESG investment has its own criteria to be exclusively called sustainable investment. Both investments encourage investors to utilize their capital in social responsibility and ethical value. Table 18.4 shows the level of application between the two investments.

ESG and Islamic finance prohibit investment in tobacco, alcohol, weapons, gambling, and human trafficking. Like Islamic finance, ESG investment has its principles. Though both have similarities, there are certain applications where they may differ. As stated in Table 18.4, the obedience to Shari'ah and avoidance of riba are a must for Islamic finance, while ESG investment does not put any restrictions on this. Furthermore, both show different levels of application in some areas, such as systematic ESG integration, engagement with environmental and social issues, voting, and other practices (CFA Institute, 2019). One of the consequences is that not every sustainable investment is Shari'ah-compliant. For example, conventional finance and investment employs riba and uses high leverage ratios. Though the sustainable criteria are met, the investment is excluded from the Shari'ah category.

Governance Issues

In this section, the focus is more on reporting and disclosure. Investors and other stakeholders should be informed by means of annual report, newsletter, website,

Table 18.4 Level of Application Between ESG and Shari'ah Investment

Practice	*ESG*	*Shari'ah Investment*
ESG integration	Medium level	Low level
Screening	High level based on client-specific/fund-specific screening policies	Shari'ah-compliant
Firms' involvement in environmental and social issues	High level	Low level
Voting	High level	Low level
Dividend	No limitation	It is subject to "purification" process
Riba (usury)	No limitation	Not allowed
Security lending	High level with lending practitioners applying rules that ensure they can vote	Not allowed
Short selling	Low level	Not allowed
Restriction on high leverage	No limitation	Shari'ah-compliant. Interest/riba should be avoided

Source: CFA Institute (2019)

or other communication channels on its sustainability and environmental, social, and governance program. This will help them understand how the business is conducted. SRI sukuk, for example, needs to abide by the ESG reporting and disclosure set by SRI Sukuk Framework. The report should contain the objectives of sukuk and a statement that the investment complies with ESG standards (Noordin et al., 2016). In equity investment, whether it is conventional or Shari'ah, the trend of ESG reporting has been popular in recent years. It makes the firms be more transparent about ESG risks and opportunities (Aziz et al., 2022). Some countries have made ESG reporting mandatory in companies such as the UK, countries in the EU, the US, Canada, and countries in Asia, such as Malaysia and China. Krueger et al. (2021) examined the effect of mandatory ESG disclosure around the world. The result is that mandatory ESG disclosure regulations provide benefits in terms of cheaper funding to the companies. However, in Malaysia, there are no strict regulations on ESG disclosure because it is very new in the country. Furthermore, though it has been mandatory in the US, the firms in the country have no standardization for the report (Mohammad & Wasiuzzaman, 2021). In some countries, ESG reporting and disclosure is not mandatory. These problems could lead to ineffective and misleading ESG disclosures. This condition is considered "greenwashing", where the management fails to disclose full information about its environmental and social performance. To avoid this, standardized reporting is required, because poor reporting is a big obstacle for ESG development (Qoyyum et al., 2022a, 2022b). One of the impacts of poorly integrated ESG reporting is a low level of awareness and a knowledge gap (Luo & Tang, 2022).

Challenges

Lack of Knowledge

The effectiveness of ESG application depends on the information. The stakeholder can highlight the company's strength and vision through ESG reporting. Without this, there will be limited ESG knowledge capacity for the stakeholders (Pu et al., 2022). Zahid (2019) argued that while the knowledge and capacity building are important, a low level of awareness and understanding of sustainability practices still happen among individual and institutional practices. Understanding and managing ESG-related risks will enable the financial sector's role transition to a low-carbon and more sustainable economy. The trend of ESG has been increasing the last few years. However, the lack of knowledge does exist, so it can't adapt to the current demand. BCG-INSEAD ESG Pulse Check Survey (2021) reported that 44% of directors have a lack of knowledge, data, and capabilities in achieving ESG goals, making it the top on the list of burdens.

Philanthropy for the ESG

The existence of philanthropy acts an important role in Islamic finance. Arguably, some Islamic finance instruments are related to philanthropy and ESG, such as waqf, zakat, sadaqah, and qard hasan. In the Muslim countries, the concept of philanthropy is linked to business organizations. The funds of those instruments can be channelled for the purpose of poverty eradication, social welfare, better education, health, and protecting the environment (Hanic & Smolo, 2022). The sources of tools and instruments of Islamic finance mentioned here depend on Islamic philanthropy (Kuanova et al., 2021). Likewise, the success of SDG is associated with philanthropic contributions in the private and public sectors. In achieving sustainable development, the involvement of philanthropy plays a crucial role (Sulistyowati et al., 2022). Oussama Kaissi (2022) stated that for the purpose of Islamic philanthropic giving, even though there is no strong data to prove this claim, the total of its AUM reaches billions of dollars. In addition, the global total of $730 billion is spent every year on good deeds; however, only 2% is utilized for the purpose of climate change reduction. The same scenario occurs when it comes to Islamic philanthropy. Through the ESG-related projects, the capital of philanthropic giving can contribute more to mitigating environmental issues.

Accelerating Shari'ah and ESG investment

Integrating Shari'ah and ESG investment to gain profit and to prove its impact is going to be crucial in the coming years. It comes to its momentum as the current studies prove that when Shari'ah and ESG are combined, the performance of the companies is improved. Furthermore, the combination between Shari'ah and ESG screening might not hinder firm performance and might improve the overall risk-adjusted return (Al Ansari & Alanzarouti, 2020). Accelerating Shari'ah and ESG is a relatively new concept. Therefore, compared to the conventional ESG investment, Shari'ah-ESG is still low in terms of its global impact. The result of the UN's Principles for Responsible Investment (PRI) shows that only 1% commitment comes from the OIC countries, while the Principles for Responsible Banking (PRB) is only 10%. Furthermore, a lack of pledges and commitment are still seen for ESG Shari'ah investing (Ja'afar, 2022). Ja'afar (2022) added that to obtain green assets is a challenge for investors. In addition, Shari'ah guidelines are inadequate in policies on ESG-related investments. At the same time, Shari'ah-ESG finance needs to validate that its investment has met the standards. When it comes to the investors, the information gap should be solved by issuing standard reporting and its framework. Lastly, different jurisdictions across the world challenge Shari'ah-ESG investment in having centralized regulation. As the result, the journey of Shari'ah and ESG acceleration still has a long way to go.

Conclusion

The trend of sustainable investment has rapidly grown and developed throughout the years, and this has gained huge attention from parties due to social and environmental concerns. A massive impact of ESG issues triggers the initiative in the market to have sustainable investments. Corporations and governments have started to implement the strategy to promote social and environmental awareness. As a result, regulations and policies are established for responsible investment. Furthermore, trillions of dollars in funding has been invested and managed for this purpose. Islamic finance is not left behind in contributing to sustainability. Islamic and ESG principles philosophically share the same concept. Thus, Islamic finance is deemed to be advanced in delivering the SDGs' purpose. Through Islamic finance tools and instruments, such as zakat, waqf, and sadaqah, the initiative to integrate between Islamic and ESG principles in a form of investment is developing in the market. The most popular investment is green sukuk, which holds a big place in Shari'ah investment. The integration between Shari'ah and ESG has also been established to attract all types of investors. However, this development is followed by issues and challenges. This chapter highlights non-compliance and governance issues. In addition, Islamic sustainable finance also faces the challenge of gap knowledge, philanthropy, and integrating between ESG and Shari'ah investments. It is known that to be Shari'ah-compliant, an investment needs to pass Shari'ah screening. Similarly, ESG investment has its own screening with which to comply. However, there are certain areas where ESG does not put restrictions on its investment. The result is that not all sustainable investment complies with Shari'ah principles. Another issue is a governance-related problem. Islamic sustainable investment needs to provide the ESG reporting regarding the business activities. If the management does not comply with this rule, the issue of greenwashing will appear, where the information relating to the environment is not fully disclosed.

Lack of knowledge for stakeholders is one big challenge for Islamic sustainable investment. To have the proper knowledge and capacity building is crucial for the stakeholder because the public will assess the vision and the objectives of the investment. Unfortunately, lack of knowledge is still at the top of the list of ESG challenges. Low contributions from philanthropists is another challenge faced by Islamic sustainable finance, as they are the funding source. Only a small percentage of their cumulative fund is utilized for climate change mitigation. Lastly, accelerating between ESG and Shari'ah investment contributes to the long journey of Islamic sustainable finance. There are a lot of burdens in initiating this integration such as low commitment, an inadequate number of Shari'ah experts in establishing policies, and different jurisdictions around the world.

This chapter has two implications. Firstly, this study elaborates issues and challenges of Islamic sustainable finance in ICM, so it may assist academicians and practitioners in analysing the current situation in Islamic sustainable finance. Secondly, it raises the awareness of Shari'ah- and ESG-compliant investment. There are some limitations to this research. To combine Islamic and ESG principles in investment is a recent phenomenon in ICM. Thus, there are limited data available to support the study.

References

Abdullah, M. S., & Keshminder, J. S. (2020). What Drives Green Sukuk? A Leader's Perspective. *Journal of Sustainable Finance & Investment*, 12(3), 1–21.

Alam, M. M., Tahir, Y. M., Alyousfi, A. Y. H. S., Ali, W. B., Muda, R., & Nordin, S. (2022). Financial Factors Influencing Environmental, Social and Governance Ratings of Public Listed Companies in Bursa Malaysia. *Cogent Business & Management*, 9(2002), 1–22.

Al Ansari, R., & Alanzarouti, F. (2020). ESG and Islamic Finance: An Ethical Bridge Built on Shared Values. *Journal of Islamic Finance Studies*, 6(1), 5–11.

Al-Hiyari, A., Ismail, A. I., Kolsi, M. C., & Kehinde, O. H. (2022). Environmental, Social and Governance Performance (ESG) and Firm Investment Efficiency in Emerging Markets: The Interaction Effect of Board Cultural Diversity. *Corporate Governance*, 23(3).

Al Rahahleh, N., Bhatti, M. I., & Misman, F. N. (2019). Development in Risk Management in Islamic Finance: A Review. *Journal of Risk and Financial Management*, 12(37), 1–22.

Aziz, M. R. A., Noor, F. M., Marzuki, A., Basah, M. Y. A., Sabri, H., Ramli, N. A., & Shahwan, S. (2022). Research and Publication Trends in Environmental, Social and Governance (ESG), Sustainable and Responsible Investment (SRI) and Maqasid Shari'ah Framework between 2012–2021. *Journal of Information and Knowledge Management (JIKM)*, 12(1), 1–30.

BAZNAS. (2017). *Sebuah Kajian Zakat on SDGs*. Jakarta Pusat: Pusat Kajian Strategis.

BCG-INSEAD Board ESG Pulse Check. (2021). *Directors Can Up Their Game on Environmental, Social, and Governance Issues*. https://web-assets.bcg.com/7e/71/fc29b62542e6bac1732ebd890bbc/bcg-directors-can-up-their-game-on-environmental-social-and-governance-issues-mar-2022.pdfn

CFA Institute. (2019). *ESG Integration and Islamic Finance: Complementary Investment Approaches*. www.unpri.org/download?ac=9578#:~:text=Islamic%20finance%20and%20ESG%20investing%20are%20complementary%20capital%2Draising%20and,to%20society%20and%20the%20environment

Chin, P. N. (2022). ESG Rating and Firm Performance: Comparison among Singapore, Malaysia, Brunei, Indonesia, and Thailand. *International Journal of Accounting, Finance and Business (IJAFB)*, 7(43), 155–164.

Eliwa, Y., Aboud, A., & Saleh, A. (2019). ESG Practices and the Cost of Debt: Evidence from EU Countries. *Critical Perspectives on Accounting*. https://doi.org/10.1016/j.cpa.2019.102097

Ellili, N. O. D. (2022). Impact of ESG Disclosure and Financial Reporting Quality on Investment Efficiency. *Corporate Governance*, 22(5), 1094–1111.

Fauziah, N. N., Ali, E. R. A. E., Bashir, A. A. M., & Bacha, A. M. (2021). An Analysis of Cash Waqf Linked Sukuk for Socially Impactful Sustainable Projects in Indonesia. *Journal of Islamic Finance*, 10(1), 1–10.

Foglie, A. D., & Keshminder, J. S. (2022). Challenges and Opportunities of SRI Sukuk Toward Financial System Sustainability: A Bibliometric and Systematic Literature Review. *International Journal of Emerging Markets* (ahead-of-print).

Hanic, A., & Smolo, E. (2022). Islamic Approach to Corporate Social Responsibility: An International Model for Islamic Banks. *International Journal of Islamic and Middle Eastern Finance and Management* (ahead-of-print).

Hardiningsih, P., Januarti, I., Yuyetta, E. N. A., Srimindarti, C., & Udin, U. (2019). The Effect of Sustainability Information Disclosure on Financial and Market Performance: Empirical Evidence from Indonesia and Malaysia. *International Journal of Energy Economics and Policy*, 10(2), 18–25.

Ja'afar, N. (2022). Shari'ah-ESG: Moving from Laggard to Catch-Up and Alignment, Toward Pragmatic and Significant Impact. *Islamic Finance News*. www-islamicfinancenews-com.ezlib.iium.edu.my/Shari'ah-esg-moving-from-laggard-to-catch-up-and-alignment-toward-pragmatic-and-significant-impact.html

Jan, A., Mata, M. N., Albinsson, O. A., Martins., J. M., Hassan, R., & Mata, P. N. (2021). Alignment of Islamic Banking Sustainability Indicators with Sustainable Development Goals: Policy Recommendations for Addressing the COVID-19 Pandemic. *Sustainability*, 13(5), 1–38.

Kaissi, O. (2022). *The Dynamics, Challenges and Potential for Islamic Green Finance and Sukuk*. www-islamicfinancenews-com.ezlib.iium.edu.my/the-dynamics-challenges-and-potential-for-islamic-green-finance-and-sukuk.html

Khemir, S. (2019). Perception of ESG Criteria by Mainstream Investors: Evidence from Tunisia. *International Journal of Emerging Markets*, 14(5), 752–768.

Krueger, P., Sautner, Z., Tang, D. Y., & Zhong, R. (2021). The Effects of Mandatory ESG Disclosure Around the World. *ECGI Working Paper Series in Finance*. https://ecgi.global/sites/default/files/working_papers/documents/kreugersautnertangzhongfinal.pdf

Kuanova, L. A., Sagiyeva, R., & Shirazi, N. S. (2021). Islamic Social Finance: A Literature Review and Future Research Directions. *Journal of Islamic Accounting and Business Research*, 12(5), 707–728.

Lee, S.-P., & Isa, M. (2022). Environmental, Social and Governance (ESG) Practices and Financial Performance of *Shari'ah*-Compliant Companies in Malaysia. *Journal of Islamic Accounting and Business Research* (ahead-of-print).

Liu, F. H. M., & Lai, K. P. Y. (2021). Ecologies of Green Finance: Green *Sukuk* and Development of Green Islamic Finance in Malaysia. *Economy and Space*, 53(8), 1896–1914.

Luo, L., & Tang, Q. (2022). The Real Effects of ESG Reporting and GRI Standards on Carbon Mitigation: International Evidence. *Business Strategy and Environment*, 2022, 1–16.

Misbah, H., Johari, F., Mat Nor, F., Haron, H., Shahwan, S., & Shafii, Z. (2022). Sustainable Development, Regional Planning, and Information Management as an Evolving Theme in Waqf Research: A Bibliometric Analysis. *Sustainability*, 14(14126), 1–25.

Mohammad, W. M. W., & Wasiuzzaman, S. (2021). Environmental, Social and Governance (ESG) Disclosure, Competitive Advantage and Performance of Firms in Malaysia. *Cleaner Environmental System*, 2(2021), 1–11.

Muhamad, S. F., Zain, F. A. M., Samad, N. S. A., Rahman, A. H. A., & Yasoa, M. R. (2022). Measuring Sustainable Performance of Islamic Banks: Integrating the Principles of Environmental, Social and Governance (ESG) and Maqasid Shari'ah. *IOP Conference Series: Earth and Environmental Science*, 1102(2022), 1–8.

Musari, K. (2022). Integrating Green Sukuk and Cash Waqf Linked Sukuk, the Blended Islamic Finance of Fiscal Instrument in Indonesia: A Proposed Model for Fighting Climate Change. *International Journal of Islamic Khazanah (IJIK)*, 12(2), 133–144.

Nomran, N. M., & Haron, R. (2020). Shari'ah Supervisory Board's Size Impact on Performance in the Islamic Banking Industry: An Empirical Investigation of the Optimal Board Size Across Jurisdictions. *Journal of Islamic Accounting and Business Research*, 11(1), 110–129.

Noordin, N. H., Haron, S. N., Hasan, A., & Hassan, R. (2016). Complying with the Requirements for Issuance of SRI Sukuk: The Case of Khazanah's Sukuk Ihsan. *Journal of Accounting and Business Research*, 9(3), 415–433.

OECD Publishing. (2020). *How Islamic Finance Contributes to Achieving the Sustainable Development Goals*. www.oecd-ilibrary.org/docserver/ac1480ca-en.pdf?expires=1672109106&id=id&accname=guest&checksum=0BCFBA9E908FCBD4EE1EEB8096250D20

Oldford, E., Willcott, N., & Kennie, T. (2021). Can Student Managed Investment Funds (SMIFs) Narrow the Environmental, Social and Governance (ESG) Skills Gap? *Managerial Finance*, 48(1), 57–77.

Principal. (2022). *Shari'ah and Sustainable Investing: Two Sides of the Same Coin*. www.principal.com.my/en/node/630409

Pu, R., Chankoson, T., Dong, R. K., & Song, L. (2022). Bibliometrics-Based Visualization Analysis of Knowledge-Based Economy and Implications to Environmental, Social and Governance (ESG). *Library Hi Tech* (ahead-of-print).

Qoyyum, A., Jamil, R. A., & Sehar, A. (2022a). Impact of Green Marketing, Greenwashing and Green Confusion on Green Brand Equity. *Spanish Journal of Marketing-ESIC* (ahead-of-print).

Qoyyum, A., Sakti, M. R. P. S., Thaker, H. M. T., & AlHashfi, R. U. (2022b). Does the Islamic Label Indicate Good Environmental, Social, and Governance (ESG) Performance? Evidence from Shari'ah-Compliant Firms in Indonesia and Malaysia. *Borsa Istanbul Review*, 22(2), 306–320.

Refinitiv. (2021). *Islamic Finance Development Report 2021*. https://static.zawya.com/pdf/Islamic%20Finance%20Development%20Reports/2021%20IFDI%20Report.pdf

Rozman, A. T., & Azmi, N. A. (2022). Green Sukuk, Environmental Issues and Strategy. *IOP Conference Series: Earth and Environmental Science*, 1067, 1–8.

Septiana, E., & Dewi, G. (2022). Challenges and Opportunities for the Development of Green Sukuk in Indonesia. *Budapest International Research and Critics Institute-Journal (BIRCI-Journal)*, 5(3), 18488–18500.

S&P Dow Jones Indices. (2022). *Equity S&P Global 1200 ESG Shari'ah Index*. www.spglobal.com/spdji/en/indices/equity/sp-global-1200-esg-Shari'ah-index/#overview

Sulistyowati, Sukmana, R., Ratnasari, R. T., Ascarya, & Widiastuti, T. (2022). Issues and Challenges of Waqf in Providing Healthcare Resources. *Islamic Economic Studies* (ahead-of-print).

Trisnowati, Y., Achsani, N. A., Sembel, R., & Andati, T. (2022). The Effects of ESG Score, Financial Performance, and Macroeconomics on Stock Returns during the Pandemic Era in Indonesia. *International Journal of Energy Economics and Policy*, 12(4), 166–172.

World Bank Group. (2020). *Pioneering the Green Sukuk: Three Years On*. https://openknowledge.worldbank.org/bitstream/handle/10986/34569/Pioneering-the-Green-Sukuk-Three-Years-On.pdf

Yunita, P. (2020). Cash Waqf Linked Sukuk (CLWS) Model: For Indonesia Sustainable Food Security. *Al-Awqaf*, 13(1), 59–72.

Yusfiarto, R., Nugraha, S. S., Mutmainah, L., Berakon, I., Sunarsih, S., & Nurdany, A. (2022). Examining Islamic Capital Market Adoption from a Socio-Psychological Perspective and Islamic Financial Literacy. *Journal of Islamic Accounting and Business Research* (ahead-of-print).

Zahid, A. Z. M. (2019, December 3). *Sustainability and Challenges Ahead*. The IFN Green and Sustainable Finance Forum, Kuala Lumpur, Malaysia. www.bis.org/review/r191204b.pdf

Index

9781032743073